NEW DOCUMENTS ILLUSTRATING EARLY CHRISTIANITY

A Review of the
Greek Inscriptions and Papyri
published in 1976

by

G. H. R. Horsley

The Ancient History Documentary Research Centre
Macquarie University
1981

The Ancient History Documentary Research Centre (Director: E. A. Judge, Professor of History) has been formed within the School of History, Philosophy & Politics at Macquarie University to focus staff effort in research and professional development and to coordinate it with the work of other organisations interested in the documentation of the ancient world.

Committee for *New Documents illustrating Early Christianity*
Chairman: P. W. Barnett, Master of Robert Menzies College, Macquarie University.
Secretary: P. T. O'Brien, Head, New Testament Department, Moore Theological College, Sydney.
Members: P. Geidans, D. M. Knox, J. Lawler.

Editorial Consultants
F. I. Andersen, Professor of Studies in Religion, University of Queensland.
G. W. Clarke, Deputy Director, Humanities Research Centre, Australian National University.
W. J. Dumbrell, Vice-Principal, Moore Theological College, Sydney.
J. A. L. Lee, Senior Lecturer in Greek, University of Sydney.
K. L. McKay, Reader in Classics, Australian National University.

This volume has been produced with the support of the Macquarie University Research Grant and the Sydney Diocesan Educational and Book Society.

Editorial correspondence should be addressed to Mr G. H. R. Horsley, School of History, Philosophy & Politics, Macquarie University, North Ryde, N.S.W. 2113, Australia.

Business address: The Ancient History Documentary Research Centre, Macquarie University, North Ryde, N.S.W. 2113, Australia.

SUGGESTED CATALOGUING DATA:

Horsley, G. H. R.
    New Documents illustrating early Christianity. A review of the Greek inscriptions and papyri published in 1976.

Bibliography.
Includes index.
ISBN 0 85837 481 1
ISBN 0 85837 899 X (pbk)

1. Bible. New Testament — Language, style. 2. Inscriptions, Greek. 3. Manuscripts (Papyri). 4. Greek language, Biblical. 5. Church History — Primitive and early church.
I. Macquarie University. Ancient History Documentary Research Centre. II. Title.

PA 810   1981   487.4

Typeset by Essay Composition, 225 Miller Street, North Sydney, Australia
Printed by J. Bell and Company Pty. Ltd., 15 McCauley Street, Alexandria, Australia.

CONTENTS

LIST OF ENTRIES

A. New Testament Context

B. Minor Philological Notes

C. Biblical and Related Citations

D. Judaica

E. Ecclesiastica

F. Varia

PREFACE

By *New Documents* we refer to the hundreds of newly discovered Greek papyri and inscriptions which are published each year. Our aim is to report them in a form that will be more accessible to students of the New Testament and related fields. They provide a steadily accumulating context which illustrates early Christianity in a variety of ways.

In the early part of this century the first flush of papyrus discovery led to masterly appraisals of the new documents in relation to the language, ideas and institutions of the New Testament. For example: Adolf Deissmann, *Light from the Ancient East,* and J. H. Moulton and G. Milligan, *The Vocabulary of the Greek Testament illustrated from the Papyri and other non-literary Sources* (= MM). Their contribution has rightly built itself into the regular apparatus of New Testament scholarship. But the recovery of new sources has not stopped. Already five times as many papyrus documents have been published as were available then, and the current rate of publication is higher than ever. Three volumes of new papyri appeared in 1930, the year MM was published; in 1976, the year we report here, there were fifteen, though this seems an exceptionally prolific year. While much of this material may be repetitive, every year sees scores of items (words, names, usages, nuances) registered for the first time in the documentary record. There is a steady sharpening of focus open to students of the New Testament in these newly published texts.

But the flow of new material has also effectively swamped many items long since published. While papyrology may be relatively well served by cumulative works of reference, a systematic search of the epigraphic evidence becomes increasingly complex. There is usually no practical way by which a non-specialist, even one favoured with a comprehensive library, can secure an adequate sample of the evidence, let alone exhaust it, on any particular point. This review is therefore intended not only to report recently published texts, but also, in the course of doing so, to bring old ones once more to the surface.

In the preparation for this volume (1981) we have tried to take stock of the whole range of texts published in 1976 in *corpora* or *repertoria* or reprinted in 1976 from the journals in works such as *SEG* and *SB*. These last also reprint revised editions of texts already published. As usual, we include with the papyri the ostraca and any texts preserved in a similar way on other materials (e.g. wood, parchment), and with the inscriptions we may occasionally include other documentary artefacts (coins, engraved gemstones, etc.).

Our selection is made in the following way. One reader covered the whole body of material, noting documents which illustrate New Testament matters of any kind, or matters to do with the history of Judaism or Christianity to the sixth century (and occasionally even later), and selected for reporting a range of items which seemed interesting to him in this connection. Several other collaborators each read a small group of the 1976 publications to ensure that his choice was generally acceptable. We should welcome the collaboration of others both in sifting the material for future years, and in drawing to our notice items we have missed in the harvest of 1976.

The reports in this first number have almost all been written by Mr G. H. R. Horsley (Macquarie University), but revised in response to criticism by a number of collaborators in Australia and elsewhere. They have been deliberately composed, however, as a fresh digest of the ancient evidence, as prompted by the collections appearing in 1976. We have not attempted to take account of earlier studies, especially those readily accessible to New Testament students. We thought it better to use our limited time to help such readers find their way to the newly published sources, rather than to appraise the secondary literature. The risks in this are clear. We will have made mistakes which could have been corrected by wider reading, and we will have gone over some ground as though we were pioneers when others have already explored it. We expect to publish corrections, supplements and refinements in subsequent volumes. By expanding our circle of collaborators in this way, we hope to attune the review better to the interests of contemporary New Testament study and exegesis. The indices should progressively relate this piece-meal approach to a more orderly pattern.

The readers we have in mind are not those who are already masters of biblical or classical philology, let alone of epigraphy or papyrology. The review does not aim to make an independent contribution in any of these fields. Its purpose is to relay to a wider range of New Testament and other students the raw material that is constantly being produced by specialist editors. We report the views of editors without necessarily implying that we agree with them. Insofar as we have added comments of our own, that is to be taken simply as an attempt to promote communication between the disciplines. As with the selection of texts, such comment inevitably reflects individual interests. The artificiality of taking a single year's editorial production increases the random effect. No one supposes, for example, that we will have gathered an adequate sample from 1976 for the discussion of by-names (**55**). Yet the imagination demands that one attempt some connection if the material is not to be left a bare catalogue. We would not expect to treat such a topic substantially again for several years. Certain entries cover a range of questions, either thrown up by the text being treated, or arising tangentially in the course of discussion of it. In all these matters we have thought it more realistic to allow an individual touch to shape the presentation of the material.

We have not adopted any predetermined position about the relationship of the New Testament writings to their contemporary secular context. In particular, the appearance of this review does not constitute any judgement upon the source of New Testament ideas, nor does its concentration upon Greek documents imply any opinion on the relation of the New Testament to Judaism. We simply assume that, being written for Greek readers living in particular Greek-speaking communities, the New Testament writings will be better understood if we are aware of any other materials familiar to such readers. Nor do we mean to take up any position on how closely the papyri and inscriptions document the type of Greek used in the New Testament. They do, however, supply a growing pool of data, both linguistic and cultural, which varies the picture of the hellenistic world given by the literary sources, and this at least widens the contextual framework within which the language of the New Testament must eventually be located. We see the project partly as a documentary contribution to the *Corpus Hellenisticum Novi Testamenti.*

Why does such a review come from a School of History, Philosophy & Politics? At Macquarie University the study of the ancient world has been developed (since 1969) within this disciplinary framework. The result has been a combination of interests, linguistic and archaeological, historical and philosophical, classical and biblical, which has situated the New Testament as an object of study within a wide range of related ancient-world topics (rather than setting it within a theological or religious studies curriculum). The research efforts of the staff are linked in the Ancient History Documentary Research Centre.

At an early stage the School adopted papyrology as a point of concentration, and a systematic Corpus of Christian Papyri is being prepared. This in turn has sharpened our interest in how the contemporary documents could be brought to bear on New Testament studies (see my article, 'The Social Identity of the First Christians: a Question of Method in Religious History', *Journal of Religious History* 11 (1980), 201-217). The Rev. B. W. Winter first proposed that we should use the papyrological resources of the University to revise MM. For a short period in 1980, the University engaged Dr. C. J. Hemer, now Librarian of Tyndale House, Cambridge, as a visiting research fellow, to investigate the desirability and feasibility of this. His report on the matter is expected to appear in a forthcoming number of *Novum Testamentum* (1982). The present review may be seen as a second step towards the long-range project of revising MM. (See R. S. Bagnall, *Research Tools for the Classics* [Scholars Press 1980], p.52.) To that end, comments, mainly philological, are included in various entries which suggest qualification to, or new evidence for, MM's entry. The index of Greek words carries an asterisk beside each lemma where comment is made on MM's entry.

The financial support of the Sydney Diocesan Educational and Book Society is of particular importance. It is the oldest church society in this country, going back to the Diocesan Committee formed by W. G. Broughton after taking up the See of Australia in 1836. It was linked to the SPCK and SPG, and has by various stages like them come to concentrate its functions upon education and books. As with the Lutheran Church-Missouri Synod's support of the Chicago University Press in the production of BAGD, the Diocesan Book Society's support for us registers the common interest of church and university in promoting biblical research. In Moore Theological College the Anglican Diocese of Sydney has long fostered a lively centre of New Testament studies. Not a few of its advanced students and staff have been trained in philology and in *koine* Greek in the school of the late G. P. Shipp in the University of Sydney. The present project draws in more than one way upon this joint heritage.

For 1981 and 1982 Mr G. H. R. Horsley has undertaken to prepare this review. Our basis of working beyond that will be determined in the light of the response to the first volume. We cordially invite suggestions and criticisms, which should be addressed to Mr G. H. R. Horsley, School of History, Philosophy & Politics, Macquarie University, North Ryde, N.S.W. 2113, Australia.

December 1981   **E.A. Judge**

Introduction

This review is primarily a reporting journal, designed to make more widely known especially to biblical scholars published texts of philological and historical interest. Those who follow up the bibliographies to particular items will therefore find that much in these pages is derivative, although independent suggestions and comments are also offered.

The reader who has been mainly kept in mind during the writing of entries has been the NT researcher, teacher, and student. Readers should be clear that the review does not aim to provide definitive statements about any text treated. Undoubtedly some of the suggestions put forward in these pages will need correction or supplementation, and so **short notes** in reply (following the format of this volume) will be considered for inclusion. At present, the offer of long articles cannot be entertained.

While the main focus is upon the NT and the first four centuries, texts of later date have been included if it is judged that they may be of interest to students of that era (e.g. liturgical and homiletical texts; biblical citations). Some texts (e.g. **28,29)** have been included simply because they are representative of the times in some way, and make a general contribution to understanding NT background. It is envisaged that, as the review proceeds over a number of years, it will gradually form a *Chrestomathie* for those whose main focus of interest is the NT and Early Church History but who do not have ready access to the epigraphic and papyrological documents.

This volume treats texts published during 1976, either for the first time or as re-editions, in corpora and 'conspectus' volumes (such as *AE, SB, SEG*). Occasionally such a text will render necessary more-than-passing discussion of texts published at some earlier date, which were not re-published in 1976. Following the practice of *SEG,* we have not refrained from including occasional references to texts and discussions published after 1976, where they are relevant. The emphasis is heavily·upon Greek texts, although Latin documents and occasionally ones including Semitic words are noticed. Corpora consisting entirely of, e.g., Latin inscriptions, or hieroglyphic, demotic or Coptic papyri have not been taken into account.

Listed below are all collections for the year 1976 which have been read, arranged according to the abbreviations used in this volume. Where the abbreviation is bracketed, the work was read, but no texts were selected for noting in this volume. Unless otherwise specified, all references to texts throughout this review are to item numbers in the work whose abbreviation precedes it, not to page numbers. Volume number and date are provided throughout the review for all texts from non-1976 corpora. Where no volume number and date are given, the reference is to a publication of 1976 as listed below.

List of works read

AE   — *L'Année épigraphique 1976* [1980]

BE   — J. and L. Robert, *Bulletin épigraphique* in *Revue des études grecques* 89 (1976) 415-595 (also published separately)

BGU   — *Ägyptische Urkunden aus den staatlichen Museen zu Berlin. Griechische Urkunden* XIII. *Greek Papyri from Roman Egypt,* ed. W. M. Brashear (Berlin, 1976)

CPR   — *Corpus Papyrorum Raineri* V. *Griechische Texte* II, edd. J. Rea and P. J. Sijpesteijn (2 vols; Vienna, 1976)

I. Assos	— *Inschriften griechischer Städte aus Kleinasien* IV. *Die Inschriften von Assos,* ed. R. Merkelbach (Bonn, 1976)
I. Bankers	— *Epigraphica* III. *Texts on Bankers, Banking and Credit in the Greek World,* ed. R. Bogaert (*Textus Minores* XLVII; Leiden, 1976)
[*IG* IV 1²]	— *Inscriptiones Graecae* IV 1². *Inscriptiones Epidauri,* ed. F. Hiller von Gaertringen (Berlin, 1929; repr. Chicago, 1976)
IG Aeg.	— *Inscriptiones Graecae Aegypti* I. *Inscriptiones nunc Cairo in museo,* ed. J. G. Milne (Oxford, 1905; repr. Chicago, 1976)
IGLR	— *Inscripţiile greceşti şi latine din secolele IV-XIII descoperite in România (= Inscriptiones intra fines Dacoromaniae repertae graecae et latinae anno CCLXXXIV recentiores),* ed. E. Popescu (Bucharest, 1976)
I. Kyme	— *Inschriften griechischer Städte aus Kleinasien* V. *Die Inschriften von Kyme,* ed. H. Engelmann (Bonn, 1976)
IMS	— *Inscriptions de la Mésie supérieure, I. Singidunum et le nord-ouest de la province,* edd. M. Mirković and S. Dušanić (Belgrade, 1976)
ISE	— *Iscrizioni storiche ellenistiche* II, ed. L. Moretti (Florence, 1976)
[*I. Thess. Grab.*]	— *Thessalische Grabgedichte vom 6. bis zum 4. Jahrhundert v. Chr.,* ed. B. Lorenz (Innsbruck, 1976)
O.Amst.	— *Ostraca in Amsterdam Collections,* edd. R. S. Bagnall, P. J. Sijpesteijn, K. A. Worp (Zutphen, 1976)
O. Florida	— *The Florida Ostraca. Documents from the Roman Army in Upper Egypt,* ed. R. S. Bagnall (Durham, N. Carolina, 1976)
O.ROM	— *Ostraca in the Royal Ontario Museum* II, edd. R. S. Bagnall and A. E. Samuel (Toronto, 1976)
P.Coll. Youtie	— *Collectanea Papyrologica. Texts published in Honor of H. C. Youtie,* ed A. E. Hanson (2 vols; Bonn, 1976)
P. Köln	— *Kölner Papyri* I, edd. B. Kramer and R. Hubner (Cologne, 1976)
P. Laur.	— *Dai papiri della Biblioteca Medicea Laurenziana* I, ed. R. Pintaudi (Florence, 1976)
P. Oxy.	— *The Oxyrhynchus Papyri* XLIV, edd. A. K. Bowman, M. W. Haslam, J. C. Shelton, J. D. Thomas (London, 1976)
[*P. Saqqara*]	— *Excavations at North Saqqara. Documentary Series* I. *The Archive of Hor,* ed. J. D. Ray (London, 1976) [Mostly demotic texts; very few Greek]
P. Stras.	— *Papyrus grecs de la Bibliothèque Nationale et Universitaire de Strasbourg* V, 1-2, edd. J. Schwartz et al. (Strasbourg, 1976)
P. Tebt.	— *The Tebtunis Papyri* IV, edd. J. G. Keenan and J. C. Shelton (London, 1976)
[*P.Theon*]	— *The Family of the Tiberii Iulii Theones,* ed. P. J. Sijpesteijn (Amsterdam, 1976)
P.Vindob.Tandem	— *Fünfunddreissig Wiener Papyri,* edd. P. J. Sijpesteijn and K. A. Worp (Zutphen, 1976)
SB	— *Sammelbuch griechischer Urkunden aus Ägypten* XII, 1, ed. H. A. Rupprecht (Wiesbaden, 1976)
SEG	— *Supplementum Epigraphicum Graecum* 26 (1976/77) [1979]
[*SIA*]	— *Supplementum Inscriptionum Atticarum* I, ed. A. N. Oikonomedes (Chicago, 1976)

Abbreviations

Other abbreviations follow standard conventions, except where altered for clarity.

Journals — as in *L'Année philologique* (but note, e.g., *RAC* = *Reallexikon für Antike und Christentum,* not *Riv(ista) di Ant(ichità) Crist(iana)*).

Papyrological works — as in S. R. Pickering, *Papyrus Editions held in Australian Libraries* (North Ryde, N.S.W., 1974²), part 1, 'General List of Abbreviations'.

Epigraphical works (for which no standard guide exists) — according to generally used conventions (see LSJ), preceded where necessary by *I*. (e.g. *I. Kyme).*

Ancient authors, biblical and patristic works — generally as in LSJ, BAGD, and Lampe (see below)

Some other abbreviations used, occasionally frequently, in this volume:

BAGD	— Bauer/Arndt/Gingrich/Danker, *A Greek-English Lexicon of the New Testament and other Early Christian Literature* (Chicago, 1979²)
BDF	— Blass/Debrunner/Funk, *A Greek Grammar of the New Testament and other Early Christian Literature* (Chicago, 1961)
Bib. Pat.	— *Biblia Patristica. Index des citations et allusions bibliques dans la littérature patristique* (Centre d'analyse et de documentation patristiques; 3 vols; Paris, 1975-81)
CIJ	— J. B. Frey, *Corpus Inscriptionum Judaicarum* (2 vols; Rome, 1936, 1952); vol. 1 repr. with Prolegomenon by B. Lifshitz (New York, 1975)
CPJ	— V. A. Tcherikover, A. Fuks, et al., *Corpus Papyrorum Judaicarum* (3 vols; Cambridge [Mass.], 1957-64)
DACL	— Cabrol/Leclercq, et al., *Dictionnaire d'Archéologie chrétienne et de liturgie* (15 vols; Paris, 1907-1953)
Deissmann *LAE*	— A. Deissmann, *Light from the Ancient East* (Grand Rapids, 1980⁴)
ECL	— Early Christian Literature
fig.	— figure
Foraboschi	— D. Foraboschi, *Onomasticon Alterum Papyrologicum* (4 vols; Milan, 1966-71)
Hatch and Redpath	— Hatch and Redpath, *A Concordance to the Septuagint and other Greek Versions of the Old Testament* (Oxford, 1897; 2 vols. repr. Graz, 1954)
Lampe	— Lampe, *A Patristic Greek Lexicon* (Oxford, 1961, repr.)
LSJ/LSJ Suppl.	— Liddell/Scott/Jones, *A Greek-English Lexicon* (Oxford, 1940⁹, repr. with supplement ed. E. A. Barber 1968)
LXX	— Septuagint (Rahlfs' edition)
MM	— Moulton and Milligan, *The Vocabulary of the Greek Testament* (London, 1930; repr.)
Naldini	— M. Naldini, *Il Cristianesimo in Egitto. Lettere private nei papiri dei secoli II-IV* (Florence, 1968)
NB	— F. Preisigke, *Namenbuch . . . enthaltend alle . . . Menschennamen . . . in griechischen Urkunden . . . Ägyptens . . .* (Heidelberg, 1922)
ph./pl.	— photo/plate
Spoglio	— S. Daris, *Spoglio lessicale papirologico* (3 vols; Milan, 1968)
van Haelst	— J. van Haelst, *Catalogue des papyrus littéraires juifs et chrétiens* (Paris, 1976)
WB	— F. Preisigke, et al., *Wörterbuch der griechischen Papyrusurkunden* (Heidelberg, et alibi, 1924—)

An asterisk (*) beside a reference in the bibliography for an entry signifies, where more than one edition exists, which has been reprinted; otherwise the *editio princeps* has been followed.

Dates are AD unless otherwise marked. IV¹ = 'first half IVth century', IV² = 'second half IVth century'; etc.

Textual sigla used are as follows:—

αβ	— letters not completely legible
....	— 4 letters missing

[αβ]	— letters lost from document and restored by editor
[± 8]	— about 8 letters lost
⟨αβ⟩	— letters omitted by scribe and added by editor
(αβ)	— editor has resolved an abbreviation in the text
{αβ}	— letters wrongly added by scribe and cancelled by editor
[[αβ]]	— a (still legible) erasure made by scribe
`αβ´	— letters written above the line
α´ or ā	— letter stands for a numerical equivalent
v.,vv.,vac.	— one, two, several letter spaces left blank *(vacat)* on document
m.1, m.2	— first hand *(manus),* second hand
recto, verso	— The conventional front and back of a papyrus sheet.

The Format of most entries is as follows:—

Item no.	Short title
Provenance	date
editio princeps	
Text	
Brief descriptive comment	
Bibliography (very selective, normally including only actual references to the text)	
Translation	
Comment	

Where a text is not quoted in full or at all this format is somewhat modified, but should still be clear (e.g. Section B, *Minor Philological Notes).* Within the larger subdivisions of the review items have usually been arranged chiefly by genre (e.g., letters, epitaphs), and within that, chronologically. This arrangement does not apply to Section B, where entries are alphabetical; nor, of course, to Section F *(Varia).* In Section C entries follow canonical book order with non-biblical books at the end. Where an entry deals with a diversity of texts, it is placed in the genre grouping to which the first, usually the main, text belongs.

The **indices** are to be regarded as an integral element in the review. They will usually provide the easiest means of discovering which biblical words and passages are discussed, what ideas and institutions, etc.

Item numbers are in bold type throughout the review, for cross-referencing.

All entries are by G. H. R. Horsley, except for **9, 26, 81,** and **94** *bis,* which are by E. A. Judge. Translations have been made by the author of the entry.

For those wishing to refer to this Review, the **abbreviation** *NewDocs 1976* is suggested.

Acknowledgements

Advice from colleagues on specific matters is acknowledged in the appropriate entry. Frequent discussions with J. A. L. Lee (Sydney) and S. R. Pickering (Macquarie) have been particularly stimulating. The help of J. M. Arnold and S. Llewellyn, who volunteered their services as indexers, has been most welcome. More than all, E. A. Judge has been a constantly-available sounding board and encouragement to persevere. The trouble taken with the printing of this MS by P. Bell and D. Surtees in conjunction with our Secretary, should be placed on record. Should this volume prove useful even to some, let that be taken as a compliment to my parents, who encouraged me in my study of Classics, and to whom this work is offered in gratitude.

G. H. R. Horsley

A. NEW TESTAMENT CONTEXT

1. Invitations to the *kline* of Sarapis

Oxyrhynchos   II/III

ed. pr. — (a,b): J. F. Gilliam, *P.Coll.Youtie,* 51-5, pp.315-24 (pl.17); (c): L. Koenen, *ZPE* 1 (1967) 121-26 (pl.2) (= *P. Köln* 57, pp.175-77)

(a) ἐρωτᾷ σε Νικεφόρος δειπνῆσαι εἰς κλείνην τοῦ
κυρίου Σαράπιδος ἐν τῷ
λοχίῳ τῇ κ̅γ̅ ἀφ' ὥρας θ̅.

(b) ἐρωτᾷ σε Ἡραὶς δει-
πνῆσαι ἐν τῷ οἴκω
τοῦ Σαραπείου εἰς
κλείνην τοῦ κυρίου
Σαράπιδος αὔριον ἥ-
τις ἐστὶν ια ἀπὸ ὥρας
θ̅.

(c) καλεῖ σε ὁ θεὸς
εἰς κλείνην γεινο(μένην)
ἐν τῷ Θοηρείῳ
αὔριον ἀπὸ ὥρ(ας) θ'

Three texts to add to the small collection of very similarly-worded invitations to a banquet involving the god Sarapis. Almost certainly they were written by professional scribes.

Bib. — G. A. Deissmann, *LAE* 351; L. Castiglione, *A.Ant.Hung.* 9 (1961) 287-303 *(non vidi);* H. C. Youtie, *HTR* 41 (1948) 9-29 (= *Scriptiunculae* I [Amsterdam, 1973], 487-509; includes additional comments and bib.); L. Koenen, *ICS* 1 (1976) 154; further bib. in Gilliam, 316, n.6.

(a) **Nikephoros asks you to dine at a banquet of the lord Sarapis in the Birth-House on the 23rd, from the 9th hour.**

(b) **Herais asks you to dine in the (dining-) room of the Sarapeion at a banquet of the Lord Sarapis tomorrow, namely the 11th, from the 9th hour.**

(c) **The god calls you to a banquet being held in the Thoereion tomorrow from the 9th hour.**

The publication by Gilliam of the first two of the texts above brings to eleven the known examples of this specific type of invitation, namely to a banquet in honour of the god Sarapis. The formulae employed are notably similar to those of invitations to weddings, e.g., *P.Oxy.* 1(1898) 111(III); 3(1903) 524(II); 12(1916) 1486, 1487 (both IV); other examples listed in *P.Yale* 1(1967) 85, p.260; from 1976 texts add *P.Oxy.*

3202 (late III/early IV), an invitation to the crowning of a prytane. As for a literary allusion L. Koenen argues (*ICS* 1 [1976] 153-54) that Tib.1.7. 49-54 is an invocation to Sarapis (*qua* Osiris) to appear as a guest at Messalla's birthday party. Excepting the three reprinted above, the full list of Sarapis banquet invitations (which Gilliam tabulates) is: *P.Oxy.* 1(1898) 110(II); 3(1903) 523(II); 12(1916) 1484 (II/early III); 14(1920) 1755 (II/early III); 31(1966) 2592 (late I/II); *P.Osl.* 3(1936) 157 (II); *P.Yale* 1(1967) 85 (late II); O. Giannini, *ASNP* (ser.2) 35(1966) 18-19, no.7 (II/III). The reasonably small number extant has suggested two possibilities, that usually the invitation was merely oral (*P.Yale* 1, p.260), and that written invitations may have been sent as reminders (Gilliam, 318). Half these *kline* texts originated from Oxyrhynchos, and the others have tended to be accorded the same provenance. But these invitations were presumably not confined to Egypt, let alone that town, for we know that the cult of Sarapis spread well outside Egypt. In *CIL* XIII.8246 (= L. Vidman, *Sylloge inscriptionum religionis Isiacae et Sarapiacae* [Berlin, 1969] no.720) we are provided with epigraphical testimony to a *kline* at Cologne (II). *SEG* 967-969 prints three inscriptions related to the cult of Sarapis on Paros (III/IV; *ed. pr.* — A. K. Orlandos, *Arch.Eph.* (1975) 11-15, nos. 9, 10, 14 (cf. *BE* [1977] 342). Of special note is no. 968.9-10, εὐφράνθημεν.|εὐτυχῶς, 'nous avons banqueté dans une cérémonie rituelle' (*BE*).

Although it was a matter of some disagreement earlier in the century, there is now a clear consensus that these banquets had a fundamentally religious character: Sarapis was considered as being present for the dinner (see further below). The most clear-cut evidence for this is provided by Koenen's text, republished as *P.Köln* 57 —(c) above. This invitation is unique to the set: only here is the god himself the host who bids the guests attend. We know next to nothing about what occurred at these banquets, but there will have been some kind of sacrifice to the god as a matter of course, in addition to the meal. In another 1976 text, *P.Oxy.* 3164.3 (4/9/73 AD) ἱερὰν κλείνην occurs in a fragmentary context. In his petition (?) the priest proceeds to make clear that the sacrifices on behalf of the emperor have been performed. Here, apparently, the sacrifices are made to Sarapis (see editor's note, *ad loc.*).

Scholarly unanimity is lacking, but the view is held strongly that the cult of Sarapis was created by Ptolemy Soter in the late fourth century BC from the largely political motive that it might provide a unifying focus for the diverse peoples in that section of Alexander's empire over which he was endeavouring to assert control. This cult proved to be enormously popular — of all the pagan cults it was one of the longest-lived. By II AD its popularity had grown very much and it had spread well beyond the geographical confines of Egypt. For discussion of the cult and its expansion see Gilliam, 317, n.10 (dealing especially with Delos, where the cult was established by late III BC); more generally, F. Cumont, *Oriental Religions in Roman Paganism* (London, 1909²; repr. New York, 1956), 73-85; H. I. Bell *Cults and Creeds in Graeco-Roman Egypt* (Liverpool, 1953; repr. Chicago, 1975), 19-22; further bibliography in F. Sokolowski, *GRBS* 15(1974) 441, n.1. On the relevance of Aelius Aristides' prose-hymn to Sarapis (especially § 26-28) see Koenen, 122-23 and n.7; cf. A. D. Nock, *HTR* 37 (1944) 150-51 (= *Essays in Religion in the Ancient World* II [Oxford, 1972], 584).

The extant papyri invite guests to a variety of places, although most commonly the banquet is to be held in the Sarapeion (*P.Oxy.* 110, 2592; *ASNP* no.7), or a building/room attached to it. Of the latter we find specified a λόχιον (a, above), a hapax which

Gilliam (321) takes to refer to a shrine for Isis who was associated with women and childbirth; (b) above and *P.Oxy.* 1755 mention that the *kline* will take place in the *oikos* of the Sarapeion; this seems to mean a dining room attached to the temple complex. For this sense of *oikos* see especially L. Robert, *Arch.Eph.* (1969) 7-14, together with the other references given by Gilliam, 324. *P.Oxy.* 1484 and (c) above mention the Thoereion as the meeting-place: Koenen points out (123-24) that Thoeris was identified with the Greek Athena, and linked in a divine triad with Isis and Sarapis. All three remaining texts (*P.Oxy.* 523; *P.Osl.* 157; *P.Yale* 85) specify a private home as the venue. In like manner, a dinner in honour of Isis is held in the home of Sarapous (*P.Fouad* [1939] 76 [II; provenance unknown; pl. 1]). Similarly, wedding invitations did not request guests to attend at a religious site. *P.Oxy* 3 (1903) 524 (II) asks the invitee to come to Ischyrion's house.

Day and hour are given for the banquet, not the month. There is discernible a bunching of invitations around the middle of the month; it is possible that these banquets are being held in connection with a festival of Isis (cf. Koenen, 125-26; but Gilliam is cautious about this, 319). But despite being held in a public place, these dinners were not open to anyone. '. . . The cult meal, as a family celebration, was essentially a private affair' (*P.Yale* 1, p.264). For the possible involvement of a θίασος — the text is fragmentary at this point — see *P.Oxy.* 3164.2, alluded to above (cf. Koenen, 123). If many people were wanting to host such a gathering at a festival period in the second or third century (the time-span for the bulk of the *kline* invitations), space in the temple precinct itself may have been unattainable by some. This *may* serve to explain why some venues were private homes; and it may also suggest why the date for the *kline* was altered from the 10th to the 15th on *ASNP* no.7. There was clearly a preferred hour of the day, around 3.00 p.m. While some invitations include αὔριον in the invitation (e.g., nos. (b) and (c) above), it should not be assumed too readily that the banquets were *ad hoc* functions arranged very quickly. Youtie, *HTR* 41(1948) 15ff., publishes a text which makes plain that — at least in that instance — potential participants had two months' advance notice. So, too, in the case of the crowning of a prytane (*P.Oxy.* 3202, referred to above) it is unlikely that the date was decided only the day before.

Those invited to any particular *kline* will not have been many in number. In the archaeological excavations of the sanctuary of Demeter-Kore at Acrocorinth in Greece, some 40 dining-rooms had been discovered by the end of the 1973 season (N. Bookidis, *Hesperia* 43 [1974] 267). These vary in date of use mainly from VI - late IV BC, but also down to Mummius' sack of the city in 146 BC. Bookidis reports (p.272) that several are 5 × c. 4.5 m. square, could accommodate seven diners, and that cooking facilities in the rooms themselves were lacking. In an earlier report for the same site (*Hesperia* 38 [1969] 297-310) Bookidis discusses several of these dining-rooms in more detail. Room 13, for example (see her pl. 77b and 78a), could accommodate nine or ten banqueters at a time; a continuous couch (.80–.90m. wide, .55m high); while room 6 had similar remains around two walls (pl. 78b). Recent discussion of dining-rooms include E. Will, 'Banquets et salles de banquet dans les cultes de la Grèce et de l'Empire romain,' in *Mélanges d'histoire et d'archéologie offerts à Paul Collart* (Lausanne, 1976), 353-62; more generally, J. E. Stambrough, 'The Functions of Roman Temples', *ANRW* 16.1 (1978) 554-608.

This evidence, much earlier than and geographically distant from the Sarapeion at Oxyrhynchos, is nevertheless very relevant to our discussion, as Gilliam has intimated briefly (319-20). For the conclusion appears to be clear that the very notion of a *kline,* a banquet meal at which one reclined, is Hellenic, not Egyptian. J-M. Dentzer, *RA* (1971) 215-58, has shown that while there are Syrian illustrations of the reclining posture for meals the practice was not known in Egypt before the Ptolemaic period. (The earliest written allusion from Egypt to κλίνη = 'banquet' which I have been able to find is *PSI* 5[1917] 483, where the plural is used [258/7 BC, Philadelphia].) Nor is this practice depicted on Phoenician or Aramean pictures (Dentzer, 229). Hebrew custom was to eat sitting up: Dentzer (226-27) exploits well the evidence of Amos 6.4-7 in support of this conclusion. But in the Greek world it was entirely the norm to recline at banquets — though perhaps not at ordinary family meals — as many vase paintings show. It seems to be beyond question that the Greek world's practice gave rise to the *kline* associated with the cult of Sarapis. This is not a matter to occasion surprise. For despite the name of the god, it was a thinly-veiled Greek cult which Ptolemy I introduced (cf. Youtie, 13).

The presence of the god himself at the *kline* was alluded to earlier. This point is further supported by some extant coins from Alexandria and Egyptian terracotta which portray Sarapis reclining on a couch (Gilliam, 317). The Alexandria coins with this design would provide testimony to the importance of the cult in that Greek city in Egypt. Some of the terracottas may perhaps have had a collection-box function, to receive contributions towards the cost of the *kline* (ibid., n.9). This possibility may be strengthened by *P.Mich.* 8(1951) 511, which Youtie published earlier in *HTR.* That third-century text yields up other information about the cult of Sarapis; but suffice it to mention here that Ptolemaios refers in his letter to a fee he needs to pay as a novice attending the Sarapis *kline,* in addition to another monetary contribution which would guarantee him a place (τόπος) at the banquet. (In passing, Youtie, 17 n.38, draws attention to the use of this word in exactly the same sense at Lk. 14.9-10.)

Before we turn to consideration of the relevance of these invitations for the NT, one more detail should be observed. In (b) above a woman called Herais sends the invitation. Since it is rare for women to do the inviting — other examples, *P.Oxy.* 1(1898) 111 (wedding; presumably she is a widow); *P.Fouad* (1939) 76 (cult meal) — Gilliam plausibly infers (322-23) that Herais was 'a widow, or unmarried and the head of her household'. Her presence here proves that women certainly were present at a *kline,* and adds some weight to the view that these banquets were private meetings, not formal assemblies of members of an organised society.

There are obvious implications for the NT which flow from the discussion above about the '*kline* of Sarapis' invitations. Two matters will be considered here, both briefly: their relevance for an aspect of the Pauline communities in the Greek cities, esp. as alluded to in 1 Cor.; and the light which is thrown on the question of the Hellenisation of Palestine by some words in the gospels which deal with meal-taking.

The archaeological evidence from Corinth to which reference was made provides food for thought — at the least — about the size of the Christian groups meeting together for shared meals. We have no reason to suppose that Corinth was typical of the rest of the Greek world in its dining fashions. But it is a happy coincidence that Paul should allude to meal-invitations in his correspondence with the Christians from that city. Consider the remarkable uniformity in the wording of the papyrus invitations. καλεῖ is clearly a synonym for ἐρωτᾷ : the former appears only in (c) above of this group, though also in two marriage invitations as well as the invitation to the prytane's crowning alluded to above (*P.Oxy.* 3.1486, 1487; 3202). Of the eleven *kline* texts (c) above alone lacks the verb δειπνῆσαι. An interesting verbal affinity in the NT is 1 Cor. 10.27, εἴ τις καλεῖ ὑμᾶς τῶν ἀπίστων (εἰς δεῖπνον — these words only in D* G) κτλ. Further, the situation of 1 Cor. 8.10 may be seen in illuminating perspective when the *kline* invitations are taken into account. The latter, too, may be brought to bear on the elucidation of 1 Cor. 11.17-22. The papyrus invitations, then, document in quite a striking manner the situation which would have been known as normal and everyday by the recipient's of Paul's letters at Corinth, and no doubt elsewhere. But there is an implication of greater magnitude which emerges from the discussion.

The NT uses a number of verbs which sometimes denote reclining at a meal: ἀνάκειμαι (Mt. 26.20; Mk. 14.18; Lk. 22.27; Jn 13.23, 28 [cf. v.25 for the close proximity of the diners to one another]); κατάκειμαι (Mk. 14.3; Lk. 5.29, 7.37; 1 Cor. 8.10); ἀνακλίνω (Mt. 8.11 = Lk. 13.29; Lk. 12.37); κατακλίνω (Lk. 7.36, 14.8, 24.30; for the open-air meal for very large numbers at Lk. 9.14-15 [= Mk. 6.39, where note especially συμπόσια], cf. Hdt. 1.126.3). In the NT κλίνη (cf. κλινίδιον, κλινάριον) regularly means a 'bed'; nowhere does it refer to a dining couch. But cf. πρωτοκλισία (Lk. 14.7,8; at Mt. 23.6 a clear distinction is made between πρωτοκλισίαν ἐν τοῖς δείπνοις and πρωτοκαθεδρίας ἐν ταῖς συναγωγαῖς). In contrast, only once in the NT is καθίζω employed to refer to a meal setting (1 Cor. 10.7); and it is to be noted that this is a question from Ex. 32.6, dealing with an event well before the penetration of Greek influence into Jewish mores. Now, the most arresting aspect about this list of references is that all but one of the examples come from the gospels: all but one deal with Palestine. This evidence accords very well with the visual evidence collected by Dentzer. For if the custom of the *kline* was pre-eminently a Greek style of banqueting, it has made its appearance in a thorough-going manner in first-century Palestine, and that not merely in the cities. As with the introduction of the fashion to Egypt under the Ptolemies, so we have evidence from Palestine for the ubiquitous spread of Hellenism. Furthermore, the passages given above reveal that the custom is not confined to urban areas, and that Pharisees invite guests to meals conducted in this manner (Lk. 6.36-37). So typical must the *kline* have been that parables can be told in which this fashion is alluded to (Lk. 12.37; 14.7 ff.). Even the Heavenly Banquet at which the patriarchs will be in attendance is conceived in these terms (Mt. 8.11 = Lk. 13.29). One final inference may — perhaps — be drawn from this brief study of the words.

If the last supper (Jn. 13.22 ff.) were a Passover meal one might expect that orthodox Jews would not have reclined at least on this occasion, however much they may have done so in other situations. Either the words in vv.23 and 28 may provide minor support for the view that this was not a Passover meal; or else this passage reveals *a fortiori* how thoroughly normal this Greek fashion was felt to be by pious first-century Jews from rural Galilee. At numerous places where there are allusions to meals, the English translations (such as the RSV) obscure how perfectly usual for first-century Palestine was this once distinctively Greek fashion.

To revert to the importance for the NT background of these everyday invitations to meals from Egypt, I can do no better than quote Gilliam (314, n.1): '. . . trivial and ephemeral as the invitations may appear to be, they reflect some of the most pervasive and persistent religious ideas of their time, as well as the mutual penetration and interaction of Greek and native elements in the daily life and civilisation of Hellenistic and Roman Egypt.'

2. A personalised Aretalogy of Isis

Maroneia (Macedonia)   II²/I¹BC
ed. pr. — Y. Grandjean, *Une nouvelle arétalogie d'Isis à Maronée* (Leiden, 1975); (pls. 1-3)

ΑΥΤΗΣ

ἐλ]άμβανον γὰρ

ν] θεωρήσειν, οἵαν πρὸς τὸ μέγεθος

[τῆς σῆς εὐε]ργεσίας οἱ λόγοι τῶν ἐπαίνων μὴ ἐλλίπωσιν· ἦι δέ

5   [σε ἐ]ρωτᾶ τὸ μὲν ἐγκώμιον· τὸ δὲ προσώπου θεῶι κείμενον

[οὐκ ἀν]θρώπωι· ὥσπερ οὖν ἐπὶ τῶν ὀμμάτων, Ἴσι, ταῖς εὐχαῖς

[ἐπήκ]ουσας, ἐλθὲ τοῖς ἐπαίνοις καὶ ἐπὶ δευτέραν εὐχήν·

[κα]ὶ γὰρ τὸ σὸν ἐγκώμιον τῶν ὀμμάτων ἐστὶ κρεῖσσον,

[ὅτ]αν οἷς ἔβλεψα τὸν ἥλιον, τούτοις καὶ τὸν σὸν βλέπω κόσμον·

10   πείθομαι δὲ πάντως σε παρέσεσθαι· εἰ γὰρ ὑπὲρ τῆς ἐμῆς καλουμέ-

νη σωτηρίας ἦλθες, πῶς ὑπὲρ τῆς ἰδίας τιμῆς οὐκ ἂν ἔλθοις; θαρ-

ρῶν οὖν πορεύομαι πρὸς τὰ λοιπά, γινώσκων ὅτι τὸ ἐγκώμιον,

νοῦς μὲν θεοῦ, χεῖρες δὲ γράφουσιν ἀνθρώπου· καὶ πρῶ-

τον ἐπὶ τὸ γένος ἥξω, τῶν ἐγκωμίων ποιησάμενος ἀρχὴν

15   τὴν πρώτην σου τοῦ γένους ἀρχήν· Γῆν φασι πάντων μη-

τέρα γενηθῆναι· ταύτηι δὲ σὺ θυγάτηρ ἐσπάρης πρώτηι·

σύνοικον δ' ἔλαβες Σέραπιν, καὶ τὸν κοινὸν ὑμῶν θεμένων γάμον,

τοῖς ὑμετέροις προσώποις ὁ κόσμος ἀνέλαμψεν ἐνομματισθεὶς

Ἡλίωι καὶ Σελήνηι· δύο μὲν οὖν ἐστε, καλεῖσθε δὲ πολλοὶ παρ' ἀν-

20   θρώποις· μόνους γὰρ ὁ βίος ὑμᾶς θεοὺς οἶδεν· πῶς οὖν τῶν

ἐγκωμίων οὐ δυσκράτητος ὁ λόγος ὅταν δέηι τὸν ἔπαινον

πολλοῖς θεοῖς προναῶσαι; Αὕτη μεθ' Ἑρμοῦ γράμμαθ' εὗρεν

καὶ τῶν γραμμάτων ἃ μὲν ἱερὰ τοῖς μύσταις, ἃ δὲ δημόσια

τοῖς πᾶσιν· αὕτη τὸ δίκαιον ἔστησεν ἵν' ἕκαστος ἡμῶν,

25   ὡς ἐκ τῆς φύσεως τὸν θάνατον ἴσον ἔσχεν, καὶ ζῆν ἀπὸ τῶν

ἴσων εἰδῆι· αὕτη τῶν ἀνθρώπων οἷς μὲν βάρβαρον, οἷς δ' ἑλλη-

νίδα διάλεκτον ἔστησεν ἵν' ἦι τὸ γένος διαλλάσσον μὴ μό-

νον ἀνδράσιν πρὸς γυναῖκας ἀλλὰ καὶ πᾶσι πρὸς πάντας·

[σ]ὺ νόμους ἔδωκας, θεσμοὶ δ' ἐκαλοῦντο κατὰ πρώτας· τοι-

30   [γα]ροῦν αἱ πόλεις εὐστάθησαν, οὐ τὴν βίαν νομικὸν ἀλλὰ

[τ]ὸν νόμον ἀβίαστον εὑροῦσαι· σὺ τιμᾶσθαι γονεῖς ὑπὸ

[τ]έκνων ἐποίησας, οὐ μόνον ὡς πατέρων, ἀλλ' ὡς καὶ θεῶν

[φ]ροντίσασα· τοιγαροῦν ἡ χάρις κρείσσων ὅτε τῆς φύσε-

ως τὴν ἀνάγκην καὶ θεὰ νόμον ἔγραψεν· σοὶ πρὸς κατοίκησιν

35   Αἴγυπτος ἐστέρχθη· σὺ μάλιστα τῆς Ἑλλάδος ἐτίμησας τὰς

Ἀθήνας· κεῖθι γὰρ πρῶτον τοὺς καρποὺς ἐξέφηνας· Τριπτόλε-

μος δὲ τοὺς ἱεροὺς δράκοντάς σου καταζεύξας ἁρματοφο-

ρούμενος εἰς πάντας Ἕλληνας διέδωκε τὸ σπέρμα· τοιγαροῦν

τῆς μὲν Ἑλλάδος ἰδεῖν σπεύδομεν τὰς Ἀθήνας, τῶν δ' Ἀθη-

40 νῶν Ἐλευσῖνα, τῆς μὲν Εὐρώπης νομίζοντες τὴν πόλιν, τῆς
    δὲ πόλεως τὸ ἱερὸν κόσμον· ἔγνω τὸν βίον ἐξ ἀνδρὸς
    συνεστηκότα καὶ γυναικός· ἔγνω   τερον τὴν γυ-
    ναῖκα· πῶς ἔδει τὸ ἧσσον
    Ν ἐσφραγισ

On palaeographical grounds this is the earliest of extant aretalogies of Isis. The inscription was discovered in 1969 at Maroneia, modern Kambana, though the beginning and end of the text are lost. Three other inscriptions relating to Egyptian gods have been found in the city (Grandjean, Appendix 2, pp.118-21; pls. 4-5).

Bib. — *SEG* 821; R. Merkelbach *ZPE* 23 (1976) 234-35; F. Solmsen, *Isis among the Greeks and Romans* (Cambridge, Mass., 1979) 45. Text follows Grandjean, but incorporates some of Merkelbach's corrections to the first few lines. The reading at the beginning of *l.*9 (suggested by F. W. Danker in a note to me) replaces *ed. pr.,* and Merkelbach's ἄπ]αν'.

(*l.*3) . . . may words of praise not be lacking in the face of the magnitude of your
5   benefaction. Therefore |this encomium entreats you, and praise for my face belongs to a goddess not with a man. So, just as in the case of my eyes, Isis, you listened to my prayers, come for your praises and to hear my second prayer; for the praise of you is entirely more important than my eyes whenever with the
10 same eyes with which I saw the sun I see your world. |I am completely confident that you will come again. For since you came when called for my salvation, how would you not come for your own honour? So taking heart I proceed to what remains, knowing that this encomium is written not only by the hand of a man, but also by the mind of a god. And first I shall come to your family, making
15 as the beginning of my praises |the earliest beginnings of your family. They say that Ge was the mother of all: you were born a daughter to her first. You took Sarapis to live with you, and when you had made your marriage together the world, provided with eyes, was lit up by means of your faces, Helios and Selene.
20 So you are two but have many designations among men. |For you are the only ones whom (everyday) life knows as gods. Therefore, how would the account of your praises not be unmanageable when one must praise many gods at the outset? She with Hermes discovered writing; and of this writing some was sacred for initiates, some was publicly available for all. She instituted justice, that each
25 of us might know how to live on equal terms, |just as, because of our nature, death makes us equal. She instituted the non-Greek language for some, Greek language for others, in order that the race might be differentiated not only as between men and women, but also between all peoples. You gave laws, but they
30 were called *thesmoi* originally. |Accordingly, cities enjoyed tranquillity, having discovered not violence legalised, but law without violence. You made parents honoured by their children, in that you cared for them not only as fathers, but also as gods. Accordingly, the favour is greater when a goddess also drew up as
35 law what is necessary in nature. As a domicile |Egypt was loved by you. You particularly honoured Athens within Greece. For there first you made the earth produce food: Triptolemos, yoking your sacred snakes, scattered the seed to all Greeks as he travelled in his chariot. Accordingly, in Greece we are keen to see

40   **Athens and in Athens, Eleusis, |considering the city to be the ornament of
Europe, and the sacred place the ornament of the city. She determined that life
should cohere from a man and a woman . . .**

This is one of a small group of Greek texts which praise Isis via an evocation of
her powers, influence, and manifestations. Diodorus Siculus 1.27 is our only example
— incomplete — that has survived in the literary tradition. Four other inscriptions
have been found:

a.   Andros (I BC; very damaged; in hexameters; discovered 1842; reprinted in *IG* XII
      5, 739);

b.   Kyme (I/II; complete; discovered 1925; repub. most recently as *I. Kyme* 41 —
      reprinted below);

c.   Thessalonike (I/II; very fragmentary; discovered 1920; published 1934, repub.
      most recently as *IG* X 2,254);

d.   Ios (III, fragmentary; discovered 1877; repub. *SEG*[3] 1267; Deissmann, *LAE*,
      136-42).

These aretalogies appear to be derived from a common source in Egypt. The
opening lines of *I. Kyme* 41 state that the inscription was a copy of an original set
up in the temple of Hephaistos (= Ptah) in Memphis. Yet there has been considerable
debate in the past whether the common ancestor of these texts — for a stemma see
I. Kyme, p.101 — was written in Egyptian or Greek. The view that the original was
in Greek seems to have prevailed, due largely to the arguments of A. D. Nock,
Gnomon 21 (1949) 221-28 (= *Essays* II, 703-11), and A. J. Festugière, *HTR* 42 (1949)
209-34 (= *Etudes de religion grecque et hellénistique* [Paris, 1972], 138-63), against the
thesis of R. Harder that they are Greek translations of an Egyptian original
(*Karpokrates von Chalkis und die memphitische Isispropaganda* [Berlin, 1944]).

This small group of texts forms part of a larger body of aretalogies, invocations and
hymns for various gods — especially Egyptian ones — which survive from places as
far apart as Africa and Asia Minor, on papyri (perhaps above all, *P.Oxy.* 11 [1915]
1380), on stone, and in our literary sources (most notably Apuleius *Metamorphoses*
11.5.1-5). These texts span about 400 years, II/I-III/IV; a list is conveniently
assembled by Grandjean, 8-11. As with the cult of Sarapis, the worship of Isis spread
from Egypt throughout the Greek world in the Hellenistic period. Aretalogies such as
this recently discovered one from Maroneia (at this time part of the Roman province
of Macedonia) are to be understood on at least one level as instruments of
propaganda, designed to publicise the cult and the beneficence of the god. But
Solmsen may be right (43) to doubt that they have this as their primary function. For
it is quite evident from the personal details in this newest aretalogy for Isis that a
genuine gratitude and devotion lie behind the wording. Even in the case of *I. Kyme*
41, where the only individual touch occurs in *ll.*1-2, we should be wary of dismissing
personal piety as a motive for the setting up of the stele. These statements in praise
of Isis allow us a useful glimpse of the ideas which Hellenistic Greeks and Romans
had about Isis: she is a universal goddess who has exerted a civilising influence upon
society; she is the protector of women and the family, as well as of other groups in
society (e.g. sailors); and she offers to those initiated into her mysteries a special
relationship and a special perception of the world.

It is not surprising that these aretalogies have attracted a large secondary literature, for they are of first importance for the study of religious cult and religious attitudes in the late Hellenistic and Roman world. For bibliography about Isis see Grandjean, and Solmsen. Yet apart from Deissmann, and very recently H. C. Kee, *Christian Origins in Sociological Perspective* (Philadelphia, 1980), 155-61, there has been curiously little interest taken in these epigraphical texts by NT scholars. On the other hand literary biographies of itinerant holy men (such as Apollonius and Pythagoras) have been exploited with some considerable effect, and 'aretalogies' of this kind are now a regular element in 'Divine Man' studies. (A shift in the orientation of the term 'aretalogy' thus appears to be occurring, for while mortals are not excluded the term is more usually understood by classicists of a text in praise of a god.) Still important is L. Bieler, ΘΕΙΟΣ ΑΝΗΡ. *Das Bild des 'göttlichen Menschen' in Spätantike und Frühchristentum* (1935-36; 2 vols. repr. in one, Darmstadt, 1976). C. R. Holladay, *'Theios Aner' in Hellenistic Judaism* (Missoula, 1977), offers a critical analysis of the application of the term to NT Christology, but includes no discussion of aretalogies. Among fairly recent discussions of aretalogies one may cite M. Hadas and M. Smith, *Heroes and Gods* (1965; repr. Freeport, N.Y., 1970); M. Smith, *JBL* 90 (1971) 174-99; D. L. Tiede, *The Charismatic Figure as Miracle Worker* (Missoula, 1972; his first four pages deal with Isis aretalogies); H. C. Kee, *JBL* 92 (1973) 402-22; J. Z. Smith, in *Christianity, Judaism, and other Greco-Roman Cults, I: New Testament*, ed. J. Neusner (Leiden, 1975), 21-38. While these discussions note the Isis aretalogies, the inscriptions still await thorough treatment by students of this branch of NT studies.

The two aretalogies reprinted here have been included not simply because they are caught up in the 1976 'net', but also because of the distinctive importance of each. The example from Kyme is the most important of the whole group because of its completeness and because of its form (those from Andros, Thessalonike, and Ios are very akin in form to it). It will be treated below. In contrast the Maroneia text is quite distinct in form from the others, and is the earliest yet discovered. Readers are referred to Grandjean's monograph for detailed explication of the text; a few general points are offered here, some links with the NT suggested, and comment made on some details of the text.

Of the extant wording there is a preamble, which takes the form of an invocation (4-15), followed by the aretalogy proper, which itself treats the *genos* of Isis (15-22) and her εὑρήματα and ἔργα (22-42). For a detailed analysis of the structure, see Grandjean, 106,n.13. While written in prose the text contains numerous metrical clausulae (cf. Grandjean's analysis, App. 1, pp.115-117). This is one indicator of the rhetorical genre to which this encomiastic work formally belongs. Distinctive of the Maroneia inscription, too, is the use of second and third person statements: contrast the Kyme text below. The care with which the statements are presented in sequence to one another sets the new aretalogy sharply apart from the haphazard order in the other examples. Examples abound of anaphora, chiasmus, rhetorical use of the interrogative form of sentence, play on words (e.g., ἐνομματίζω, 18; cf. ὄμμα, 4; βίαν νομικόν ... νόμον ἀβίαστον, 30-31); particles are common (note, e.g., μὲν ... δέ ... at 15, 19, 23, 26, 39, 40-41). There are three *hapax legomena*: ἐνομματίζω (18), προναόω (22), ἀρματοφορέω (37-38). Yet it is a matter for some surprise that the language of such a text is so 'pure': Koine influence is scarcely felt, and even hiatus is avoided (cf. Grandjean, 109). This abundance of rhetorical features and the concern for logical sequence point to some public occasion — a festival of Isis, perhaps — at which the text will have been declaimed (Grandjean, 109). This need not be inconsistent with the author's reason for writing this praise of Isis, namely his gratitude for the miraculous healing of an eye complaint (3-9).

Adherence to Greek rhetorical conventions in this aretalogy shows clearly that, whatever its ancestry may have been in Egypt, in the form in which they survive these aretalogies were written by and for Greeks in Greek cities. They are to be seen as a Greek interpretation of Isis. The only unequivocally Egyptian allusion in the Maroneia text occurs in *ll.* 34-35 (though cf. 23). It is noteworthy that there should be less Egyptian 'colouring' in this earliest example and more in the later ones. But this may have to be attributed to the very idiosyncratic nature of this newest one. Distinctive features there may be, but Grandjean shows (App. 3, pp.122-124) how indisputably related by a common ancestry is this text with the Kyme aretalogy (and hence with the others which closely adhere to it in form). Further confirmation of this view of the text as a Greek interpretation of Isis may be found in the assimilation of Isis and Demeter, and the emphasis on Athens and the Eleusinian mysteries (35-41; cf. τοῖς μύσταις, 23). The inscription confirms that there were mystery rites associated with Isis in Greece (and in Egypt?) before the Roman period.

Our text bears witness to the writer's personal faith in Isis, and is comparable in this respect with the document concerning the cult of Saturn (**4**). The person who composed this encomium of Isis, 'initié sans aucun doute aux mystères éleusiniens, nous apparait comme un homme profondément religieux, confiant dans la toute puissance de la déesse. Ses convictions se manifestent non seulement à travers son comportement — glorification du dieu, humilité personnelle, gratitude, foi en l'aide divine — mais encore dans le choix de termes ou d'expressions empruntées au vocabulaire religieux ... Ainsi ce texte, expression d'une foi véritable, porte témoignage des relations, d'ordre mystique, qui pouvaient unir à cette époque le croyant et son dieu' (Grandjean, 105). Grandjean's point about religious vocablulary raises sharply for us a distinction to be made with the NT. For Paul in particular avoids using cultic terms in what might be thought cultic contexts, but appears to use them by design in passages of the letters which certainly have no cultic significance (e.g. μνέω, μυστήριον). For philological points of contact with the NT note the following. θεωρέω (3) of 'spiritual' perception, Jn. 14.17, 19; 17.24; εὐεργεσία (4), Acts 4.9; ἐπακούω (7), 2 Cor. 6.2 (quoting Is. 49.8); κόσμος (9, 18), examples in BAGD, s.v., 2; for the sense at *l.*41, 1 Pet. 3.3; πάρειμι (10), see **35**; σωτηρία (11) of physical preservation is not a NT sense (though cf. Acts 27.34; Heb. 11.7); but see **4**; σύνοικος (17), not NT, but cf. συνοικέω at 1 Pet. 3.7. Solmsen (127, n.4) believes that the word refers not to marriage but to Sarapis as the 'sharer of Isis' temple'. διάλεκτος (27, cf. *I. Kyme* 41.31, below) Acts 1.19; 2.6, 8; 21.40; 22.6; 26.14; διαλλάσσω (27), middle at Mt. 5.24 ('reconcile'); Grandjean (83-84) thinks this sense is required in the inscription, but the active has to be taken as 'differentiate'; νομικός (30), cf. Tit. 3.9; χάρις (33), frequent in NT; ἀνάγκη (34), frequent but usually impersonal in NT; κατοίκησις (34), Mt. 5.3. The following words occur in ECL (for references see BAGD, s.vv.): ἐλλείπω (4), εὐσταθέω (30); στέργω (35).

At the most general level, perhaps the nearest equivalent to an aretalogy like this in the NT is the Magnificat (Lk. 1.46-55) — leaving aside its OT associations. More specifically, while the NT statements about children honouring their parents (Eph. 6.1-2; Col. 3.20) hark back to the Decalogue (Ex. 20.12), this same sentiment is present in the inscription at *ll.*31-32. Such an attitude was well-known and accepted by non-Jews throughout the Greek world and elsewhere, well before the Hellenistic age. As one example of how basic this was, a potential magistrate at Athens in the fourth century could be rejected from assuming office if witnesses could show that he did not treat his parents well (Arist. *Ath.Pol.* 55.3-4).

Several points should be made about the particular contents of the inscription.

(i)   Isis is not only a goddess who cures eye diseases (6-7); she also inflicts blindness (Grandjean, 25-26).

(ii)   The (restored) verb ἐπακούω (7) is very appropriate for her, for the epithet ἐπήκοος is often attached to her name. *I. Kyme* 43 (III pl.12) is a dedication to Isis, above which are carved two ears: Δωροθέα κατὰ πρόσ|ταγμα τῆς Εἴσεως. See Engelmann's n. to that inscription, p.109. The standard treatment of the epithet is O. Weinreich, 'θεοὶ ἐπήκοοι', *Ath.Mitt.* 37 (1912) 1-68 (= *Ausgewählte Schriften* I [Amsterdam, 1966], 131-95). Other attestations from 1976 publications include *SEG* 1143 (Pisa, II¹), above which are three pairs of ears, symbolising the Alexandrian triad, Harpokrates, Sarapis and Isis: θεοῖς ἐπηκόοις ἀνέ|θηκεν Τ. Φλάουιος Φαρνουτιάνους Ῥούφους. *SEG* 1149 is a dedication from Ostia, Διὶ Ἡλίω μεγάλω ἐπη[κόῳ Σα]ράπ[ιδι] (reign of Hadrian). T. Drew-Bear, *GRBS* 17 (1976) 267-68, no.20 (pl. 10) published a text on an altar in Phrygia on which the dedication is to ἐπη|κόῳ | θεῷ Ἀπό|λωνι (= *SEG* 1389; cf. *BE* [1977] 485).

(iii)   Although the rhetoricians made a distinction between ἔπαινος and ἐγκώμιον, the words are synonymous in this aretalogy (4, 5, 7, 8, 14; cf. Grandjean, 24, n.5).

(iv)   As with the particular meaning of θεωρέω (3) in religious contexts, so βλέπω at the end of *l.*9 refers not to physical perception but to spiritual contemplation (Grandjean, 32).

(v)   The writer seeks divine aid to write his eulogy (10-13): notions of divine inspiration implied here are discussed at length by Grandjean, 34-37, 39-43. This attitude had a long tradition in the Greek world, from Homer onwards, and is discussed most fully by Plato. See R. Harriott, *Poetry and Criticism before Plato* (London, 1969), esp. 78-91; most recently, P. Murray, *JHS* 101(1981) 87-100. It may be worth raising the question, if only in passing, to what extent Greek ideas about divine aid for the composition of written work meshed with Jewish views, and whether Christians were influenced at all by the former. This matter may be relevant in the case of the NT *locus classicus,* 2 Tim. 3.16-17 (cf. 2 Pet. 1.21), but of more significance for patristic commentators, especially those strongly influenced by Middle Platonism (e.g., Clement of Alexandria) and for the question of the formation of the NT Canon.

(vi)   For the παρουσία of a god (10), see **35**; Grandjean provides several further examples (34, n.45).

(vii)   Isis is frequently invoked as *soteira* (11), Grandjean 26-30, 37-38.

(viii)   θαρρέω (11-12) has a technical connotation in religious contexts, especially those involving initiation into mystery cults where the death and resurrection of a god is celebrated. Grandjean (43, n.66) cites Firmicus Maternus, *de errore* 22.1, θαρρεῖτε μύσται τοῦ θεοῦ σεσωσμένου· |ἔσται γὰρ ἡμῖν ἐκ πόνων σωτηρία. The verb is particularly relevant in our inscription, therefore, in view of allusions to mystery cults with which Isis is associated (29, 39-41).

(ix)   The aretalogy proper (15ff.) exhibits numerous differences from the standard form, insofar as that can be reconstructed from the other examples. First, this author has chosen his own order of treatment of the topics, and has tidied up the haphazard sequence visible in the others which their putative common ancestor must have shared (see discussion above). Second, the genealogy differs markedly, for elsewhere Isis is daughter of Kronos (= Egyptian Geb, god of earth). The reason for this change is at least partly to make the Maroneia aretalogy more distinctively Greek and less obviously Egyptian in 'colouring'; partly, too, because the cult of Ge was important in Attika and was linked with the Eleusinian mysteries (in some mythic accounts Ge = Demeter). On all this, see Grandjean, 44-53.

(x)   Isis' active role in her relationship with Sarapis is marked by ἔλαβες (17). The union of these two deities (17) was regarded as a symbol of legitimate marriage. Isis' concern with marriage, childbirth, and the family is more explicit in *I. Kyme* 41, but in the Maroneia inscription note *ll*.31-33, 41-42.

(xi)   These two gods are here personified by the Moon and the Sun (19); and the notion of lighting up the world is to be understood on the level of Isis and Sarapis as the divine bestowers of civilising influences upon humanity. A somewhat different point is in view in Jesus' claim to be τὸ φῶς τοῦ κόσμου (Jn. 8.12). A strikingly close parallel to this statement in the Fourth Gospel occurs in an inscription from Bithynia (I AD) in which Isis is spoken of as a φῶς πᾶσι βροτοῖσι (L. Vidman, *Sylloge inscriptionum religionis Isiacae et Sarapiacae* [Berlin, 1969] no.325; cited by Grandjean, 61). A good deal of the remainder of the aretalogy is devoted to enumerating the beneficent interest which Isis has taken in human society (invention of writing, allocation of languages, provision of law for cities ensuring their peaceful existence, etc.). An inscription in honour of the goddess Roma speaks of Θεὰ[ν Ῥώ]μην [τ]ὴν εὐεργέτιν τοῦ κόσμ[ου] (*I. Assos* 20.2; principate of Augustus or Tiberius). For further references to this notion see Merkelbach's n., *ad loc.* cf. εὐεργεσία in the Isis aretalogy above, *l*.4.

(xii)   Isis and Sarapis as universal gods is the point being made at *ll*.19-20. The epithets πολυώνυμος and μυριώνυμος were commonly attached to them; and the author alludes to this in a restrained manner, by avoiding listing all those other names by which they were known, such as is done in *P.Oxy.* 11 (1915) 1380 (early II). One may wonder whether the ascription of such epithets to deities in the late Hellenistic and Roman world is one element behind the thinking of Phil. 2.9-11. The universality of these two gods is suggested further in *l*.20 when the author says that they are 'the only ones to preside over all the moments of human life' (Grandjean, 69).

(xiii)   With *ll*.22-24 begins the enumeration of Isis' 'virtues'. At this point the author abandons second-person address in favour of third-person narration. There is a return to second person at *l*.29; at *l*.41 third person resumes again. Isis as the inventor of writing with Hermes is a notion common to the other aretalogies. The reference to hieroglyphic and demotic scripts is not to be taken simply as an allusion to the Egyptian situation, but together with τοῖς μύσταις it looks forward primarily to the praise of Eleusis later in the text.

(xiv)   Isis is occasionally identified with Dikaiosyne (cf. *ll*.24-26; Grandjean, 79).

(xv)   It is an Egyptian idea — found also in the Near East (Gen. 11) — that the plurality of languages is a divine creation (26-28); but another indication of the Hellenic orientation of this aretalogy is that the author makes a distinction between Greek and non-Greek speakers (cf. Grandjean, 82-83). At Col. 3.11 Paul seems to be alluding to two fundamental distinctions in the one breath: that between Jews and Greeks (i.e. non-Jews?), and that between Greeks and Barbarians. The former is a distinction on the basis of religious outlook, the latter due to language. (Skythians are mentioned as an expansion of the allusion to Barbarians, since they were popularly

held to be the most barbaric of non-Greek peoples. Lightfoot's note on the word —
Comm., ad loc. — is still the best.) There is no need for διαλλάσσω in the aretalogy
here to mean 'harmonise, reconcile', as Grandjean thinks (83-84). It can have its
ordinary active sense 'differentiate' without implying at all that Isis is exercising a
divisive influence. We are to perceive Isis here as the giver of enriching diversity to
the creation.

(xvi)   Isis' civilising role is also to the fore in her capacity as lawgiver and legislator
(29-31). These statements are thoroughly Greek (note that it is the *polis* which is in
view), and may be compared with other aretalogies in which Isis brings tyranny to an
end (e.g. *I. Kyme* 41.26-27). The text from Kyme repeatedly mentions Isis' legislative
function.

(xvii)   Isis' requirement of filial duty towards parents (31-34) features also in the
other related texts: the goddess has made people respect a natural principle. The
phrase τιμᾶσθαι γονεῖς is an echo of an Eleusinian precept (γονεῖς τιμᾶν) which will
have been familiar to the author if he were an initiate, as seems reasonable to infer
(Grandjean, 89). The notion of likening a parent to a god does occur elsewhere in
popular Greek thinking, usually after the death of the parent where it becomes blurred
with the notion of the Hero (e.g., from Greek tragedy, Soph. *El.* 184; A. *Pers.* 634,
641ff., 711, 854f. — see H. D. Broadhead's commentary [Cambridge, 1960], xxviii.
On the synonymy of δαίμων with θεός, suggested by comparison of *Pers.* 634 and
854f., cf. E. *Phoen.* 413f.). Grandjean (88-89) cites a papyrus letter from the Roman
period (= *SB* 3 [1926] 6263.27-28) in which one brother writes to another about their
mother: ὀφίλομεν γὰρ σέβεσθαι (-εσθε, Grandjean) τὴν τεκοῦσαν ὡς | θε[όν], μάλειστα
τοιαύτην οὖσαν ἀγαθήν, 'For we ought to respect as a god her who bore us, especially
since she is a person of such goodness.'

(xviii)   The identification of Isis with Demeter has been alluded to above: this
merging is attested as early as Herodotos (2.59, 156). Yet another of Isis' aspects is
here mentioned, for she had a function as an agrarian god in the Graeco-Roman
world. Hence the claim that she revealed such matters first to people at Athens (36).

(xix)   The inscription provides an insight into the view of Athens as the 'centre of
everything' in the late Hellenistic world. That Athens still exercised some kind of
'intellectual primacy' in Greece in this period cannot have been merely nostalgia —
although that was no doubt a factor. For Romans like Cicero sent their sons to Athens
to complete their education, and this raised no eyebrows. Nor should it be a matter
for surprise that Paul included this city on his itinerary. As with cities like Corinth
and Ephesos, Athens had a constant stream of visitors from many places, and this
may have made it strategically attractive.

   To conclude discussion of this new aretalogy, two comments on the text *per se* are
appended. The very last word, ἐσφραγισ-(44), looks like part of σφραγίζω. That may
imply that we are very near to end of the text. Yet against this is the all-too-brief
lacuna in *ll.*42-44; it is hard to imagine how the writer could have effected a
rhetorically appropriate conclusion commensurate with the care taken in the rest of
the text. Finally, this is our earliest example of an aretalogy of Isis, one which clearly
belongs to the tradition of the others, yet conforms to their style least of all. This
raises a question about the ancestor of these texts. If the author of the Maroneia
inscription was not simply a 'maverick', writing by design something which could be
his own and no-one else's version, two possibilities suggest themselves:

(i)   The original, conforming largely to the Kyme text, goes back to early Ptolemaic

Egypt. The cult of Isis was fostered by the Ptolemies for similar reasons as was that of Sarapis. Personal and distinctive treatment of the original version was perfectly acceptable; thus, in addition to this newest text, the Andros inscription was *sui generis* because it was in verse. But by the turn of the era Isis religion had gained considerable acceptance outside Egypt, and a closer adherence to the original was required — even in form, a sort of orthodoxy was expected. Thus, the texts from Kyme, Thessalonike, and Ios.

(ii)   No standard form existed in Egypt at the time when the Maroneia text was written. The common material which it shares with the later aretalogies (which do imply the existence of a standard form) reflects the existence of a 'pool' of statements about Isis which only later were crystallised into the format represented by *I. Kyme* 41.

These alternatives prompt the suggestion that there is some kind of credal quality to be observed in these aretalogies, most noticeably in *I. Kyme* 41 (our only complete example), in view of the same text being employed in quite different localities in different centuries (Kyme, I/II; Thessalonike, I/II; Ios, III). But it is not to be thought of as a carefully worded philosophical statement; the jumble of statements of which it is comprised underlines this (cf. Solmsen, 43). But credal element there is, reflecting the essential belief of a popular religious movement, not merely that of diverse individuals. First edited in the 1920's — A. Salač, *BCH* 51 (1927) 378-83; cf. P. Roussel, *REG* 42 (1929) 137-68 — the inscription from Kyme in Asia Minor has received considerable attention, and is most recently reprinted by H. Engelmann as *I. Kyme* 41, pp. 97-108 (pl. 11); see his introduction to the text for bibliography. In view of the size of that bibliography only brief notes will be appended here. (Note that parts of the text are often referred to by section numbers, rather than by line number; section numbers are included in brackets in the text.)

        (1)Δημήτριος Ἀρτεμιδώρου ὁ καὶ Θρασέας Μάγνη[ς]
        ἀπὸ Μαιάνδρου Ἴσιδι εὐχήν·
        (2)Τάδε ἐγράφηι ἐκ τῆς στήλης τῆς ἐν Μέμφει, ἥτι-
        ς ἔστηκεν πρὸς τῷ Ἡφαιστιήωι· (3a)Εἶσις ἐγώ εἰ-

5   μι ἡ τύραννος πάσης χώρας· (3b)καὶ ἐπαιδεύθην ὑπ[ὸ]
        Ἑρμοῦ καὶ (3c)γράμματα εὗρον μετὰ Ἑρμοῦ, τά τε ἱερὰ
        καὶ τὰ δημόσια γράμματα, ἵνα μὴ ἐν τοῖς αὐτοῖς
        πάντα γράφηται. (4)Ἐγὼ νόμους ἀνθρώποις ἐθέμην,
        καὶ ἐνομοθέτησα ἃ οὐθεὶς δύναται μεταθεῖναι.

10   (5)Ἐγώ εἰμι Κρόνου θυγάτηρ πρεσβυτάτηι. (6)Ἐγώ εἰμι γ[υ-]
        νὴ καὶ ἀδελφὴ Ὀσείριδος βασιλέως. (7)Ἐγώ εἰμι ἡ καρπὸν
        ἀνθρώποις εὑροῦσα. (8)Ἐγώ εἰμι μήτηρ Ὥρου βασιλέως.
        (9)Ἐγώ εἰμι ἡ ἐν τῷ τοῦ Κυνὸς ἄστρῳ ἐπιτέλλουσα. (10)Ἐγώ
        εἰμι ἡ παρὰ γυναιξὶ Θεὸς καλουμένη. (11)Ἐμοὶ Βούβαστος

15   πόλις ᾠκοδομήθη. (12)Ἐγὼ ἐχώρισα γῆν ἀπ' οὐρανοῦ.
        (13)Ἐγὼ ἄστρων ὁδοὺς ἔδειξα. (14)Ἐγὼ ἡλίου καὶ σελήνη[ς]
        πορέαν συνεταξάμην· (15)Ἐγὼ θαλάσσια ἔργα εὗρον. (16)Ἐ-
        γὼ τὸ δίκαιον ἰσχυρὸν ἐποίησα. (17)Ἐγὼ γυναῖκα καὶ ἄνδρα
        συνήγαγον. (18)Ἐγὼ γυναικὶ δεκαμηνιαῖον βρέφος εἰς

20 φῶς ἐξενεγκεῖν ἔταξα. ⁽¹⁹⁾Ἐγὼ ὑπὸ τέκνου γονεῖς
ἐνομοθέτησα φιλοστοργῖσθαι. ⁽²⁰⁾Ἐγὼ τοῖς ἀστόρ-
γως γονεῦσιν διακειμένοις τειμωρίαν ἐπέθηκα.
⁽²¹⁾Ἐγὼ μετὰ τοῦ ἀδελφοῦ Ὀσίριδος τὰς ἀνθρωποφα-
γίας ἔπαυσα. ⁽²²⁾Ἐγὼ μυήσεις ἀνθρώποις ἐπέδε[ι-]
25 ξα. ⁽²³⁾Ἐγὼ ἀγάλματα θεῶν τειμᾶν ἐδίδαξα. ⁽²⁴⁾Ἐγὼ
τεμένη θεῶν ἱδρυσάμην. ⁽²⁵⁾Ἐγὼ τυράννων ἀρ-
χὰς κατέλυσα. ⁽²⁶⁾Ἐγὼ φόνους ἔπαυσα. ⁽²⁷⁾Ἐγὼ στέρ-
γεσθαι γυναῖκας ὑπὸ ἀνδρῶν ἠνάγκασα. ⁽²⁸⁾Ἐγὼ
τὸ δίκαιον ἰσχυρότερον χρυσίου καὶ ἀργυρίου ἐποίη-
30 σα. ⁽²⁹⁾Ἐγὼ τὸ ἀληθὲς καλὸν ἐνομο[θέ]τησα νομίζε[σ-]
θαι. ⁽³⁰⁾Ἐγὼ συγγραφὰς γαμικὰς εὗρον. ⁽³¹⁾Ἐγὼ διαλέκτους
Ἕλλησι καὶ βαρβάροις ἔταξα. ⁽³²⁾Ἐγὼ τὸ καλὸν καὶ αἰσχρὸ[ν]
διαγεινώσκεσθαι ὑπὸ τῆς Φύσεως ἐποίησα. ⁽³³⁾Ἐγὼ
ὅρκου φοβερώτερον οὐθὲν ἐποίησα. ⁽³⁴⁾Ἐγὼ τὸν ἀδίκως
35 ἐπιβουλεύοντα ἄλλοις {ἄλλῳ} ὑποχείριον τῷ ἐπιβου-
[λ]ευομένῳ παρέδωκα. ⁽³⁵⁾Ἐγὼ τοῖς ἄδικα πράσσουσιν
τειμωρίαν ἐπιτίθημι. ⁽³⁶⁾Ἐγὼ ἱκέτας ἐλεᾶν ἐνομοθ[έ-]
τησα. ⁽³⁷⁾Ἐγὼ τοὺς δικαίως ἀμυνομένους τειμῶ. ⁽³⁸⁾Πα-
ρ’ἐμοὶ τὸ δίκαιον ἰσχύει. ⁽³⁹⁾Ἐγὼ ποταμῶν καὶ ἀνέμων
40 [κ]αὶ θαλάσσης εἰμὶ κυρία. ⁽⁴⁰⁾Οὐθεὶς δοξάζεται ἄνευ τῆς ἐ-
μῆς γνώμης. ⁽⁴¹⁾Ἐγώ εἰμι πολέμου κυρία. ⁽⁴²⁾Ἐγὼ κεραυ-
νοῦ κυρία εἰμί. ⁽⁴³⁾Ἐγὼ πραΰνω καὶ κυμαίνω θάλασσαν.
⁽⁴⁴⁾Ἐγὼ ἐν ταῖς τοῦ ἡλίου αὐγαῖς εἰμί. ⁽⁴⁵⁾Ἐγὼ παρεδρεύω τῇ
τοῦ ἡλίου πορείᾳ. ⁽⁴⁶⁾Ὃ ἂν ἐμοὶ δόξῃ, τοῦτο καὶ τελεῖτα[ι].
45 ⁽⁴⁷⁾Ἐμοὶ πάντ’ ἐπείκει. ⁽⁴⁸⁾Ἐγὼ τοὺς ἐν δεσμοῖς λύωι. ⁽⁴⁹⁾Ἐγὼ
ναυτιλίας εἰμὶ κυρία. ⁽⁵⁰⁾Ἐγὼ τὰ πλωτὰ ἄπλωτα ποι[ῶ ὅ-]
ταν ἐμοὶ δόξῃ. ⁽⁵¹⁾Ἐγὼ περιβόλους πόλεων ἔκτισα. ⁽⁵²⁾Ἐ-
γώ εἰμι ἡ Θεσμοφόρος καλουμένη. ⁽⁵³⁾Ἐγὼ νήσσους ἐγ β[υ-]
[θ]ῶν εἰς φῶς ἀνήγαγον. ⁽⁵⁴⁾Ἐγὼ ὄμβρων εἰμὶ κυρία. ⁽⁵⁵⁾Ἐγὼ
50 τὸ ἱμαρμένον νικῶ. ⁽⁵⁶⁾Ἐμοῦ τὸ εἱμαρμένον ἀκούει.
⁽⁵⁷⁾Χαῖρε Αἴγυπτε θρέψασά με

**Demetrios son of Artemidoros, also called Thraseas, from Magnesia on the
Maeander, made this dedication to Isis. This was written from the stele in**
5 **Memphis which stands before the Hephaistieion. Isis am I, |the ruler of every
land. I was educated by Hermes and I invented with Hermes sacred and public
writing in order that everything might not be written in the same script. I laid**
10 **down laws for men and legislated what no one can alter. |I am the eldest
daughter of Kronos. I am the wife and sister of King Osiris. I am the one who
discovered fruit for men. I am the mother of King Horos. I am the one who rises
in the constellation of the Dog. I am the one who is called goddess among**
15 **women. For me the city of Boubastis |was built. I separated earth from sky. I
pointed out the routes of the stars. I arranged the course of the sun and moon.
I invented maritime activities. I made justice strong. I united woman and man.**

20   I arranged for a woman to bring forth her unborn child into the light after nine
months. |I legislated that parents should be loved tenderly by their child. I
inflicted vengeance on those disposed without natural affection towards their
parents. I with my brother Osiris stopped cannibalism. I revealed initiations to

25   men. |I taught them to honour the statues of the gods. I built sacred precincts
of the gods. I destroyed the government of tyrants. I stopped murders. I
compelled wives to be loved by their husbands. I made justice stronger than gold

30   and silver. |I legislated that truth should be considered beautiful. I invented
marriage contracts. I assigned languages to Greeks and non-Greeks. I made
beauty to be distinguished from ugliness by Nature. I made nothing more to be

35   feared than an oath. I handed over the man who plots unjustly |against others
into the hands of the person plotted against. I inflict vengeance on those who
do unjust things. I legislated for mercy to be shown to suppliants. I have regard
for those who defend themselves with justification. On my account justice is

40   strong. I am mistress of rivers and winds |and sea. No one is glorified without
my consent. I am mistress of war. I am mistress of the thunderbolt. I lull and
trouble the sea. I am in the rays of the sun. I concern myself with the course

45   of the sun. Whatever I decide, this also is accomplished. |To me all things yield.
I release those in fetters. I am mistress of seamanship. I make the navigable
unnavigable whenever I decide. I founded the walls and cities. I am the one who
is called Lawbringer. I brought up islands out of the depths to the light. I am

50   mistress of storms (inundations?). I |conquer fate. It is to me that fate listens.
Hail, Egypt who nurtured me!

The single most arresting point of comparison between this inscription and the NT
is its form. The plethora of 'I am' statements takes us immediatly to the Fourth
Gospel. This was noticed long ago by Deissmann who remarks, when treating the Ios
aretalogy (*LAE*, 136-42), 'How easy it must have been for Hellenistic Judaism and
Christianity to adopt the remarkable and simple style of expression in the first person
singular' (41). Deissmann concentrated on points of similarity with the LXX; in the
text from Kyme note for example *l*.15 (cf. Gen. 1.4, διαχωρίζω), *l*.18 (cf. Gen. 2.22),
and *ll*.28-30 (cf. Ps. 19.9-10). For the NT *ll*.27-28 will make one think of Paul at Eph.
5.25, 28; *ll*.39-40, 42, will be suggestive of several passages in the gospels (Mt. 8.23-27;
Mk. 6.45-52, cf. Lk. 8.22-25).

For particular words note the following: εὐχή (2), Acts 18.18; 21.23, see also
comment in item **4**; νομοθετέω (9, 21, 30, 37-38), Heb. 7.11 (of Moses), 8.6 (of the
covenant); χωρίζω (15), not NT in this sense, but cf. comment in previous paragraph;
πορεία (17, 44), not quite the same sense in NT at Lk. 13.22; Jas. 1.11; συντάσσω (17),
different sense in NT; συνάγω (19), not quite this sense in NT at Mt. 22.10; Jn. 11.47;
Acts 15.30; cf. BAGD, s.v., 2; βρέφος (19), Lk. 1.41, 44; γονεῖς (20, 22; cf. the
Maroneia text above, *l*.31), frequent in NT; φιλοστοργέω (21), not NT, nor is the noun
in -ία though there are various contemporary parallels (cf. BAGD), to which add *P.
Stras.* (626.9; end I BC?) — a fragmentary document dealing with an inheritance in
which occurs the phrase σῴζων φιλοστο[ργ (φιλοστοργίαν, quite possibly). The
adjective -γος occurs at Rom. 12.10; ἄστοργος (21-22), Rom. 1.31; 2 Tim. 3.3 μύησις
(24), not NT, but note the non-technical use of μυέω at Phil. 4.12; διαγιγνώσκω (33),
different sense in Acts 23.15, 24.22; ἐλεάω (37; later form of ἐλεέω), frequent in NT;
δοξάζω (40), frequent in NT; αὐγή (43), Acts 20.11 ('daybreak'); παρεδρεύω (43)

different sense at 1 Cor. 9.13. στέργω (27-28) occurred in the Maroneia text also, but here of the love between spouses as in the Apostolic Fathers (see BAGD, s.v.) συγγραφή (31) is also found in *Ep. Barn.* but not with the specific sense accorded to it here.

2 *bis*. A *thiasos* named after its founder (*I. Kyme* 30).

The concluding few lines of a decree (the remainder is lost) of the association of Menekleides from Kyme (II BC) states where the stele is to be placed (*ll.* 1-4), provides the date (6-8), and declares ἔμμεναι δὲ τὰν στά[λ]|λαν ταύταν ἱρὰν τῶ Διονύσω τῶν Θια|σωτᾶν τῶν Μενεκλέιδα (4-6), 'this stele belonging to the members of the association of Menekleides is sacred to Dionysos.' We may infer from the way that the members of this *thiasos* call their group after Menekleides that he was its founder (so Engelmann, n. *ad loc.*).

3. Exclusiveness in a Zeus cult at Sardis

Sardis   I/II
ed.pr. — L. Robert, *CRAI* 1975, 306-30 (ph. 307,309)

```
        ἐτέων τριήκοντα ἐννέα Ἀρτα-
        ξέρξεω βασιλεύοντος, τὸν ἀν-
        δριάντα Δροαφέρνης vac.
        Βαρ⟨ά⟩κεω Λυδίης ὕπαρχος Βαρα-
   5    δατεω Διί. (leaf) προστάσσει τοῖς
        εἰσπορευομένοις εἰς τὸ ἄδυ-
        τον νεωκόροις θεραπευ- vac.
        ταῖς αὐτοῦ καὶ στεφανοῦσι τὸν θε-
        ὸν μὴ μετέχειν μυστηρίων Σαβα-
  10    ζίου τῶν τὰ ἔνπυρα βασταζόν-
        των καὶ Ἀνγδίστεως καὶ Μᾶς. προσ-
        τάσσουσι δὲ Δορατη τῷ νεωκόρῳ τού-
        των τῶν μυστηρίων ἀπέχεσθαι.
```

Discovered mid-1974. Text complete and unbroken: no readings in doubt. Size of stone: roughly .45m. high x .58 wide. Date based on letter style.

Bib. — J. Reynolds, *JRS* 66(1976) 195; C. J. Hemer, *Buried History* 12(1976) 36-37; A.T. Kraabel in *Paganisme, Judaïsme, Christianisme. Mélanges offerts à Marcel Simon* (Paris, 1978), 31.

In the thirty-nine years of Artaxerxes' reign, Droaphernes son of Barakis,
5 **governor of Lydia, dedicated the statue to Zeus the Legislator. | He (Droaphernes) instructs his (Zeus') temple-warden devotees who enter the innermost sanctum and who serve and crown the god, not to participate in the**

10   **mysteries of Sabazios |with those who bring the burnt offerings and (the mysteries) of Agdistis and Ma. They instruct Dorates the temple-warden to keep away from these mysteries.**

The continuity of religious tradition makes this an inscription which will attract the attention of those interested in the history of ideas and in the general religious milieu in which the Christian groups were spawned.

We have here a Greek translation of an Aramaic edict promulgated c.365 BC (during the reign of Artaxerxes II Memnon) by the Persian monarch's satrap of Lydia, one of the westernmost provinces of the Persian Empire. Our inscription is a copy made some 500 years afterwards. The existence of an Aramaic original appears to be inferred by Robert from the Persian character of this cult.

Droaphernes dedicates a statue to Ahura Mazda (*ll.* 1-5). In the Greek translation the name of the Persian divinity is given as Zeus, and Robert suggests (314) that the epithet *Baradates* is an Iranian term applied to him, "the legislator". The form Βαραδατεω ought to be a normal Ionic genitive (others in this inscription at *ll.* 1-2,4); and Photius, *Bibl.* 248a, ad fin., attests it as a man's name (I owe this reference to G. Mussies). But Robert (313) does not see how that way of construing the word could fit in here. The Ionic dialect features in these lines confirm the antiquity of the Greek of this part of the inscription. Hemer (36) suggests that the odd wording in *l.*1 ('39 years' for '39th year') bespeaks 'translation Greek, the reproduction of an early archetype whose Greek was translated from an original in the official Aramaic of the Persian Empire'.

Since a statue is being set up for the god, we may suppose that there existed at Sardis a temple in his honour: this temple had a secret inner sanctum *(adyton)*. A temple is also implied by the allusion to cult officials. A *neokoros* was a subordinate official closely involved with the cultic acts of such a centre; the reference to *therapeutai* alludes to those devotees who perform some special service and have special privileges granted them which are forbidden to others. In this case they are permitted to enter the *adyton* where the god's statue is located, and crown it. But these members have certain constraints placed upon them: they are forbidden to participate in the mysteries of various native gods of Asia Minor. Sabazios and Agdistis are in origin Phrygian deities, while Ma is a Cappadocian goddess. One other 1976 text refers to Agdistis, an altar from Phrygia on which is the dedication Αγδιστι εὐχήν (T. Drew-Bear, *GRBS* 17[1976] 259-60, no.14; = *SEG* 1382). The text clearly implies that cults of these gods exist at Sardis in Lydia, far distant from Cappadocia. The presence in one locale of such diverse religious cults was a product of the breadth of the dominion of the Persian Empire. The very existence of the prohibition upon participation in these other mystery cults reflects the polytheistic situation in Persian-dominated Asia Minor in the fourth century BC. Only an inner group is directed to be exclusive in its religious attachments, presumably in order to preserve and transmit the purity of the Zeus/Ahura Mazda cult. The contrast implied between the two compounds of ἔχω (9,13) is noteworthy: to be present for the mysteries constituted participation in the rites. Both verbs occur in the NT; for ἀπέχεσθαι note Acts 15.29; but especially Ignatius, *Letter to the Smyrnaeans* 7.1 (cited BAGD, s.v., 3).

Yet what gives this inscription special interest is that it was deemed worthwhile/ necessary to re-inscribe it half a millennium later. The cult must still be in existence, and it continues to guard itself jealously against contamination; for the exclusivity clause for *neokoroi therapeutai* is repeated. In the first two centuries of our era such exclusivity is particularly noticeable among Jews and Christians, but it is not confined to those groups. The particular occasion which led to the re-cutting of this text on to stone appears to have involved Dorates (a Greek, not a Persian, name) who apparently stepped out of line vis-à-vis this exclusivity requirement, though a *neokoros* (*ll.* 11-13). These lines are a later addition to the fourth-century BC text. Yet this addition is curious; who are the people who give the directive to Dorates ($\pi\rho o\sigma\tau\acute{a}\sigma\sigma o\upsilon\sigma\iota$ 11-12)? Presumably those who now control the cult, but their anonymity is tantalising.

Robert (320-21) refers to another inscription (I BC) for a Zeus cult from Sardis (Buckler and Robinson, *Sardis* 7.1 [1932]22). There $o\acute{\iota}$ $\tau o\hat{\upsilon}$ $\Delta\iota\grave{o}\varsigma$ $\theta\epsilon\rho a\pi\epsilon\upsilon\tau a\grave{\iota}$ $\tau\hat{\omega}\nu$ $\epsilon\grave{\iota}[\varsigma]$ | $\tau\grave{o}$ $\check{a}\delta\upsilon\tau o\nu$ $\epsilon\grave{\iota}\sigma\pi o\rho\epsilon\upsilon o\mu\acute{\epsilon}\nu\omega\nu$ crown a certain man described as $\tau\grave{o}\nu$ $\pi\rho\hat{\omega}\tau o\nu$ $\tau\hat{\eta}\varsigma$ $\pi\acute{o}\lambda\epsilon\omega\varsigma$ for his piety $\pi\rho\grave{o}\varsigma$ $\tau\grave{o}$ $\theta\epsilon\hat{\iota}o\nu$. The similarity of wording used to refer to those allowed to enter the *adyton* leads Robert to conclude that the two inscriptions are dealing with the same cult. This new text thus witnesses to the persistence of a religious cult and its ideas over a lengthy period. This may not seem unusual, but it should not be forgotten that what we are looking at here is one voluntary religious association in one particular locality which has retained alive — and apparently in not too contaminated a form — Iranian religious traditions long after the Persian Empire had disappeared. If at first the cult was established for Persian colonists who settled in cosmopolitan Sardis (soldiers, bureaucrats), after 500 years Persian and local Greek and indigenous blood will have intermingled. Small wonder, then, that the text as we have it was inscribed in Greek, the *lingua franca,* and that a man with a non-Persian name is mentioned as a member.

A cult group like this one from Sardis offers a useful yardstick against which to measure some features of the early Christian assemblies. Like the latter by the time of the Pastoral epistles, the religious leaders of this Zeus cult are subject to certain special regulations; though nothing is said about the ordinary members in general. Considered more generally against the long pedigree of such cult groups, it is no wonder that the Christians were viewed as a new phenomenon, and *ipso facto* suspect. It fell to the Apologists of the second and later centuries to argue that Christianity's roots were ancient and therefore respectable. Finally, those to whom cult associations like this one in honour of Ahura Mazda were the norm must have found the Christians distinctly peculiar in their religious habits, if not downright irreligious. Where were their specially set-aside cult centres, their statues of the god, their cultic acts (mysteries, sacrifices, etc.), and their official hierarchy? These were all aspects to which Christianity gradually made concessions in the second and later centuries in the difficult process of accommodation and acclimatisation.

4. Personal piety in the cult of Saturn

Chul (Medeïna), Africa Proconsularis   11/6/283 or 13/7/283
ed.pr. — A. Beschaouch, *CRAI* (1975) 111-18 (fig. 7, p.114)

Pos(uit) Car[o et Carino cos(ulibus)]
III idus i[un]ias (or i[ul]ias).

> *Saturno Aug(usto) sac(rum).*
> *C(aius) Manius Felix Fortu-*
> 5 *natianus sacerdos,*
> *in somnis monitus, Satur-*
> *ni numine iussus —*
> *Manius hic votum solvi*
> *sacrumque dicavi,*
> 10 *pro comperta fide et pro ser-*
> *vata salute —*
> *V(otum) s(olvit) l(ibens) a(nimo).*

One of a series of inscriptions dedicated to Saturn, found in the god's sanctuary at this site. The lettering of the last line has a palm before and following it. A clumsy drawing of a man follows the lettering of this last line immediately before the right-hand palm.

Bib. — *AE* (1975) 874; J. Reynolds, *JRS* 66 (1976) 195.

He set it up in the consulship of Carus and Carinus, the third day before the Ides of June [or, July]. Sacred to Augustan Saturn. Gaius Manius Felix
5 **Fortunatianus, |priest, warned in dreams, ordered by the divine will of Saturn.**
10 **I Manius discharged my vow and dedicated a sacrifice |for the proving of my faith and the preservation of my health. He discharged his vow with a willing spirit.**

This is no merely conventional dedication made to mark the fulfilment of a vow. The most striking feature of the text is its tone: implied is the close personal dealing which Manius has with his god (cf. Beschaouch, 117). His trust in Saturn has not been found wanting in a time of sickness (*salus* need mean no more than physical health here); similarly σωτηρία in **2** and **19**. Such a relationship between the sick and the gods who heal them appears to be characteristic: Aelius Aristides' *Sacred Tales* comes to mind immediately. Cf. **2**, the new Isis aretalogy; perhaps, too, Paul's relationship with God over his 'thorn in the flesh' (2 Cor. 12.7-10). The attitude to Jesus engendered by the healing miracles reported in the gospels may be worth viewing in this context. For divine warnings conveyed through dreams, cf. **6**; and in the NT note Mt. 2.12, 13.

The Isis aretalogy from Kyme was set up in fulfilment of a vow (I. *Kyme* 41.2; = **2**). For dedications resulting from a vow by a Christian note the bronze tablet reprinted as *IGLR* 434 (Biertan in Transylvania, IV?): *Ego Zenovius votum posui.* An inscription from a Christian church at Antioch (March, 387) records the donation of a mosaic *exedra* by Dorys the presbyter, in fulfilment of a vow (εὐξάμενος); text republished in W. A. Meeks and R. L. Wilken, *Jews and Christians at Antioch* (Missoula, 1978), 56. *IMS* contains 27 inscriptions which include the words *votum soluit* or some variant; of these one (no. 83; cf. **89**) may possibly be Christian. Paul's vow (Acts 18.18) may appear to reflect his Jewish background in view of the decision to cut his hair. But it may be rather a standard Greek cultural reaction to some dream through which came divine guidance; cf. **6**. For Torah regulations about vows, see Deut. 23.21-22.

For some examples of more usual inscriptions involving the cult of Saturn see *Inscriptions latines de l'Algérie* II, 2 (Algiers, 1976), ed. H.-G. Pflaum, nos. 4398(with note), 4643, 6093, 6344, 6347, 7238.

5. Dedications to 'The Most High God'

Near Akmonia, Phrygia   Imperial Period?
ed.pr. — T. Drew-Bear, *GRBS* 17(1976) 247-49, nos. 1 and 2 (pl.7)

(1) Ἐβίκτητος
ἐπύησε-
ν Θεῷ
Ὑψίστῳ
εὐχήν

(2) Ἀγαθῇ Τύχ[η]·
Αὐρ. Τατις Ὀ-
νησίμου χαλ-
κέος σύνβιος
5 σὺν τῷ συμβί-
ῳ Ὀνησίμῳ Θε-
ῷ Ὑψίστῳ ἐκ τ-
ῶν ἰδίων ἀνέ-
[θ]ησαν

Two inscriptions, no.1 found on a small altar at Yenice Köy, no.2 at Çorum, published together with eighteen others (pp.247-68, pl. 7-10). All twenty texts are dedications to various gods from Graeco-Roman Phrygia.
Bib. — *SEG* 1355, 1356. No.1 originally published in W. M. Ramsay, *Cities and Bishoprics of Phrygia* I, ii (Oxford, 1897), 652, no.563.

(1) Epiktetos fulfilled his vow to the most high god.
(2) With good fortune. Aurelia Tatis, spouse of Onesimos the blacksmith, set up
5 **(this monument)| along with her spouse Onesimos, to the most high god, at their own expense.**

One of the most frequently-discussed aspects of texts which mention Zeus *Hypsistos, Theos Hypsistos,* or *Hypsistos,* is whether they indicate Jewish or Jewish-Christian influence. The view early this century was affirmative, e.g. F. Cumont, *Oriental Religions in Roman Paganism* (ET, London 1909[2]; repr. New York, 1956) 227, n.30: '. . . Theos Hypsistos, that is to say the god of Israel.' So, too, A.B. Cook, *Zeus* II, 2 (Cambridge 1925) 889. The provenance of the first of these inscriptions printed above suggests to Drew-Bear (248) that Epiktetos may have had links with the Jewish community in this part of Akmonian territory. From the same place he reprints an 'indubitably Jewish' curse epitaph which alludes to the LXX (text printed below at **61**). See also L. Robert, *J.Sav* (1975) 158-60 (cf. *BE* 674), who discusses briefly the Jewish community at Akmonia and its romanisation. Certain other *Hypsistos* texts reprinted in 1976 are similarly to be classed as Jewish. S.M. Sherwin-White, *ZPE* 21 (1976) 183-88 (cf. eadem, *Ancient Cos* [Göttingen, 1978], index s.v. 'Jewish

Community'), identifies three inscriptions from the Paton/Hicks corpus, *Inscriptions of Cos* (Oxford, 1891), as emanating from the Jewish community on the island. Her third text (Paton/Hicks, no.63; cf. *SEG* 949) is a I AD dedication, Θέανος | Θεῷ Ὑψίστῳ εὐ|χήν. She holds that Theanos is a Jew or a Judaizing Greek — a 'Godfearer', perhaps? Again, A. Negev, *Eretz-Israel* 12 (1975) 136, no.9 (English summary, 123; cf. *SEG* 1697), published a rock engraving from the Sinai, dated c.299/300, whose first line reads Εἶς Θεὸς ΤΥΘ (i.e. *Hypsistos Theos,* with Heb. *dalet* between the words). A menorah (or palm branch?) is drawn at the end of the second line of this text. The editor takes the *dalet* to stand for *ḥd,* 'One' (although the letter is not clear on the photograph); is it rather an early example of the use of this letter to refer to the Divine Name?

Yet as long ago as the mid-1930's A. D. Nock argued against assuming Jewish influences in the bulk of such texts. In his fundamental discussion of the cult of Zeus *Hypsistos, HTR* 29 (1936) 39-88 (pl.)— the article was jointly authored with C. H. Roberts and T. C. Skeat, and is largely reprinted in Nock's *Essays on Religion and the Ancient World* I (Oxford, 1972) 416-43 — he argued that while certain of these texts undoubtedly do betray 'the impact of Jewish or Judaizing culture' *(Essays,* 425), the guild of Zeus *Hypsistos* (which was the subject of the papyrus published in that article) certainly did not. On this text, see further below. A recently published inscription from Macedonia may appear — at first sight — to show that the mention of Zeus *Hypsistos* (as opposed to *Theos Hypsistos,* or *Hypsistos* alone) does not automatically prove a text to be non-Jewish. J.M.R. Cormack, in *Mélanges offerts à Georges Daux* (Paris, 1974) 51-55 (pl., p.53), presents a dedication to Zeus *Hypsistos* by a guild of worshippers (250 AD). This inscription names the posts of five officials of the cult (9-16), including an ἀρχισυνά|γωγον (12-13), and proceeds to list the members of the association (29 of them, men, women, slaves, freedmen; the Roman citizens are mostly Aurelii, presumably deriving their citizenship from the *constitutio Antoniniana* of 212). Several other *Hypsistos* texts have been found in Macedonia (Cormack, 54; Cook, 878), though this is the first from this particular locality (Pydna).

ἀγαθῇ τύχη·
ἔτους ·Β·Π·Ε· Σεβ.
τοῦ καὶ ·Η·Ρ·Τ· Δαισί-
ου ·Η̄·Ι·, ἐν Πύδνῃ
5 οἱ συνελθόντες
θρησκευταὶ ἐπὶ θεοῦ
Διὸς Ὑψίστου ἔθεν-
το τήνδε τὴν στήλην,
λογιστεύοντος Οὐρ-
10 βανιανοῦ Βιλίστου,
ἄρχοντος Αὐρ. Νιγερ[ί]-
ωνος ὑπὸ ἀρχισυνά-
γωγον Αὐρ. Κηπίωνα τὸν
πρὶν Πιερίωνος καὶ προστάτου

15   Αὐρ. Σεβήρου καὶ γραμματέως
     Αὐρηλίου Θεοφίλου τοῦ πρὶν
     Πιερίωνος καὶ οἱ λοιποὶ θρησκευ-
     ταὶ οἱ ὑπογεγραμμένοι· εὐτυχῶ[ς]·
20   Αὐρήλιος Ἐρωτιανὸς, |Αὐρήλιος Βόηθος, Τ. Ὀκτάβιος Ζώσιμος,
     Ἀτάνιος Τατιανὸς, Αὐρήλιος Τρόφιμος, Κλαύ. Φιλουμενὸς,
25 |Αὐρηλία Σαβεῖνα, Αὐρήλιος Ἀρτεμίδωρος, Αὐρηλία Παρθενόπη,
30   Αὐρήλιος Ἐλπίνεικος, Τ. Φλάβιος Ἰουλιανὸς, |Τ. Αἴλιος Ἰουλιανὸ⟨ς⟩,
     Κορνήλιος Ὠφελίων, Φιλοκύρις οἰκονόμος, Ἐλευσείνις οἰκέτης,
35   Κλαύδιος Ἀμβρόσις, |Αὐρήλιος Ἐπάγαθος, Αὐρήλιος Ἀλέξανδρος,
     Αὐρήλιος Κόπρυλλος, Κορνιφ. Καλλίμορφος, Ἀντώνιο⟨ς⟩ Παράμονος,
40 |Αὐρήλιος Πολύξενος, Αὐρηλία Ἀθηνώ, Αὐρήλιο⟨ς⟩ Ἡρακλείδης,
45   Αἴλιος Φίλων, Αὐρήλιος Μάξιμος, |Αὐρήλιος Θεόδουλος,
     Αἴλιος Καλοφρόνιος, Αὐρήλιος Λεοντίσκ[ος]

     On side of stele
5,10   δει᾽ ἐπι-με-λη-|τοῦ Θεο-φί-λου κέ |Αὐ-ρη-λί-ου
15,20,25 Κη-|πί-ων-ος το-ῦ π-|ρὶν Πι-ερ-ίω-νο-|ς.

(l.5) The assembled worshippers set in place this stele for the god Zeus
10 *Hypsistos,* **in the year when | Urbanianus Vilistus was auditor, Aurelius Nigerion**
    was archon, Aurelius Kepion (formerly of Pieria) was leader of the assembly,
15 **|Aurelius Severus was patron, and Aurelius Theophilos (formerly of Pieria) was**
    secretary. The remaining worshippers are recorded below . . .

Is this body a Jewish diaspora synagogue? Almost certainly not; for surely we have here a fairly rare example of the use of *archisunagogos* in a pagan context. By way of contrast note two decidedly Jewish epigraphical references to such an official: Ramsay, *Cities and Bishoprics* I, ii, 649-51 (no. 559); and Deissmann, *LAE,* 439-41. Even so, the Pydna inscription merits close attention, particularly for what the list of names may yield about the mixed composition of the group. A mystery cult for the god Mandros is the subject of the long but damaged *I.Kyme* 37; at the end of the text is appended a list of members, many more being men than women.

As further examples to illustrate the correctness of Nock's view, note the following. D.M. Pippidi, *Stud.Clas.* 16(1974) 260-63 (in Rumanian; French summary, 265), republishes (cf. *SEG* 839) a fragmentary dedication from Tomis, which at *l.*2 reads Ὑψίστ[ῳ θεῷ...]. A Jewish connection is very unlikely here in view of θιασ – – – (6), almost certainly referring to a *thiasos.* Similarly, M. Taceva-Hitova, *Thracia* 4 (1977) 271-301 *(non vidi),* rejects the idea of Jewish diaspora influence upon the 22 known Zeus *Hypsistos* and *Theos Hypsistos* inscriptions from Thrace. L. Robert, *Opera Minora Selecta* I (Amsterdam, 1969) 411-18, argues that an inscription from Lydia (181/2) is clearly not Jewish in view of its reference to another local goddess. Whereas *CIJ* I.727-29 are clearly Jewish (from a synagogue on Delos), yet *CIJ* I.690 (Bosporos, 41) may well not be. This text used to be considered Jewish (e.g., Cook, 884); but *l.*14 mentions Zeus, Ge, and Helios. Nor are the non-Jewish *Hypsistos* inscriptions confined to Eastern Europe and Macedonia. *CIJ* II.1532 (Fayum) is 'not Jewish' according to D.M. Lewis, who republishes the Egyptian texts from *CIJ* in an appendix to *CPJ* III (pp. 163-64). The epithet *Hypsistos* occurs elsewhere in Egypt, e.g., of Isis: see the references collected by G. Ronchi, *Lexicon theonymon rerumque sacrarum et divinarum ad Aegyptum pertintentium quae in papyris, titulis, Graecis Latinisque in Aegypto repertis laudantur* (Milan, 1977), 1120-22. For Jewish examples from Egypt, see Nock, 427. There are no literary attestations of the term from Asia Minor, according to M. Santoro, *Epitheta deorum in Asia Graeca cultorum ex auctoribus Graecis et Latinis* (Milan, 1974).

Theos Hypsistos is common in the later OT books to refer to the God of Israel. There is no reason to doubt the Jewish background to the epithet as used in the NT: Lk. 1.32, 35,76; 6.35; 8.28; Mk. 5.7; Heb. 7.1; Acts 7.48. Perhaps at Acts 16.17 it may be possible to see the overlapping of the Jewish and Greek influences: Paul and Silas at Philippi are announced to be δοῦλοι τοῦ θεοῦ τοῦ ὑψίστου.

SB 5.2 (1938) 7835 is reproduced below since the Greek text was omitted from the reprint of the *HTR* (1936) article in Nock's *Essays*. A translation was included in that volume. Possibly from the Fayum, this papyrus is dated mid-I BC (c.69-57). The editors estimate that c.15 lines are lost; the accounts on the *verso* are so scrappy as to be of little intelligible use.

Recto

Ὠρίων Ἀρυώτου αγελ(   ) αι..
τριάκοντα δύο / λβ

ἀγαθῆι τύχηι.
νόμος ὃν ἔθεντο [κα]τὰ κοινὸν οἱ ἐκ τῆς τοῦ Διὸς Ὑψίστου συνόδου τοῦτον εἶναι κύριον,
5 καὶ ποιοῦντες καθ᾿ διαγ[ορ]εύει πρῶτον μὲν προχειρισάμενοι ἐπ᾿ ἑαυτῶν
ἡγούμενον Πετεσοῦ[χον] Τεεφβέννιος, ἄνδρα λόγιον, τοῦ τόπου καὶ τῶν ἀνδρῶν
ἄξιον, εἰς ἐ[ν]ιαυτὸν [ἀπὸ τοῦ] προ[γ]εγρ[ρ]αμένου μηνὸς καὶ ἡμέρας συνεισ-
φ[ό]ρ[οι]ς δὲ πᾶσι π[οιεῖσθ]ε κατὰ μῆινα πόσι[ν] μίαν ᾱ ἐν τῶι τοῦ Διὸς
ἱερῶι ἐν αἷς ἐν ἀνδ[ρῶνι] κοινῶι σπένδοντες εὐχέσθωισαν καὶ τἆλλα τὰ νο-
10 μιζό[μεν]α ὑπέρ τε τ[ο]ῦ θεο(ῦ) καὶ κυρίο(υ) βασιλέ(ω)ς· ὑπακούσειν δὲ πάντας τοῦ τε
ἡγουμέ-
νου καὶ τ[οῦ] τούτου ὑπηρέτου ἐν τε ταῖς ἀνήκουσι τῶι κοινῶι καὶ παρέσονται ἐπὶ τὰ[ς]
δοθει[σομ]έναις αὐτοῖς παραγγελίας καὶ [σ]υνλόγους καὶ συναγωγὰς καὶ ἀποδημί[ας]
καὶ μ[η]ι[δ]ενὶ αὐτῶν ἐξέστωι συντευματαρχήισειν μηιδὲ σχίματα συνίστασ[θαι]
μηιδ᾿ ἀπ[ο]χωρήισε[ιν ἐκ] τῆς τοῦ ἡγ[ου]μένου φράτρας εἰς ἑτέραν φράτραν
15 καὶ μὴι γ[ε]νεαλογ[ήσειν ἔ]τερος τὸν ἕτερον ἐν τῶι συμποσίωι μηδὲ κακο-
λογ[ήσειν] ἕτερος [τὸν] ἕτερον ἐν τῶι συμποσίωι μηιδὲ λαλήσειν μηιδὲ ἐπ[ικα]λήσειν καὶ μὲ κατηιγορή[σ]ειν [[α]] τοῦ ἑτέρου μηιδὲ ἀπόρρησιν
διδ[όναι] ἐπὶ τὸν ἐνι[αυτ]ὸν καὶ μηιδ᾿ ἀ[φα]ριεῖν τὰς συμποσίας μηιδὲ ἐπεργες
θ·[·]·ντ[·]·πον εκτολ(   ) [μη]ιδ᾿ ἀποκλέψειν τ ἑτέραν καὶ μὴι κωλύσειν τὸν
20 [.................. δη]μοσίω[ι] καὶ ἀ[ντ?]ὶ το[ῦ] πρός τε τὰς συμβολ(ὰς) καὶ τἆλλα ἐπι
[*c. 28 letters*   ]ηπει καὶ εἰσενεγκεῖν ἕκαστος αὐτῶν
[*c. 35 letters*   ] ε[...] ἐὰν δέ τις αὐτῶν πατὴρ
[*γένηται? c. 44 letters in all*   ] η[·]χ[·]κη

Read καθά ... ἐφ’ ἑαυτῶν(5); προγεγραμμένου μηνὸς(7); ποιεῖσθαι, μῆνα(8); εὐχέσθωσαν(9); κυριο,pap.(10); τοῖς(11); δοθησομένας(12); μηδενὶ, ἐξέστω, μηδὲ(13); μηδ’, ἀποχωρήσειν(14); μὴ(15); μηδὲ bis(16); ἐπικαλέσειν, μὴ, κατηγορήσειν, μηδὲ, ἀπόρρησιν(17); μηδ’, μηδὲ(18); μη(19); συμβο^,pap.(20).

Verso

	Πνεφερῶ(ς) β̄ τῆς ἀνὰ χειρο( )	ἀσ
γ̄	Ἀπολλώνιο(ς)	ω
	Σωκράτης γ̄ τῆς ἐνεστ(ώσης)	ἀσ
δ̄	Πετοσεῖρις	ἀσ
5	Πε[τ]εσοῦχο(ς) β̄ τῆς ἐπὶ χει( )	ἀ[σ]
γ̄	[··]·ρ Καλειβις	[[ἀρ]]

NT philologists may note the following words which appear in this text. προχειρίζομαι (5), figuratively at Acts 3.20, 22.14, 26.16; ὑπακούω + genitive (10), + dative at Eph. 6.1, Col. 3.20 (parents); Eph. 6.5, Col. 3.22, Rom. 6.16 (master); 1 Pet. 3.6 (husband); Heb. 5.9 (Christ); ὑπηρέτης (11) of a cult official, cf. Lk. 4.20; παραγγελία (12), cf.Acts 5.28, 16.24, et al.; συναγωγή (12), common in NT, but nowhere in this general, non-Jewish sense; σχί(σ)ματα (13), 1 Cor. 12.25; γενεαλογέω (15), not quite the same sense at Heb. 7.6; κακολογέω (15-16), Mk. 9.39, Acts 19.9 (τὴν ὁδόν); συμπόσιον (15, 16; cf. συμποσία,18). Mk. 6.39; λαλέω (16), 1 Cor. 14.34; ἐπικαλέω (17), frequent in NT; κατηγορέω (17), frequent in NT; ἀφανίζω (18), Mt. 6.19 f. (but intransitive here). Note also that ἀποδημία appears in Hermas (see BAGD, s.v.).

One other *Theos Hypsistos* text deserves to be kept in view. There exist two almost identical Jewish prayers for vengeance against the killer of two Jewish girls. Both inscriptions are originally from Delos and are dated II/I BC. The recent reprinting of Deissmann *LAE* makes this text readily accessible (his discussion in App. 1, pp. 413-24, is quite full and valuable). The text is also printed in Cook, 880-81 (fig. 817); *SIG*[3] 1181; *CIJ* I.725 a, b; and is briefly discussed by Pippidi, 261.

6. A 'letter from heaven'

Thessalonike   I
ed.pr. — *IG* x 2,255 (pl.10)

               − − − − − ιλιο ....
         − − − − οαεσα ... κατὰ τὰν πρεσβείαν
[------] κομίζεσθαι ἐν οἶκον, ἔδοξε καθ’ ὕπ⟨ν⟩ον ἐπιστάντα
[ν παρ’ αὐ]τὸν Σάραπιν ἐπιτάξαι ὅπως παραγενόμενος ἐν Ὀποῦντα

5 ν ἀναγγείλη Εὐρυνόμῳ τῷ Τειμασιθέου ὑποδέξασθαι αὐτόν τε καὶ
   νν τὰν ἀδελφὰν αὐτοῦ Εἶσιν, τάν τε ἐπιστολὰν τὰν οὖσαν ὑπὸ τῶι ποτι-
   ννν κεφαλαίῳ ἀναδῷ αὐτῷ· τὸν δὲ ἐγερθέντα θαυμάξαι τε τὸν
   [νν ὄ]νειρον καὶ διαπορεῖν τί πο⟨ι⟩ητέον ἐστὶν διὰ τὸ ὑπάρχει⟨ν⟩ αὐτῷ ἀντιπο-
   ν λειτείαν ποτὶ Εὐρύνομον· καθυπνώσας δὲ πάλιν καὶ τὰ αὐτὰ ἰδών,
10 ν καὶ ἐπεργεθεὶς τάν τε ἐπιστολὰν εὖρε ὑπὸ τῷ ποτικεφαλαίῳ
   ν καθὼς αὐτῷ ἐτεκμάρθη· ἐπανελθὼν δὲ ἀνέδωκε τὰν ἐπιστολὰν
   Εὐρυνόμωι καὶ ἀνήγγειλε τὰ ὑπὸ τοῦ θεοῦ ἐπιταχθέντα· Εὐρύνομος δὲ
   τὰν ἐπιστολὰν λαβὼν καὶ ἀκούσας τὰ ὑπὸ Ξεναινέτου λεγόμενα
   ν παρ' αὐτὸν μὲν τὸν καιρὸν ἀπόρως εἶχε διὰ τὸ καθὼς ἐπάνω
15 [διασ]αφεῖται εἶμεν αὐτοῖς ἀντιπολειτείαν ποτ' αὐσωτούς· ἀναγνοὺς δὲ
   [νν τὰν ἐπιστ]ολὰν καὶ ἰδὼν τὰ γεγραμμένα σύμφωνα τοῖς π[ρό]-
   [νν τερον ὑπ' αὐτ]οῦ εἰρημένοις ὑπεδέξατο τὸν Σάραπιν καὶ τὰν Εἶσιν
   [καὶ μετὰ τὸν ξενισμ]ὸν ἐν τᾶι οἰκίαι τᾶι Σωσινείκας ἐν τοὺς οἴκ[ου]-
   [ν ρους θεοὺς παραλαβοῦσα ἔ]θνε Σωσινείκα τὰς θεσίας χρόν[ον τινά·]
20 [νν μετὰ δὲ τὸν αὐτᾶς θάνατον Εὐν]όστα ἀ Σωσιβίου θυγατριδᾶ π[αρε]-
   [ν δίδου καὶ διεξᾶγε τὰ μυστήρια τῶ]ν θεῶν ἐν τοὺς κ[αὶ] ἀμετό[χ]ους
   [ν τῶν ἱερῶν· Εὐνόστας δὲ ὕστερον ἐν ἀρρωστ]ίαν ἐμπεσο[ύσα]ς προέθνε
   [ὑπὲρ αὐτᾶς τὰς θυσίας — — — — — — — — — — — — — — — — — —] ιο.ρμ ..μ..

Part of a much longer, damaged inscription (which includes an aretalogy of Sarapis), found at Thessalonike c.60 years ago, but first published in 1972 by C. Edson in *IG*.

Bib. — R. Merkelbach, *ZPE* 10 (1973) 49-54; *F. Sokolowski, *GRBS* 15 (1974) 441-45; *BE* (1973) 278; (1976) 394; L. Vidman, *Sylloge inscriptionum religionis Isiacae et Sarapiacae* (Berlin, 1969), catalogues a list (nos. 107-26) of epigraphical texts from Macedonia dealing with Sarapis and Isis.

(*l.* 3) . . . to come into the shrine, it seemed that in his sleep Sarapis was standing
5 **beside him and instructing him, upon arrival at Opous, | to report to Eurynomos the son of Timasitheos that he should receive him (viz., the god) and his sister Isis; and to give to Eurynomos the letter which was under his pillow. Waking up he (viz., Xenainetos) was amazed at his vision and perplexed about what he should do because of the political hostility which he had towards Eurynomos.**
10 **But falling asleep again, he had the same dream, | and when he awoke he discovered the letter under his pillow, just as was indicated to him. When he returned home, he handed over the letter to Eurynomos and reported the god's instructions. Eurynomos took the letter and after hearing what Xenainetos said he was perplexed during the occasion itself, because of the existence of the**
15 **political hostility between them (as is mentioned above). | But when he read the letter and saw that its contents were consistent with what had been said beforehand by Xenainetos, he accepted Sarapis and Isis. After he provided hospitality (for the gods) in the house of Sosinike, she received them among her**

20 **household gods and performed the sacrifices for some time. | After her death, Eunosta the grand-daughter of Sosibios transmitted the (cult) and administered the mysteries of the gods among those who also were non-participants in the rites. Later, when Eunosta fell ill . . . performed the sacrifice on her behalf.**

The Sarapeion at Thessalonike was originally built in the third century BC (C. Edson, *HTR* 41 [1948] 181-82). The excerpt printed above was set up at least two hundred years later, and reveals one way in which such a cult was disseminated. For this text is a piece of religious propaganda, designed to make plain the divine authorisation for the establishment of the cult of Isis and Sarapis in the Lokrian city Opous. (The text is written in Lokrian dialect: αὐσωτούς[15] = ἑαυτούς.) Not everywhere was the cult of these gods accepted readily, e.g., at Histria (Sokolowski, 447), and perhaps implied in the inscription from Magnesia on the Maeander which Sokolowski republishes (445-46). The text above states that while consulting (via incubation, 3) Sarapis at Thessalonike, a certain Xenainetos received a divine vision, not once, but twice, in which the god gave him certain instructions. The reality of this dream was brought home by the discovery of a letter under his pillow. Such *Himmelsbriefe* are discussed by Merkelbach (53) and Sokolowski (443), who assemble other references to the phenomenon, literary (Paus. 10.38.13; Ael. Arist. *Sacred tales* 2.394 Keil), epigraphical (*IG* XI 4, 1299,56-58; cf. A.D. Nock, *Conversion* [Oxford, 1933; repr. 1972] 50-54; this text from Delos is another Sarapis aretalogy, discussed at length by H. Engelmann, *The Delian Aretalogy of Sarapis* [Leiden, 1975]), and papyrological (*P.Cairo Zen.* 1 [1925] 59034). S.R. Pickering points out to me that this same motif occurs in later Christianity. According to Palladius, *Hist. Laus.* 32 (1099C), while Pachomius was sitting in his cave ὤφθη ἄγγελος καὶ λέγει αὐτῷ ... καὶ ἐπέδωκεν αὐτῷ δέλτον χαλκὴν ἐν ᾗ ἐγέγραπτο ταῦτα (viz. the Pachomian Rule). Sozomen derives his account (*HE* 3.14) from Palladius. Instances continue to occur in the mediaeval world, e.g., the letter from Christ which the eighth-century Aldebert received (see J. B. Russell, *Church History* 33[1964] 231-47, especially 238-40 and n.43). The best treatment of this phenomenon in antiquity is W. Speyer, *Bücherfunde in der Glaubenswerbung der Antike* (Göttingen, 1970), esp. 17-19, 23-42. On divine instructions conveyed through dreams which result in the recipient taking some particular action, such as making a dedication or establishing a cult, see the useful survey by F. T. van Straten, *BVAB* 51(1976) 1-38 (cf. *SEG* 953). One such inscription (*SIG*³ 985) is discussed in relation to the NT churches by S.C. Barton and G.H.R. Horsley, *JbAC* 24(1981) 7-41.

Clearly implicit in this inscription is the conversion of Eurynomos: in accepting the god's injunctions which came to him via Xenainetos, and setting up the cult at Opous, he may be presumed to have become an adherent of the god. Merkelbach, who makes this point briefly (54), points to the Saul/Paul parallel in the NT. On this phenomenon generally, see Nock, op. cit., *passim*.

For discussion of the word *oikos* = shrine, see Barton and Horsley *art.cit.* 15-16. The NT uses it in this sense at Lk. 11.51 (cf. Mt. 23.25). Sokolowski, 444, discusses the notion of providing hospitality (ὑποδέχεσθαι, 5, 17) to a god; in the NT the word occurs in a similar sense, 'receive hospitably into one's home, entertain' (Lk. 10.38, 19.1; Acts 17.7; Jas. 2.25). Sokolowski argues (ibid.), from *ll.*18-19, 21-22, that this cult was originally confined to the family of the first priestess but that some time later access was provided to others (καὶ ἀμετόχους, 21). The verb ἐφίστημι (3) also finds analogous use in the NT; in our text here, the god appears in the vision and, standing beside him, gives him instructions. Note Acts 12.7-10, ἄγγελος κυρίου ἐπέστη...εἶπεν...πρὸς αὐτόν...(Πέτρος) ἐδόκει δὲ ὅραμα βλέπειν; Acts 23.11, τῇ δὲ ἐπιούσῃ νυκτὶ ἐπιστὰς αὐτῷ ὁ κύριος εἶπεν...; cf. Lk. 2.9 (not a dream). While the verb τεκμαίρομαι (11) does not occur in the NT, Merkelbach (50,n.4) has pointed to the use of the noun in a similar sense in Acts 1.3.

7. Two confession texts from Graeco-Roman Phrygia

(a) Eumeneia; (b) Provenance Uncertain   Late Roman?
ed.pr. — T. Drew-Bear, *GRBS* 17 (1976) 260-61, no.15 (ph.); 262-66, no.17 (ph.)

(a)	[Ἀπόλλω]-	(b)	[Τε]λέσφορος καὶ Ἑ[ρμ]-
	[νι Προ]-		ογένης Σταλλα-
	[πυ]λαίῳ		ηνοὶ παρορκή-
	[Ἐπ]ιτύν-		σαντες ἀνέθη-
5	[χ]ανος κολα-	5	καν
	ζόμενος		
	[ἀ]νέθηκεν		

Part of a votive tablet (a) and a broken altar (b). The former has a double axe engraved on it, the symbol of Apollo Propylaios. Depicted on the latter stone are two figures, one holding a pair of scales, the other a measuring rod.
Bib. — *SEG* 1376, 1386.

(a) **To Apollo Propylaios, Epitynchanos, while under chastisement, set up (a dedication).**
(b) **Telesphoros and Hermogenes, the Stallaenoi, perjurors, set up (the dedication).**

Confession texts like these are common in Asia Minor. A wrongdoer finds himself impelled, perhaps by a disease which now afflicts him, to place on public record his action. This takes the form of a dedication to the god whom he believes is punishing him and whom he hopes will now being relief from his troubles. The longer inscription is the first yet found in which confession is made to this particular god (Drew-Bear, 261), and the present participle is hitherto unattested on dedications of this type (usually κολασθείς, Drew-Bear, 261, n.54). For Apollo Propylaios see Drew-Bear, 260. In text (b) Σταλλαηνοί presumably refers to the village where the dedicants live; but its location is uncertain (ibid., 263). While not named, the figures depicted on this altar are the gods Hosion and Dikaion (or -ios and -ios), Purity and Justice (ibid., 263-64). This is the first confession text to these deities found thus far. Drew-Bear,

264-65, discusses other examples of these documents where perjury is admitted. The dedication provides our first epigraphical attestation of the verb παρορκέω (cf. the much commoner ἐπιορκέω), ibid., 265.

8. A love charm and 'the keys of Hades'

Region of Antinoopolis III/IV
ed.pr. — S. Kambitsis, *BIAO* 76 (1976) 213-23 (pl. 30 and 31)

Παρακατατίθεμαι ὑμῖν τοῦτον τὸν κατάδεσμον θεο[ῖ]ς καταχθονίοις, Πλούτωνι καὶ
    Κόρῃ Φερσεφόνῃ
Ἐρεσχιγαλ καὶ Ἀδώνδιι τῷ καὶ Βαρβαριθα καὶ Ἑρμῇ καταχθονίῳ Θωουθ φωκενσεψευ
    ερεκταθου μισον-
κταικ καὶ Ἀνούβιδι κραταιῷ ψηριφθα, τῷ τὰς κλεῖδας ἔχοντι τῶν κατὰ Ἅ̣δ̣ους, καὶ
    δαίμοσι κατα-
χθονίοις θεοῖς, ἀώροις τε καὶ ἀώραις, μέλλαξι καὶ παρθένοις, ἐνιαυτοῖς ἐξ ἐνιαυτῶν,
    μήνασι
5   ἐκ μηνῶν, ἡμέραις ἐκ ἡμερῶν, ὥρασι ὡρῶν, νύκτες ἐκ νυκτῶν· ὁρκίζω πάντας τοὺς δαί-
    μονας τοὺς ἐν τῷ τόπῳ τούτῳ συνπαραστῆναι τῷ δαίμονι τούτῳ Ἀντινόῳ. Διέγειραί
    μοι σε-
αυτὸν καὶ ὕπαγε εἰς πᾶν τ[όπο]ν, εἰς πᾶν ἄμφοδον, εἰς πᾶσαν οἰκείαν καὶ κατάδησον
    Π̣τολε-
μαίδα, ἣν ἔτεκεν Ἀϊᾶς, τὴν θυγατέρα Ὡριγένους, ὅπως μὴ βινηθῇ, μὴ πυγισθῇ μη-
δὲν πρὸς ἡδονὴν ποιήσῃ ἑταίρῳ ἀνδρὶ εἰ μὴ ἐμοὶ μόνῳ τῷ Σαραπάμμωνι, ὃν ἔτε-
10 κεν Ἀρ̣έ̣α, καὶ μὴ ἀφῇς αὐτὴν φαγεῖν, μὴ πεῖν, μὴ στέ⟨ρ⟩γειν μήτε ἐξελθεῖν μήτε
    ὕπνου τυχεῖν ἐκτὸς ἐμοῦ τοῦ Σαραπάμμωνος, οὗ ἔτεκεν Ἀρ̣έ̣α̣. Ἐξορκίζω σε,
    νεκύδαιμον
Ἀντίνοε, κατὰ τοῦ ὀνόματος [τοῦ] τρομεροῦ καὶ φοβεροῦ, οὗ ἡ γῆ ἀκούσασα τοῦ ὀνόματος ἀνυγήσεται, οὗ οἱ δαίμονες ἀκούσαντες τοῦ ὀνόματος ἐνφόβως φοβοῦνται,
οὗ οἱ ποταμοὶ καὶ πέτραι ἀκούσαντες ῥήσσ[οντα]ι· ὁρκίζω σε, νεκύδαιμον Ἀντίνοε,
15 κατὰ τοῦ Βαρβαραθαμ χελουμβρα βαρου[χ] Ἀδωναὶ καὶ κατὰ τοῦ Ἀβρασὰξ
    καὶ κατὰ τοῦ Ἰαω πακεπτωθ πακεβραωθ σαβαρβαραει καὶ
    τοῦ Μαρμαραουωθ καὶ κατὰ τοῦ Μαρμαραχθα μαμαζαγαρ̣. Μὴ παρα-
    κούσῃς, νεκύδαιμον Ἀντίνοε, ἀλλ' ἔγειραί μοι σεαυτὸν καὶ ὕπαγε εἰς πᾶν τό-
    πον, εἰς πᾶν ἄμφοδον, εἰς πᾶσαν οἰκείαν καὶ ἄγαγέ μοι τὴν Πτολεμαίδα,
20 ἣν ἔτεκεν Ἀϊᾶς, τὴν θυγατέρα Ὡριγένους· κάτασχες αὐτῆς τὸ βρωτόν,
    τὸ ποτόν, ἕως ἔλθῃ πρὸς ἐμὲ τὸν Σαραπάμμωνα, ὃν ἔτεκεν Ἀρέα,
    καὶ μὴ ἐάσῃς αὐτὴν ἄλλου ἀνδρὸς πεῖραν λαβεῖν εἰ μὴ ἐμοῦ μόνου
    τοῦ Σαραπάμμωνος. Ἕλκε αὐτὴν τῶν τριχῶν, τῶν σπλάγχνων,
    ἕως μὴ ἀποστῇ μου τοῦ Σαραπάμμωνος, οὗ ἔτεκεν Ἀρέα, καὶ ἔχω
25 αὐτὴν τὴν Πτολεμαίδα, ἣν ἔτεκεν Ἀϊᾶς, τὴν θυγατέρα Ὡριγένους,
    ὑποτεταγμένην εἰς τὸν ἄπαντα χρόνον τῆς ζωῆς μου,
    φιλοῦσάν με, ἐρῶσ[ά]ν μου, λέγουσάν μοι ἃ ἔχει ἐν νόῳ. Ἐὰν τοῦτο
    ποιήσῃς, ἀπολύσω σε.

This rolled-up lead tablet (roughly 11 cm. square) containing the complete text of a love-charm was found in Egypt inside a clay vase, together with a clay statuette of a kneeling woman, her hands bound behind her back, pierced with needles.
Bib. — *SEG* 1717; *BE* (1978) 34; H.D. Jocelyn, *LCM* 6(1981)45.

> **I entrust this binding-charm to you gods of the underworld: Pluto and Kore-Persephone, Ereschigal, Adonis also called Barbaritha, Hermes Katachthonios-Thoth,** *phokensepseu erektathou misonktaik,* **Anoubis the strong,** *pseriphtha,* **who holds the keys of Hades, divine daimones of the underworld, youths and**
> 5 **maidens who died before their time, year by year, month | by month, day by day, hour by hour, night by night. I conjure all daimones in this place to assist this daimon Antinoos. Rouse yourself for me and go to every place, to every quarter (of the town), to every house, and bind Ptolemais whom Aias bore, the daughter of Horigenes, so that she may not 'submit to intercourse' or buggery or provide pleasure to another [read ἑτέρῳ] man except me alone, Sarapammon whom**
> 10 **| Area bore. Do not let her eat or drink or be content or go out or find sleep apart from me, Sarapammon whom Area bore. I conjure you, daimon of the dead Antinoos, by the name of the Terrible and Aweful one, at the sound of whose name the earth will open up, at the sound of whose name the daimones are struck with fear and hearing it the rivers and rocks will shatter. I conjure you,**
> 15 **daimon of the dead Antinoos, | by** *Barbaratham cheloumbra barouch* **Adonai, and by Abrasax, and by Iao** *pakeptoth pakebraoth sabarbaraei* **and by** *Marmaraouoth* **and by** *Marmarachtha mamazagar.* **Do not disregard me, daimon of the dead Antinoos, but rouse yourself for me and go to every place,**
> 20 **to every quarter, to every house, and bring to me Ptolemais | whom Aias bore, the daughter of Horigenes. Restrain her from eating and drinking until she comes to me Sarapammon whom Area bore; and do not allow her to gain experience of another man except me alone, Sarapammon. Drag her by the hair, tear at her guts, until she does not reject me, Sarapammon whom Area bore,**
> 25 **and I have | Ptolemais herself whom Aias bore, the daughter of Horigenes, obedient for the rest of my life, loving me, desiring me, telling me her thoughts. If you do this, I will release you.**

The appearance in 1928 of K. Preisendanz' first volume of *Papyri Graecae Magicae* (Leipzig; repr. 1973), while not the first publication of magical texts, nevertheless marked an important advance. A.D. Nock, writing soon afterwards (*JEA* 15 [1929] 219-35) emphasised the importance of such texts 'for proper understanding of the religious history of the Empire' (219). Written on a variety of surfaces (papyrus, lead, wood, gemstones, etc.) and ranging enormously in length (a few letters, to over 3000 lines in the case of *PGM* 4) these magical works span many centuries, though of extant papyri the bulk appears to fall between II-V or VI. The large books of spells (such as *PGM* 4) belong to late III-V. That there was plenty of work available for the writers and practitioners of spells is clear from the incident at Ephesus reported in Acts 19.13-19.

That this charm was inscribed professionally is clear not only from the clarity of the script, but also from the very great resemblance in content which this text bears to certain other spells of similar intent. Kambitsis shows how this charm, together with the accompanying figurine, is modelled on the contents of *PGM* 4.296-434. The figurine has clearly been made in accordance with the instructions of *ll.* 296-334 of the latter; but while related, the wording on our lead tablet is closer to other magical texts than to the incantation in *PGM* 4.335-434. Those with the closest affinity are two lead tablets from Oxyrhynchos (III/IV): D. Wortmann, *Bonn. Jahrb.* 168 (1968) 57-80, nos. 1 and 2; and a lead tablet from the Fayum (not later than III) published by C.C. Edgar, *Bull. Soc. Arch. Alexandrie* 21 (1925) 42ff. (*non vidi;* [= *SB* 4 (1931) 7452 = *SEG* 8 (1937/8) 544]). The relationship between these three texts and *PGM* 4 is discussed by Wortmann, 57-59; cf. Nock, 233-35.

Sarapammon has had the text incised in order to secure the love of Ptolemais. He appeals to the spirit of a dead man, Antinoos, and seeks the help of various underworld powers — gods, the spirits of prematurely deceased young people, and spirits which frequent the place where the charm has been deposited (viz., the grave of Antinoos). The dead man's *daimon* is required to seek out Ptolemais and 'bind' her in various ways in the name of the supreme god, and bring her henceforth loving and submissive to Sarapammon. Only then will Antinoos' spirit be released from Sarapammon's demands.

A text like this demonstrates how thoroughly Greek and Egyptian magic has been blended, at least in Egypt. For in addition to various magical names, Egyptian and Greek gods are named 'in the same breath'. See Wortmann, 68-75, for passages with very similar invocations, and for comment on the magical names (which are *italicised* in the translation above). The presence of semitic names for God is to be noted: Ἰαώ and Ἀδωναί (15-16) appear on other magical texts quite frequently. Examples include Wortmann, no.8 (p.106), where the first two lines of the lead tablet used as an amulet (VI, Oxyrhynchos) contain ἰα[ὼ|Ἀδωναίε Σαβ[αώθ]. These three words appear again at *PGM* 7.311. In a posthumously published article on magical gems Wortmann, *Bonn. Jahrb.* 175 (1975) 63-82, includes a considerable number which contain Ἰαώ (nos. 1, 2, 3, 4, 5, 10, 15 — this last being Ἰαώ Σαβαώθ). B. Lifshitz discusses briefly the use of Ἰαώ in magical texts (*Rev. Bib.* 77 [1970] 82) and argues that *CIJ* 2.849 (IV-VI, Damascus) is not to be treated as a Jewish amulet: Ἰαώ was simply taken over and used by pagans who believed in the magical potency of names. For this common notion, that power resides in knowledge of the name of a person or god, cf. the incident in Acts 8.9-24 (further discussed at **68**), and the Acts 19 passage alluded to above. For a useful brief discussion of the magical papyri see H. I. Bell, *Cults and Creeds of Graeco-Roman Egypt* (Liverpool, 1953; repr. Chicago, 1975), 71-74.

Wortmann shows (1968:70) that the notion of Anoubis as the custodian of the keys of Hades (*l.*3) is a standard element in magical charms (cf. *PGM* 4.341-42). Kambitsis follows him by understanding πυλῶν with τῶν in our lead tablet. This phraseology concerning Anoubis finds a striking parallel in Rev. 1.18 where the risen Christ describes himself thus: ἔχω τὰς κλεῖς τοῦ θανάτου καὶ τοῦ Ἅιδου. Here is an example of the figurative use of κλεῖς for which MM could find no parallel ouside the NT. The commentaries of Swete and Charles refer to Targum passages which speak of God having power over the keys of death. It is possible that the phrase had a popular currency, and the similarity may be merely co-incidental. Alternatively it may imply knowledge of magical formulae by the writer of Rev. (cf. the use of ΑΩ and 'the beginning and the end' — **22**), or less probably (in view of the date) a borrowing from the latter by the magical tradition.

The variety of words for love is conspicuous in this charm (cf. **17**). Here we find φιλοῦσάν με, ἐρῶσ[ά]ν με (27) being clearly distinguished. στέργειν (10) may mean rather less than 'love' here. Two very explicit words for sexual activity are juxtaposed at *l*.8, the first of which is the equivalent of the English 'four-letter word' (cf. A. H. Sommerstein, *LCM* 5 (1980) 47). It may be only modern expectation that πυγίζεσθαι would not be used with any frequency of women; cf. J. Henderson, *The Maculate Muse* (Yale, 1975) 202. L. Koenen tells me in a note that the practice was far from uncommon in the Greek world, referring to several pieces of evidence including J. Boardman, *Athenian Red Figure Vases. The Archaic Period* (London 1975), fig.219. F.I. Andersen suggests to me that πυγίζεσθαι of women may be a contraceptive strategy such as was practised in Mesopotamia (a clear example quoted in *Chicago Akkadian Dictionary,* vol.E,.s.v., *erû,* 1a). At *l*.22 πεῖραν λαβεῖν appears to be a euphemism for sexual relations: for the construction cf. LSJ s.v. πεῖρα although this sense is not attested there.

Finally, Sarapammon's demand that Ptolemais should be ὑποτεταγμένην (26) provides a clear illustration of the word's used with reference to marital relations in the NT (cf. especially 1 Cor. 14.34; Eph. 5.22; Col. 3.18; Tit. 2.5; 1 Pet. 3.1,5). Of course, this claim is exclusive: she is to be submissive to him, not to anyone else. Fidelity to Sarapammon is implied. A common non-NT use of ὑποτάσσω, 'append, attach below', discussed by MM, s.v., is attested in a letter of 114 B.C. (*P. Tebt.* 1100).

9. The regional *kanon* for requisitioned transport

Region of Sagalassos (Pisidia)   18-19
ed. pr. — S. Mitchell, *JRS* 66 (1976) 106-31 (pl.8-10)

> *Sex. Sotidius Strabo Libuscidianus leg.*
> *Ti. Caesaris Augusti pro pr.* (vac) *dic.*
> *Est quidem omnium iniquissimum me edicto meo adstringere id quod Augusti*
>   *alter deorum alter principum*
> *maximus diligentissime caverunt, ne quis gratuitis vehiculis utatur, sed quoniam*
>   *licentia quorundam*
> 5 *praesentem vindictam desiderat, formulam eorum quae* [*pra*]*ẹstari iudico*
>   *oportere in singulis civitatibus*
> *et vicis proposui servaturus eam aut si neglecta erit vindicaturus non mea tantum*
>   *potestate sed*
> *principis optimi a quo ịd ip[s]um in mandatis accepi maiestate.* (vac)
> *Sagalassenos* {*o*} *ministerium carrorum decem et mulorum totidem praestare*
>   *debent ad usus neces-*
> *sarios transeuntium, et accipere in singula carra et in singulos schoenos ab iis qui*
>   *utentur aeris denos, in mulos autem singulos*

10   *et schoenos singulos aeris quaternos, quod si asinos malent eodem pretio duos*
          pro uno mulo dent.
      Aut, si malent, in singulos mulos et in singula carra id quod accepturi erant si
          ipsi praeberent (vac)
      dare praestent iis qui alterius civitatis aut vici munere fungentur, ut idem
          procedant.
      Praestare autem debebunt vehicula usque Cormasa et Conanam. Neque tamen
          omnibu-
      s huius rei ius erit, sed procuratori principis optimi filioque eius, usu da[*to*
          us]*que ad carra decem aut*
15   *pro singulis carris mulorum trium aut pro singulis mulis asinorum binorum*
          quibus eodem te-
      mpore utentur soluturi pretium a me constitutum; praeterea militantibus, et iis
          qui diplomum hab-
      ebunt, et iis qui ex alis provincis militantes commeabunt ita ut senatori populi
          Romani non plus quam
      decem carra aut pro singulis carris muli terni aut pro singulis mulis asini bini
          praestentur soluturis id quod
      praescripsi; equiti Romano cuius officio princeps optimus utitur ter carra aut in
          singula terni muli aut
20   *in singulos* [*mu*]*los bini asini dari debebunt eadem condicione, sed amplius quis*
          desiderabit conducet
      arbitrio locantis; centurioni carrum aut tres muli aut asini sexs eadem
          condicione. Iis qui frumen-
      tum aut aliudq < u > id tale vel quaestus sui caussa vel usus portant praestari nihil
          volo, neque cuiquam p-
      ro suo aut suorum libertorum aut servorum iumentu. Mansionem omnibus qui
          erunt ex
      comitatu nostro et militantibus ex omnibus provincis et principis optimi libertis
          et servis et iumentis
25   *eorum gratuitam praestari oportet, ita ut reliqua ab invitis gratuita non*
          e(x)sigant. (vac)
      Σέξτος Σωτίδιος Στράβων Λιβουσκιδιανὸς πρεσβευτὴς Τιβερίου Καίσαρος Σεβαστοῦ
          ἀντιστρα-
      τηγὸς λέγει· ἔστιν μὲν ἄδικον τὸ ἀκριβέστατα ἠσφαλισμένον ὑπὸ τῶν Σεβαστῶν τοῦ
          μὲν
      θεῶν τοῦ δὲ αὐτοκρατόρων μεγείστου ἐμὲ διατάγματι ἐπισφείνγειν· ἐπεὶ δὲ ἡ τινῶν
          πλεο-
      νεξία τὴν παραυτίκα ἐκδικίαν αἰτεῖ, κατὰ πόλιν καὶ κώμην ἔταξα κανόνα τῶν
          ὑπηρεσιῶν ὃν τη-
30   ρήσω οὐ μόνον δι' ἐμαυτοῦ ἀλλὰ ἐὰν δέῃ καὶ τὴν τοῦ σωτῆρος Σεβαστοῦ δεδωκότος μοι
          περὶ τούτων ἐντολ[ὰς] προσπαραλαβὼν θειότητα. Σαγαλασσεῖς λειτουργεῖν δεῖ μέχρι
          δέκα κάρ-
      ρων ἕως Κορμάσων καὶ Κονάνης, νωτοφόροις δὲ ἴσοις· ἐπὶ τῷ λαμβάνειν ὑπὲρ μὲν
          κάρρου

(*vac*) κατὰ σχοῖνον ἀσσάρια δέκα, ὑπὲρ δὲ νωτοφόρου κατὰ σχοῖνον ἀσσάρια τέσσαρα, ὑπὲρ δὲ

ὄνου κατὰ σχοῖνον ἀσσάρια δύο· ἢ εἰ προκρείνουσιν χαλκὸν διδόναι τοῖς ὑπηρετοῦσιν ἐξ ἄλ-

35   λων τόπων προσθέτωσαν αὐτοῖς ὅσον αὐτοὶ ὑπηρετοῦντες ἔμελλον λ⟨α⟩μβάνειν· οὐ πᾶ-

σιν δὲ τοῖς βουλομένοις τὴν τοιαύτην ὑπηρεσίαν παρέχεσθαι δίκαι⟨όν⟩ ἐστιν, ἀλλὰ τῶ τοῦ

Σεβαστοῦ ἐπιτρόπω καὶ τῶ υἱῶι αὐτοῦ μέχρι κάρρων δέκα ἢ νωτοφόρων εἰς λόγον ἑνὸς κάρρου τριῶν ἢ ὄνων εἰς ἑνὸς ἡμιόνου λόγον δυεῖν οἷς ὑπὸ τὸν αὐτὸν καιρὸν χρῆσ{εσ}ονται ἀποδιδόντες τὸν ὡρισμένον μισθόν· ἐπὶ τούτοις καὶ τοῖς

40   στρατευομένοις, καὶ τοῖς διπλώματα ἔχουσιν, καὶ τοῖς ἐξ ἄλλων ἐπαρχειῶν διοδεύου-σιν, ἐξ ὧν τοῖς μὲν συνκλητικοῖς οὐ πλείονα τῶν δέκα ζευκτῶν, ἢ ὑπὲρ ἑνὸς τρεῖς ἡμι-όνους, ἢ ὑπὲρ ἑνὸς ἡμιόνου δύο ὄνους, ἀποδιδοῦσιν τὸν ὡρισμένον μισθὸν παραστῆσαι ἀνάγκην ἕξουσιν· τοῖς δὲ ἱππικῆς τάξεως ἐάν τις ἐν ταῖς τοῦ Σεβαστοῦ χρή[αις] ᾖ κάρρων τριῶν, ἢ εἰς τὸν ἑκάστου λόγον ἡμιόνων τριῶν,

45   ἢ ὄνων ἓξ ἐπὶ τῇ ἰδί[α]ι αἱρέσει· ἑκατοντάρχη κάρρον ἢ νωτοφόρους τρῖς, ἢ ὑπὲρ ἑκάσ-του ὄνους δύο, [τοῖς] τὸν μισθὸν διδοῦσιν, ἐὰν δέ τις τούτοις μὴ ἀρκῆται τὰ λοι-πὰ μισθώσε[ται παρ]ὰ τῶν βουλομένων. τοῖς σεῖτον ἢ ἄλλο τι τοιοῦτο ἐπ᾽ ἐμπορία ἢ χρήσει διακομίζουσιν ὑπηρετεῖσ[θ]⟨αι⟩ οὐ βούλομαι· ὑπὲρ ἰδίων ἢ ἀπελευθερικῶν ἢ

δουλικῶν κτηνῶν λαμβάνεσθαί τι ἀποδοκιμάζω. σταθμὸν πᾶσιν τοῖς τε με-

50   θ᾽ ἡμῶν καὶ τοῖς στρατευομένοις ἐν πάσαις ἐπαρχείαις καὶ τοῖς τοῦ Σεβαστοῦ ἀπε-λευθέροις καὶ δούλοις καὶ τοῖς κτήνεσιν αὐτῶν ἄμισθον παρασχεθῆναι δεῖ, τᾶλ-
(*vac*) λα δὲ...ΡΝ − − *c.* 5 − − \ ΝΠΑΡΑϹ..ΟΝΤΩΝ (*vac*)

A grey marble stele (1.25 x 0.79m.) said to have been found at Burdur (? = ancient Praetoria, in the territory of Sagalassos) and now in the archaeological museum there. *Bib.* — *AE* 653; *SEG* 1392; *BE* (1977) 510; J.H. Oliver, *ZPE* 32 (1978) 280; P. Frisch, *ZPE* 41 (1981) 100. Text follows Mitchell, incorporating Frisch's reading of *l*.7 (see below).

(*The following translation is based on the presumably original Latin version, with notable variations in the Greek indicated. Italicised phrases are unique to the Latin.*)

Sextus Sotidius Strabo Libuscidianus, legate of Ti. Caesar Augustus acting as praetor, declares:- It is indeed of all things most inequitable that I should be tightening up by my edict what the two Augustuses, the one the greatest of gods, the other the greatest of leaders (*Gk:* commanders), most carefully guarded against, *namely that no one should make use of transport free,* **but since the**
5   **licence of certain people | demands immediate action, I have promulgated in the individual cities and villages a schedule of what I judge desirable to be supplied, it being my intention to maintain it** *or if neglected enforce it* **not merely by my own powers but by the supremacy (*Gk:* divinity) of the excellent leader (*Gk:* saviour Augustus) from whom I accepted this very thing in my mandate. The**

10

Sagalassenes are obliged to supply a service of (*Gk:* up to) ten carts and as many mules *for the necessary uses of those passing through,* and to accept ten bronze (asses) per cart per schoenus *from those who use them,* or per mule |per schoenus, four, but if they prefer donkeys they are to supply two for one mule at the same rate. Or if they prefer they are to pay over what they would have received per mule and per cart, if they themselves had provided them, to those who perform the obligation of another city or village, *so that they can fulfil it.* They shall be obliged, moreover, to supply transport as far as Cormasa and Conana. However, not everyone (*Gk adds:* wishing it) has the right to this, but to the procurator of the excellent leader (*Gk:* of the Augustus) and to (*sc.* of?)

15

his son *is granted the use of it* up to ten carts, or |three mules in place of a cart, or two donkeys in place of a mule when used at the same time, subject to their paying the price established by me; and likewise, to those on military service, or who hold a certificate, and to those who are travelling from other provinces *on military service,* on the basis that to a senator of the Roman people are supplied no more than ten carts or three mules in place of a cart or two donkeys in place of a mule subject to their *(sic)* paying what I have prescribed (*Gk adds:* to those having the obligation to supply them); to a Roman knight whose services the excellent leader is using (*Gk:* involved in the needs of the Augustus) three carts

20

or three mules for a cart or |two donkeys for a mule must be given on the same terms *(Gk adds:* at his own discretion), *while anyone who desires more shall have it at the contractor's discretion (Gk has the equivalent of this phrase at the end of the sentence);* to a centurion a cart or three mules or six donkeys on the same terms. To those who carry grain or any such thing for their own profit or use I do not wish anything to be supplied, nor (anything) for anyone (*Gk adds :* do I tolerate being taken) for his own beasts of burden or those of his freedmen or slaves. Accommodation for all those who belong to my staff and for those on military service from all provinces and for the freedmen and slaves of the

25

excellent leader (*Gk:* the Augustus) and their beasts |ought to be supplied free, but without their demanding the rest (of their costs) free from those who are unwilling (to supply them).

Historical importance and form of the document

The imposition of transport and billeting services upon local communities was a constant source of friction in the Roman provinces. Mitchell (111-12) lists 21 documents from the first two and a half centuries which illustrate the problems it gave rise to. This new text both provides the earliest epigraphic evidence for the system, and is the first to register the comprehensive schedule (*formula,* καυών) of requirements for a particular region. It is also 'apparently the earliest complete bilingual document which has survived' (110), to be compared therefore in linguistic value with the *Res Gestae* of Augustus which is preserved in several inscriptions of Asia Minor from the same period. For an analysis of the Greek text in the latter case see A.P.M. Meuwese, *De rerum gestarum divi Augusti versione graeca* (diss. Amsterdam, 1920), evaluated along with subsequent publications in H. Volkmann, *Bursians Jahresbericht* (1942) 54-63.

The style and function of the imperial edict has now been analysed by M. Benner, *The Emperor Says: Studies in the Rhetorical Style in Edicts of the Early Empire* (Gothenburg, 1975). As the name implies, an edict is the proclamation of a magistrate.

It is used to regulate the behaviour or thinking of the community under his jurisdiction. It differs from a letter in being essentially an oral statement and in not making reference to particular individuals. The 'letters' to the seven churches (Rev. 2.1, etc.) are edicts, and open, as here, with the characteristic verb of declaration, λέγει. A wide range of extant examples contemporary with the New Testament (not exploited in BAGD or MM, s.v. λέγω) may be seen in V. Ehrenberg and A.H.M. Jones, *Documents Illustrating the Reigns of Augustus and Tiberius* (Oxford, 1954²), and E.M. Smallwood, *Documents Illustrating the Principates of Gaius, Claudius and Nero* (Cambridge, 1967), in either case under the section, 'Administration of the Empire'. For English translations see A.C. Johnson et al., *Ancient Roman Statutes* (Austin, 1961).

Date and political setting

Mitchell argues from internal evidence that Sotidius must have been appointed governor of Galatia under Augustus (in say 13 AD) and continued under Tiberius (till say 15). 'Tiberius is never referred to as *princeps optimus* or as σωτὴρ Σεβαστός without further qualification, and it would be intolerably ambiguous if he were in a context where Augustus had just been mentioned' (113). All three instances of the phrase are therefore taken as references to Augustus. But while one may be the freedman (*l.*24) of a dead man, I do not see how he can be said to have either slaves (24) or a procurator (14) once his property has passed to his heir, nor how Roman knights can be said to be still used in his service (19). Mitchell takes these phrases to allude to 'Augustan appointments', perhaps relying upon the coupling of 'his son' (14) with the 'excellent leader' to safeguard the dignity of Tiberius. But the latter is certainly now in charge of them all, whenever they were appointed, and the *princeps* referred to ought therefore to be Tiberius.

What could it mean, moreover, for the legate of Galatia to invoke the *maiestas* (7)/θειότης (31) of a deceased *princeps* as a source of punishment? R.A. Bauman, *Impietas : A Study of Treason Against the Roman Emperor with Special Reference to the First Century A.D.* (Munich, 1974), 15-17, discusses the confusing expansion of the law of *maiestas* that followed the deification of Augustus, so that it even embraced 'criticising anything Augustus had ever said or done' (Suetonius, *Tiberius* 58). But this was an unplanned phenomenon. At the most Sotidius could only be unconsciously anticipating it. I take it rather that he is threatening to refer the matter to his present superior (Tiberius). Indeed one may imagine from the frustrated *iniquissimum* (3)/ἄδικον (27) of the preamble that Tiberius had given him only general *mandata* (8)/ἐντολαί (31) on the subject, perhaps refusing to supply such specific advice as Augustus had to the proconsuls in the Cyrene edicts (Ehrenberg & Jones, 311) or Trajan to Pliny (*Ep.* X), but had left open the possibility of his seeking help if he failed to assert control on his own authority. So, in a similar matter, Germanicus explicitly required his secretary to report offenders if he could not curb them himself (Ehrenberg & Jones, 320.24). It is conceivable (though the Greek plural in *l.*31 does not support it) that it is the obligation to refer intractable offenders, rather than the duty of regulating the system as a whole, which is meant by the 'id ip[s]um' now read by Frisch in *l.*7 from the photograph published by D. French and Mitchell in *Türk Arkeoloji Dergisi* 24 (1977) 220. (Frisch also corrects EN on the stone to 'in'.)

F. Millar, on the other hand, in *JRS* 56 (1966) 156-66 at 159, lists the cases in this century where *legati* sent prisoners to their superior to be judged. They were all involved in much more serious matters, relating to subversion or a threat to the Caesar himself. The prefect of Egypt in 68, Tiberius Julius Alexander, distinguishes between matters which it is in order for him to determine and execute, and 'greater ones needing the power and majesty of the *imperator*' (E.M. Smallwood, *Documents . . . ,* 391.9).

Either way, we must envisage the *princeps* of the day behind Sotidius' threat. It is surely in any case doubtful whether Augustus could have been spoken of as *princeps* at all after his death and deification. The preamble to our own text makes the distinction very clear (3, 28).

Nor was Augustus ever called *princeps optimus* during his lifetime, so far as our evidence goes. The closest approach to it is Horace, *Odes* 4.5.1: *optime Romulae custos gentis,* 'excellent guardian of the house of Romulus'. R. Frei-Stolba, *MH* 26 (1969) 18-39 at 21-28, reports the view of J. Vogt, *Hermes* 68 (1933) 84ff., especially 91, that Augustus must have avoided the phrase because it would have suggested the senatorial partisanship of the preceding era. But in spite of the *optimates* our phrase was not featured then. Cf. E. Lepore, *Il princeps ciceroniano e gli ideali politici della tarda repubblica* (Naples, 1954), 201-18.

By contrast, it is precisely with Tiberius that the slogan first appears and even wins general currency.

> *Nam facere recte civis suos princeps optimus faciendo docet, cumque sit imperio maximus, exemplo maior est.*
>
> ('For the excellent leader teaches his citizens to do the right by doing it himself, and though the greatest in power, he is yet greater in example.')

Velleius Paterculus here (2.126.5) uses *princeps optimus* of Tiberius 'without further qualification'. His book was published in 30 AD. Velleius was a military officer who had been legatus under Augustus and praetor under Tiberius, no doubt a slightly older peer of Sotidius. They share the complete loyalty of their class to the Caesars.

It would be a mistake to suppose that calling Tiberius *princeps optimus* could be construed as making an invidious contrast between him and Augustus, any more than calling him *princeps maximus* (*ll.*3-4) does. The superlatives are a courtesy to the supreme leader of his day. (Cf. Ch. Wirszubski, *Libertas as a Political Idea at Rome during the Late Republic and Early Principate* (Cambridge, 1960),153-4.) They do not set up a comparison with the past, but with the other leaders of the moment. So when Horace celebrates the victories of Tiberius *before* the death of Augustus the latter must be shown as the superior, and is hailed as *maxime principum* (*Od.* 4.14.6). It is only a modern convention which has reduced *princeps* to a term which can only apply to one leader at a time, in a chronological succession — our (anachronistic) 'emperors'. The *fasti* of Amiternum for 13 September (Ehrenberg & Jones, p.52) celebrates the deliverance of 'Tiberius and his children and the other leaders *(principes)* of the state' from the conspiracy of Libo (16 AD). Cf. Velleius Paterculus 2.115.3: 'the senate's will agreeing with the judgement of the leaders *(principum)*'.

After the suppression of Seianus (31 AD) there seems to have been quite a vogue for calling Tiberius *princeps optimus:* Valerius Maximus 2 (praef.), *CIL* 6.93, 902, 904; 11.3872. (The documentary sample used by Mitchell unfortunately excluded all these references except the last, where the phrase is 'qualified', as it also is in 6.93, by coupling with it the epithet *iustissimus.* For Tiberius called σωτήρ, with εὐεργέτης, see Ehrenberg & Jones 88, 320.38.) But this is certainly too late for Sotidius. R.K. Sherk, *ANRW* 2.7.2 (1980) 954-1052, shows that he can hardly have been legate in

Galatia later than 23, while the nearest points for which other incumbents are attested prior to that are c. 6 AD and c. 5-3 BC. Mitchell holds that he was praetor probably before c.20, and so far as we know never consul.

If we reject Mitchell's identification of the *princeps optimus* with Augustus, the date of the inscription is neatly settled with the aid of another of his conjectures. The reference on the stone to the procurator's son (14, 37) cannot stand if we assume that nepotism would hardly be explicitly provided for as part of the tightening-up. Mitchell proposes to take the dative as a slip for the genitive, introduced in the original draft and prior to the translation into Greek, which reinforces the error. He then takes the phrase to register an appointment which began under Augustus and continued under Tiberius, his son. But in that case it was pointless to specify Augustus, since the authority resided in the incumbent leader alone. We need a situation when a procurator may be acting either for the leader or for his son. In 18 Germanicus, the son of Tiberius, shared the consulship with him, and was sent to take control of the eastern provinces, with his command taking precedence (the so-called *maius imperium*) over that of all other governors. He was formally on equal terms with his father. Disorders and dynastic changes led Germanicus to assert direct Roman control over Cappadocia and Commagene (Tac. *Ann.* 2.42.5; *CAH* X, 744-6), no doubt causing a great intensification of military traffic in Pisidia and other regions on the way there. Our inscription may most plausibly be dated between Germanicus' appointment in 18 and his death the following year.

Public transport and the New Testament

The edict of Sotidius sets out a basic pattern for the transport system which affected all travellers in NT times. Local communities were collectively responsible for the transport and billeting services that were required by official personnel passing through their territory. The same services were available on a commercial basis to other travellers. The latter had an interest in securing for themselves the privileged official treatment, while the government had to maintain the system against collapse by ensuring that local communities were protected against this and adequately compensated for legitimate requisitioning. For a collection of other sources on the subject see A.C. Johnson, *Roman Egypt* = T. Frank, *Economic Survey of Ancient Rome,* II (Baltimore, 1936), 403ff. N. Lewis, *Inventory of Compulsory Services in Ptolemaic and Roman Egypt* (New Haven, 1968), cites Demetrius Phalereus' τύποι ἐπιστολικοί on how to excuse oneself because all the boats had been taken up with liturgies; and for the Roman period lists the various forms of liturgical service connected with official visits — s.v. παρουσία (on this word cf. **11**).

NT vocabulary reflects both the Persian and Roman stages in the development of the system. The verb ἀγγαρεύω, used of Simon's being required to carry the cross (Mt. 27.32, Mk 15.21), and of the one in the saying of Jesus who requires you to go one mile (Mt. 5.41 carrying his baggage on your donkey?), is derived from the vocabulary of the Persian postal service : evidence in A.H. McNeile's commentary on Mt. The Latin loan-word μίλιον reflects the new era.

Sotidius still uses the σχοῖνος, apparently a measure of travel time (not distance), and perhaps corresponding to the Persian parasang. Miles would however be expected on a measured Roman road (see **30**). This surely confirms the general assumption that the via Sebaste, the road built under Augustus to link the arc of new colonies that contained the difficult high country area of Pisidia, ran up the west side of Lake

Ascania, opposite Burdur, and was not the responsibility of the Sagalassenes. For the location of Augustan milestones see D.H. French, *ANRW* 2.7.2 (1980) 698-729, especially map on p.708, and for other maps of the contemporary province of Galatia, ibid., facing pp.960, 1057. B. Levick, *Roman Colonies in Southern Asia Minor* (Oxford, 1967), appends a map of Pisidia showing elevations and the alternative road up the east side of the lake through Burdur. G.E. Bean, *AS* 9 (1959), 81, raises the question whether this may not have been after all the main road. If the name Burdur is derived from *praetoria,* it signifies that the place was a major station on the Roman road system; cf.L. Casson, *Travel in the Ancient World* (London, 1974), 185. But if so, it perhaps came later. Mitchell (127) holds that there was as yet no regular system of *mansiones* (23). Although Sotidius' edict provides for Roman officials passing through from other provinces (17,40), and thus might seem to imply a major Roman road, only light traffic is implied by the small total outlay of the Sagalassenes, 10 carts in all (8, 31), or only enough for one senator, or for three Roman knights at a time (18-19, 41-44). Compare also the 20 donkeys of the Sagalessenes (10,34) with the 22 δημόσιοι ὄνοι kept by the village of Philadelphia in Egypt : *P.Hamb* 1.2 (1913) 33 (II).

The episode of Jesus commandeering a donkey for the entry into Jerusalem (Mt. 21.2-7; Mk. 11.2-6; Lk. 19.30-34) is to be explained in relation to the system of official transport; cf. J.D.M. Derrett, *NT* 13 (1971), 241-58. The ambiguities of the term κύριος ('master', 'owner') are apparent in Lk. where it is used both of Jesus and of the donkey's owners; cf. I.H. Marshall's commentary (Exeter, 1978), *ad loc.*: 'the implication is that a higher authority is recognised who has the right to impress the animal'. This perhaps accounts for the absolute use of κύριος for Jesus in the corresponding passages in Mt. and Mk., a usage unique in either gospel (though common in Lk.) and troublesome for commentators; cf. V. Taylor's commentary (London, 1966[2]), ad loc. We are not then forced to choose between taking it as a reference to Jesus as God or as the donkey's 'true' owner, if the transport system allows us to take it as referring to an (unspecified) legitimate claimant ('the master'), who promises to return the animal when finished with it (Mk. 11.3). Derrett demonstrates how the disciples of a rabbi might assert this right on behalf of their master.

Other 1976 texts, all from Egypt, illustrating the donkey-driving trade and associated public transport service are:—

P.Tebt. 1102:   116/115 BC, regulations specifying distances and charges involved in transporting grain from Kerkeosiris (Fayum) to a river-port, for shipment to Alexandria.

P.Köln 54 :   4BC, from Arsinoe (Fayum), the earliest attested donkey sale, the dearest price (40 *drachmae*) and the earliest bank-negotiated sale of its type.

P.Stras. 608 :   II[1], a fragmentary text, partly dealing with transport costs.

BGU 2364 :   mid-II, list of donkey-drivers with as many as six donkeys each, though most have only ½ share in one donkey (the minimum for registration was supposed to be three).

O.ROM 242 :   Roman period, the number of donkeys used (rented out?) on various days of the month at Thebes.

SB 10802 :   III (?), probably relating to the monthly pay of donkey-drivers.

P.Oxy. 3192 : 307, X swears he had never engaged in donkey-selling, having been
accused by the donkey-sellers' union of selling donkeys to the
government (they presumably hoped to have him forced to share their
obligations).

P.Coll.   VII, receipts and payments from a large estate, probably in the the
Youtie 95 :   Fayum, including fees to donkey-drivers.

For further reference see bibliographies attached especially to *P.Tebt.* 1102 and *BGU*
2364.

For the transport of Paul to Rome, the authorities took passages on private ships,
including two belonging to state-contractors on the Alexandrian grain-run (Acts 27.2,
6;28.11). But there is nothing to indicate how Paul might have been affected by the
official transport system on his earlier journeys. The edict of Sotidius at least gives us
a scale by which to estimate the style in which people travelled. Senators (including
the senior governors) are three times better provided for than knights (engaged in
lesser administrative or financial appointments), yet the procurator (manager of
imperial estates) travels in senatorial state though presumably of equestrian rank.
Knights are three times better off than a centurion with his single cart, or three mules,
or six donkeys. What was he carrying on them, and did Paul need such paraphernalia
too? His associations rate him clearly above the level of a centurion. Did he have
freedmen and servants travelling with him, as other private travellers are assumed to
have in the edict (23,48-9)? Sotidius requires hospitality (*mansio,* 23/σταθμός, 49) to
be supplied free to all official travellers, although he had insisted upon fees for
transport. What does this contribute to the obviously ambiguous web of obligations
that developed around the provision of Paul's accommodation? A key word in the
edict, however, discloses that Paul sees himself as having obligations akin to the
liturgical services of the civil community.

The crux of Paul's *kanon* in 2 Cor. 10.13-16

An immediate gain for NT studies from the new edict is the long-despaired of
solution to the meaning of the κανών alluded to by Paul in 2 Cor. 10. 13,15,16. No
relevant documentary attestation has hitherto been cited in the standard works of
reference earlier than its common use in the papyri from IV onwards for the periodic
schedule of tax assessments. *WB* III, Abschnitt 11, cites only one prior instance, in
a heavily restored document (II). MM say 'we can cite no passage from our sources
in support of the meaning "a measured area" or "province" (RV), which κανών
apparently has in 2 Cor. 10. 13,15', and quote Rouse's conjecture, based on a modern
Greek phrase, that it meant the 'official description' of anything. *BAGD* refer to 1
Clement 1.3, 14.1, for the meaning 'sphere of action or influence, province, limits',
and Clement strikingly discloses the fact, now established by the edict of Sotidius, that
κανών relates to the system of liturgical services : μὴ παρεκβαίνων τὸν ὡρισμένον τῆς
λειτουργίας κανόνα (41.1). H.W. Beyer in *TDNT* rejects the possibility of a
geographical distinction between Paul and the other apostles, interpreting the
'measure' as rather 'the blessing which God has caused to rest on his missionary
activity'. 'The measure given to Paul is not, then, a sphere marked out in space in
which he alone is to work ... The fact is that κανών never bears this sense.' C.K.
Barrett, however, in his commentary, prudently draws back from the attempt to
exclude geography.

The edict uses κανών (29) to translate *formula* (5), for which only διάταγμα and γνώμων are cited in H.J. Mason, *Greek Terms for Roman Institutions: A Lexicon and Analysis* (Toronto, 1974). It means therefore the official schedule, in this case of the transport services to be supplied by the local community. This explains the dilemma of those who, without benefit of such evidence, have tried to explain the framework of reference in 2 Cor. 10.13-16. The κανών in itself is not a geographical concept, but the services it formulates are in this case geographically partitioned (13, 32). It is reasonable to envisage that other governors were publishing similar definitions within their provinces. Paul and his colleagues who travelled the Roman roads will have been familiar with notices such as our edict, and took over from them the term which neatly expressed their understanding of the way God had measured out their respective territorial commitments. The Sagalassenes were free to negotiate an exchange of responsibilities with another contributor (12, 34-5). It is the sensitivities aroused by just such an issue which lie behind Paul's rather complex protestations about the requirements of the κανών under which he was serving. He reflects the older spirit of the liturgical system as a competition in honour through duty fulfilled. To go beyond one's limit would deprive the next man of his turn. The Sagalassenes, however, like most others by this stage, are assumed to be anxious to divest themselves of their own responsibilities.

Some other terms for which the edict usefully supplements MM/BAGD are:—

ἀκριβέστατα (27), cf. Acts 26.5 (though the term there is adjectival); no parallel cited for the superlative.

ἐντολή (31), a more closely dated epigraphic parallel than MM supply for this common NT word.

θειότης (31), cf. Rom. 1.20, only paralleled in MM from documents dated IV.

λειτουργεῖν (31), for civil services, counteracting the over-emphasis in MM/BAGD on the new 'religious' connotation; it is noteworthy that Paul uses the idea only in its 'secular' sense, Rom. 15.27, Phil. 2.17.

διοδεύω (40), cf. Acts 17.1, a more closely dated parallel.

ἀνάγκην ἔχω (43), translating *id quod praescripsi* (18/19), makes clear that when used with the infinitive it refers to orders received, cf. Lk.14.18; 23.17; Heb. 7.27; also 1 Cor. 7.37; 9.16; 2 Cor. 9.7; and surely also Jude 3 (in spite of the translations).

ἐμπορία (47), cf. Mt. 22.5, a more closely dated parallel.

(E.A. JUDGE)

10. A proconsul of Cyprus during Claudius' principate

Mentioning an inscription republished as *SEG* 18 (1962) 587, J. Devreker, *Epigraphica* 38 (1976) 180, suggests that *l*.3 should be restored as Κλαυδ]ίου Καίσαρος Σεβαστοῦ, instead of Γα]ίου Κ.Σ. The text is an honorific inscription from Paphos for T. Clodius Epirius, proconsul of Cyprus, and is dated 59? in *SEG* 1484. Whether his office fell near to the time of Sergius Paulus, whom Barnabas and Paul met at Salamis on their first journey in 47-48(?) (Acts 13.6-12), is unclear. T. B. Mitford, *The Inscriptions of Kourion* (Philadelphia, 1971), 169-70, states that the names of 46 proconsuls of Cyprus are known from 22 BC to the end of the Severan era, roughly ⅙ of the total.

11. The 'coming' of a prefect

Alexandria   c.192
ed.pr. — W. M. Brashear, *BGU* 2211, pp.1-2 (pl. 1)

$$
\begin{array}{ll}
& [\quad\quad \pi\rho\acute{o}]\nu o\iota\alpha\nu \ \dot{\epsilon}\pi o\iota\eta\sigma\acute{\alpha}\mu\eta\nu \ \tau o\hat{v} \ \pi[\quad \pm 8 \quad]o\upsilon\varsigma \\
& [\quad\quad\quad] \ (m.2) \ \dot{\epsilon}\gamma \ \tau\acute{o}(\mu o\upsilon) \ a \ \dot{\epsilon}(\pi\grave{\iota}) \ \kappa o\lambda(\lambda\acute{\eta}\mu\alpha\tau o\varsigma) \ [\quad\quad] \\
(m.1) \ \ & [\sigma\tau\rho(\alpha\tau\eta\gamma o\hat{\iota}\varsigma) \ \tau]\hat{\omega}\nu \ \dot{\upsilon}\pi o\gamma\epsilon\gamma\rho\alpha\mu\mu\acute{\epsilon}\nu\omega\nu \ \nu o\mu\hat{\omega}\nu \ \chi\alpha\acute{\iota}\rho\epsilon\iota\nu\cdot \\
& [\Lambda\alpha\rho\kappa]\acute{\iota}o\upsilon \ M\acute{\epsilon}\mu o\rho o\varsigma \ \mu\acute{\epsilon}\lambda\lambda o\nu\tau o\varsigma \ \check{\eta}\delta\eta \ \dot{\epsilon}\pi' \ \dot{\alpha}\gamma\alpha\theta o\hat{\iota}\varsigma \ \tau\hat{\eta} \ A\dot{\iota}\gamma\upsilon\pi[\tau\acute{\iota}\omega\nu \\
5 \ \ & [\chi\acute{\omega}\rho\alpha] \ \pi\alpha\rho\epsilon\hat{\iota}\nu\alpha\iota \ [\check{o}\pi]o\upsilon \ \dot{\epsilon}\grave{\alpha}\nu \ \check{\hat{\eta}}\nu \ \phi\rho o\nu\tau\acute{\iota}\sigma\alpha\tau\epsilon, \ \dot{\epsilon}\pi\iota\sigma\tau\acute{\alpha}\mu\epsilon\nu o[\iota \ \check{o}\tau\iota] \\
& [e.g. \ \dot{o} \ \dot{\alpha}\mu\epsilon\lambda\hat{\omega}\nu \ \delta\acute{\iota}\kappa\eta\nu \ \dot{\upsilon}]\phi\acute{\epsilon}\xi\epsilon\iota\cdot \ \tau\alpha\hat{v}\tau\alpha \ \gamma\rho\acute{\alpha}\phi\omega \ \dot{\alpha}[\xi\iota\omega]\theta\epsilon\grave{\iota}\varsigma \ \dot{\upsilon}\pi' \ \alpha\dot{\upsilon}\tau o\hat{v} \ \gamma\lambda[\\
& [\quad\quad\quad\quad] \\
& [\quad\quad\quad\quad]\iota\sigma\kappa[..] \ \Phi\theta\epsilon\mu\phi o\upsilon\theta(\iota\tau\text{-})
\end{array}
$$

Two writers have contributed to this very fragmentary portion of a letter. On the back of the papyrus appears *BGU* 2357, a private account (III).

> *l.2 (Second hand)* . . . **from the first roll at the -th column.** *(First hand)* **[To the strategoi] of the nomes listed below, greetings. Make provision for [Lark]ios**
> 5 **Memor who is now intending | to be present wherever he may in the land of the Egyptians for their good, knowing [that he who disregards this] will pay [the penalty]. I write this at his request . . .**

Such prior notifications of a prefectural visit were sent in order that due preparations could be made (accommodation, food, etc.) not merely for the individual himself, but for his entourage. Brashear (p.191) thinks it unlikely, but not impossible, that *BGU* 2357 (which occurs on the *verso* of this letter) is related to this request to make preparations for the visit. There, tallies are given for various foodstuffs. For a similar letter see *SB* VI, 5(1963) 9617 (19/12/129) referring to a visit to Egypt by Hadrian. The verb πάρειμι (5) with something approaching this technical sense occurs in the NT only at Jn. 11.28, but the cognate noun occurs, mostly of Christ, in Mt. 24.3, earlier Pauline letters (1 and 2 Thes.; 1 Cor.) and various non-Pauline epistles (1 and 2 Pet., 1 Jn., Jas.). 2 Thes. 2.9 refers to the *parousia* of the Antichrist. On παρουσία and related forms in NT letters, see K. Thraede, *Grundzüge griechisch-römischer Brieftopik* (Munich, 1970), 95-106. Neither MM nor BAGD offer any references to the verb in this sense of an official's coming. For fuller discussion of the notion see the old but still valuable treatment in Deissmann, *LAE*, 368-73. For the verb used of gods from Homer onwards, see L. Robert, *Hellenica* 13 (1965) 129-31; also *SEG* 821.10 (= **2**).

For ὅπου ἐάν (ἄν) + indicative (5) in the Koine, see examples collected in BDF, § 372,1a. cf. *CPR* 20.5 (**18** below). The phrase ἐπ' ἀγαθοῖς (4) occurs with some frequency in other texts dealing with prefectural visits (references in Brashear, p.2). In the NT note Eph. 2.10, ἐπὶ ἔργοις ἀγαθοῖς; and cf. the use of εἰς (τὸ) ἀγαθόν at Rom. 8.28, 13.4, 15.2.

12. A prefect's circular forbidding magic

Provenance unknown 198/9
ed.pr. — G. M. Parássoglou, *P.Coll.Youtie* I 30, pp.261-74 (pl.12)

[ἐντυχὼν πολλοῖ]ς οἱ[ηθ]ε̣ῖσιν μαντείας τρόποις ἐξαπατᾶσθ[αι]
[ε]ὐ̣θ[έως ἀναγκ]α̣ῖ[ον ἡγη]σάμην περὶ τοῦ μηδένα κίνδυνο̣[ν]
τῇ ἀ[νο]ίᾳ αὐ[τ]ῶν ἐπακολουθήσῃ σαφῶς πᾶσιν ἐνταῦθ̣α̣
διαγ[ορ]εῦσαι εἴ̣ρ̣[γεσ]θ̣[α]ι̣ τῆς ἐπισφαλοῦς ταύτης περιεργίας.
5   μήτ' οὖν διὰ χρη[σμῶ]ν ἤτοι ἐγγράφων διὰ γραφῶν ὡς
ἐπὶ τοῦ θείου διδομένων μήτε διὰ κωμασίας ἀκαλμάτω[ν]
ἢ τοιαύτης παγγανίας τὰ ὑπὲρ ἄνθρωπόν τις εἰδένα[ι]
προσποιείσθω καὶ τὴν τῶν μελλόντων ἀτηλείαν ἐπαγγε[λ-]
λέσθω μέτε τοὺς περὶ τ[ού]του πυνθανομένους ἑαυτὸν
10 ἐπιδιδότω ἢ ὅλως ἀπ[ο]κρινέσθω. ἐὰν δέ τις τῇ{ν} ἐπαγγελίᾳ{ν}
ταύτῃ{ν} παραμένων [φ]ωραθῇ, πεπίσθω ὅτι τῇ ἐσχά[τ]ῃ
τιμωρίᾳ{ν} παραδοθήσεται. τῆς ἐ[π]ιστολῆς ταύτης τὸ ἀντίγραφον δημοσίᾳ ἔν τε ταῖς μητροπ[ό]λεσιν καὶ κατὰ κώμην
φανεροῖς καὶ εὐαναγνώστοις τοῖς γράμμασιν ἕκαστος
15 ὑμῶν [εἰς λε]ύκωμ[α] προθῖ[ν]αι προνοησάτο, καὶ διὰ παντὸς πολυπραγμονίτω ⟨καὶ⟩ ἐάν τι[ν]α παρὰ τὰ ἀπηγορευμένα
πράσσον⟨τα⟩ εὕρον, δεδεμ[έ]νον ἐπὶ τὴν ἐμὴν διάγνωσιν
πεμψάτω. οὐδὲ γὰρ [ὑμῖν] ἀκίνδυνον ἔσ{ }ται, εἰ μάθοι
αὖ τοιοῦτον τινὸν ἐν [τοῖς ὑ]φ' ὑμᾶς νομοῖς περιορομένον,
20 ἀλλὰ τὴν ἴσην κόλασι[ν τοῖ]ς̣ σκεπομένοις ὑποστήσεσθαι.
ἐκεῖνον μὲν γὰρ ἕκα[στος], εἰ καὶ τὰ παρὰ ⟨τὰ⟩ ἀ̣π̣ιρημένα τολμ[ᾷ],
εἷς γέ ἐστιν, ὁ δὲ μὴ παντ[αχό]θεν αὐτοὺς ἐπε̣[ι]σχὼν πολλοῖ[ς]
κινδύνου αὐτὸς αἴτιο[ς γεγ]ένηται.   (vac.)
                                          (vac.)
(m.2)   (ἔτους) ζ Αὐτοκ[ρατόρ]ων Καισάρων Λουκ[ίου Σεπτιμίου] Σεουήρου Εὐσεβ[οῦς]
        Περτίνακος Ἀραβικοῦ Ἀδιαβηνικοῦ Παρθικοῦ
25 Μεγί[στου καὶ Μάρκου Αὐρηλίου] Ἀντωνίνου Σεβαστῷ[ν.....]...[

A nearly complete papyrus sheet with all margins partly surviving. Several consonantal and other confusions by the scribe occur: read ἐπακολουθῆσαι (3), ἀγαλμάτων (6), μαγγανείας (7), ἀδηλίαν (8), μήτε τοῖς ... πυθανομένοις (9), πεπείσθω (11), προθεῖναι (15), προνοησάτω (15), πολυπραγμονείτω (16), εὕρῃ (17), πυθοίμην, perhaps, for μάθοι (18), τοιούτων τινῶν ... περιορωμένων (19), ὑποστήσεσθε (20), ἐκείνων (21), ἀπειρημένα (21), ἐπισχών (22).

Bib. — N. Lewis *Chr.d'Ég.* 52 (1977) 143-46; *J. Rea, *ZPE* 27 (1977) 151-56 (list of divergences from the first edition at 152-53).

[Since I have come across many people] who consider themselves to be beguiled by the means of divination [immediately I thought it essential], so that no risk should follow from their foolishness, to state explicitly here to all to
5　abstain from this misleading curiosity. | Therefore neither through oracles, viz., written documents ostensibly emanating in the presence of the divinity, nor by means of the procession of images or similar trickery, let anyone lay claim to have knowledge of the supernatural, or give himself out as an expert about the obscurity of future events. Nor let anyone give himself over to those who (wish
10　to) learn about this | or offer any reply at all. But if anyone is discovered sticking to this undertaking, let him be sure that he will be handed over for capital punishment. The copy of this letter let each of you make provision to set up in public both in the nome capitals and in each village on a white board with
15　lettering that is clear and easy to read. | And let each continually make enquiries and if he finds anyone acting contrary to the prohibitions let him send him as a prisoner for my determination. For neither shall you be free of danger if I should learn once more of any like these being disregarded in the nomes under
20　your control. | But you will be laid under the same chastisement as the ones who are detected. For each of those people, even if he is bold to do things contrary to what has been banned, at least he is a single person; but he who does not keep in check those from everywhere (in his nome?) is himself responsible for much danger to many. *(2nd hand)* During the seventh year of Imperatores Caesares Lucius Septimius Severus Pius Pertinax Arabicus Adiabenicus Parthicus
25　| Maximus and Marcus Aurelius Antoninus, Augusti, . . .

This text represents an attempt to suppress magic and divination in Egypt. Although the opening formula is lost almost certainly the circular emanated from the office of the prefect of Egypt, who in 199 was Q. Aemilius Saturninus. The overall tone of authority and the particular mention of διάγνωσις (17), together with analogous phraseology in other documents from such a source, all point to this. The first editor postulated a column of text prior to what is extant, since there is insufficient space at the top of this sheet for the usual opening phrases of a prefect's edict. If that were right, given the number of lines in the extant column, this topic may not have been the only one dealt with in the circular; or the postulated first column may have contained merely a covering note. Rea suggests that such brief wording as ἀντίγραφον ἐπιστολῆς may have been all that was needed, thus dispensing with the theory of a previous sheet.

The circular is addressed to the nome *strategoi* (19), from whose copy each official would have to make his own copies of *ll.* 1-12 for posting up in his area. Parássoglou's brief survey of the anti-divination legislation under the Empire makes clear how ineffective such edicts were. Augustus' fundamental edict in 11 AD was the basis for all prosecutions of magicians and 'prophets' (its terms are summarised in Cassius Dio 56.25.5). Contrast the ninety-year period from 319 during which twelve edicts were issued by the Christian emperors beginning with Constantine. With particular reference to Rome and Italy emperors during the first and second centuries tried by means of senatorial decrees to expel astrologers and 'philosophers' (for the ancient sources see Parássoglou, 263, n.8). On this subject generally, see F.H. Cramer, *Astrology in Roman Law and Politics* (Philadelphia, 1954); R. MacMullen, *Enemies of the Roman Order* (Harvard, 1966), 128-62.

Two things are particularly intriguing about this new ban. First, it was put out during the time of Septimius Severus, notorious before his accession for his consulting of astrologers, and notorious after it for his aversion to others doing so, lest they ask the same question that he used to ask, the date of the emperor's death. Such an enquiry was tantamount to a conspiracy to supersede the ruler. In this very year, 199, Septimius visited Egypt; but the loss of the date on our papyrus, and uncertainty about just when he entered the province, leaves us in doubt whether the circular reflects the emperor's own 'displeasure at the proliferation of magic and divination in the provinces' (Parássoglou, 265), or whether the prefect has initiated the ban in anticipation of Septimius' arrival. Second, the question should at least be raised whether this circular was an entirely local initiative confined to Egypt, or whether it was part of a renewed drive to curb magic throughout the Empire. Parássoglou, 265-66, mentions the doubtful authority of the *Historia Augusta,* in which Septimius Severus is said to have issued an edict while en route to Egypt, prohibiting Jews from proselytising and Christians from making converts: *in itinere Pal⟨a⟩estinis plurima iura fundavit. Iudaeos fieri sub gravi poena vetuit. idem etiam de C⟨h⟩ristianis sanxit* (*Scriptores Hist. Aug., Sev.* 17.1). Whether or not we should give any credence to this claim (for a denial of it see A. Birley, *Septimius Severus. The African Emperor* [New York, 1972], 209-10) there does appear to be evidence for a pogrom against Christians in Egypt immediately after Septimius' departure from the province. For bibliography on this, see Parássoglou, 266, n.16.

For NT usage the following may be noted: ἐξαπατάω (1), especially Rom. 16.18; κίνδυνος (2), Rom. 8.35, 2 Cor. 11.26; ἐπακολουθέω in figurative sense with dative (3), 1 Tim. 5.10; ἐπισφαλής (4), only at Acts 27.9; περιεργία (4), cf. Acts 19.9 where τὰ περίεργα πράσσειν means 'practise magic', and 1 Tim. 5.13 where the adjective means 'inquisitive, meddlesome'. The noun and adjective both occur in patristic texts: see Lampe, s.vv., 6. τὸ θεῖον (6), with the sense 'divine being, divinity', Acts 17.27D, 29, Tit. 1.9 *(v.l.);* προσποιεῖσθαι + infinitive (8), with not quite this sense at Lk. 24.28; ἐπαγγέλλομαι (8-9), with this sense at 1 Tim. 2.10, 6.21; ἐπιδίδωμι (10), Acts 27.15 (where a reflexive needs to be understood with the participle); ἐπαγγελία (10), not in this sense in the NT; τιμωρία (12), Heb. 10.29; παραδίδωμι + dative (12), cf. Eph. 4.19; μητρόπολις (13), only in the subscript to 1 Tim; κώμη (13), frequent in gospels; perfect passive participle of δέω (17), 'as a prisoner', Mk. 15.7, Jn. 18.24, Acts 9.2, 21, 22.5, 24.27; cf. Col. 4.3; ἐπὶ ... διάγνωσιν (17), cf. εἰς δ., Acts 25.21. This word is the equivalent to Latin *cognitio,* the full judicial trial (in Egypt, before the Prefect) which included the admission of evidence and the handing down of the judgement. On *cognitio* see A.N. Sherwin-White, *Roman Society and Roman Law in the New Testament* (Oxford, 1963; repr. Grand Rapids, 1978), index, s.v. The noun κόλασις (20) is frequent in the NT, but mainly of divine retribution. ἔγγραφος (5) occurs in patristic texts (see BAGD). On the phrase διὰ κωμασίας ἀγαλμάτων (6), Rea comments (154-55): 'The sanctuary of an Egyptian Temple was normally inaccessible to the laity so that the god could only be consulted during a festival procession when his cult statue was carried outside'. The verb πολυπραγμονέω (16) occurs here in its less common, good sense.

The mention of prefectural διάγνωσις in this papyrus offers a point of contact with another recently published text whose content makes it also unique to published papyri. N. Lewis, *RD* 50 (1972) 5-12 and *RD* 51 (1973) 5-7 (cf. E. Seidl, *SDHI* 38 [1972] 319-20; *SB* 10929), published three columns of a text — the first very poorly preserved — whose provenance is unknown but which is dated 133-37.

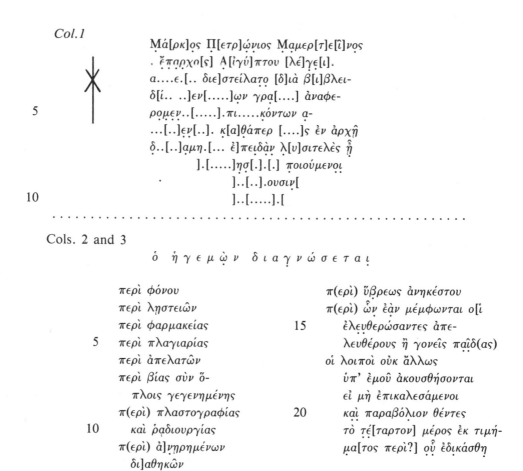

Col.1

Μά[ρκ]ος Π[ετρ]ώνιος Μαμερ[τ]ε[ῖ]νος
. ἔπαρχο[ς] Α[ἰγύ]πτου [λέ]γε[ι].
α....ε.[.. διε]στείλατο [δ]ιὰ β[ι]βλει-
δ[ί.. ..]εν[.....]ων γρα[....] ἀναφε-
ρομεν..[.....].πι.....κόντων α-
...[..]εν[..]. κ[α]θάπερ [....]ς ἐν ἀρχῇ
δ..[..]αμη.[... ἐ]πειδὰν λ[υ]σιτελὲς ᾖ
].[.....]ησ[.].[.] ποιούμενοι
]..[..].ουσιν[
]..[.....].[

Cols. 2 and 3

ὁ ἡγεμὼν διαγνώσεται

περὶ φόνου   π(ερὶ) ὕβρεως ἀνηκέστου
περὶ ληστειῶν   π(ερὶ) ὧν ἐὰν μέμφωνται ο[ἱ
περὶ φαρμακείας   15   ἐλευθερώσαντες ἀπε-
5 περὶ πλαγιαρίας   λευθέρους ἢ γονεῖς παῖδ(ας)
περὶ ἀπελατῶν   οἱ λοιποὶ οὐκ ἄλλως
περὶ βίας σὺν ὅ-   ὑπ' ἐμοῦ ἀκουσθήσονται
πλοις γεγενημένης   εἰ μὴ ἐπικαλεσάμενοι
π(ερὶ) πλαστογραφίας   20   καὶ παραβόλιον θέντες
10 καὶ ῥᾳδιουργίας   τὸ τέ[ταρτον] μέρος ἐκ τιμή-
π(ερὶ) ἀ]νηρημένων   μα[τος περὶ?] οὗ ἐδικάσθη
δι]αθηκῶν

(Col.1) **Marcus Petronius Mamertinus, prefect of Egypt, says: ...**
(Col.2) **The prefect will give judgement concerning homicide, robbery (piracy?),**
5,10 **poisoning, |kidnapping, cattle-rustling, armed violence, forgery |and fraud, the**
annulment of wills, *(Col.3)* aggravated assault, complaints in which patrons
15 **bring a charge against |their own freedmen or parents against their children. The**
20 **rest will not otherwise be heard by me unless they make an appeal |and lodge**
as deposit a quarter of the fine applied concerning the case which was judged
(i.e., in the previous trial).

This text is a Greek translation of a Latin original: the criminal charges listed here
all have their Latin equivalents. πλαγιαρία (5), for example, is a Latinism attested only
once in LSJ Suppl. *Plagiarius* occurs in 1 Tim. 1.10 (Vulgate) as a translation of
ἀνδραποδίστης (BAGD suggests 'procurer' as the meaning here, but that is not
necessary; 'kidnapper' fits quite satisfactorily into this NT vice list since by no means
all the words given relate to sexual misdemeanours). ἐπικαλοῦμαι (19) renders *appello*,
or *provoco*. Lewis points out that while Latin was the language used by the prefect's
office, in civil law, and in the army, this text was promulgated in Greek for use by
local and regional officals, since Greek was the language of provincial administration.

Lewis holds that the prefect of Egypt announces the criminal charges the trial of which he will hear personally. Seidl, however believes that ἡγεμών refers not to this official but to the emperor: it would thus translate *princeps* in a Latin original. Whether or not Seidl's interpretation be accepted, the papyrus offers illuminating background evidence of Roman legal arrangements in the provinces less than three generations after Paul's experience (Acts 23.23 — 26.32). The procedure set out in this papyrus will have applied only to Roman citizens in Egypt: it was clearly not envisaged for the general populace (Lewis, 12). At a verbal level a number of links with the Acts passage may be noted: ἡγεμών for the prefect, 23.24, 26, 33; 24.10 etc.; elsewhere in the NT at Mt. 27.2. One may compare ἀκουσθήσονται (18) with Acts 23.35; and Paul's formal appeal to Caesar uses ἐπικαλοῦμαι (25.11, 12; 26.32) for which cf. *l.*19 of the new papyrus.

The 'appeal to Caesar' is mentioned in *IGRR* 4.1044.13-16, a letter to the people of Kos from Gn. Domitius Corbulo, proconsul of Asia in Claudius' principate. Those lines read: δέ|[ον τ]οίνυν, εἰ μὲν ἐπὶ τὸν Σεβαστὸν | [ἡ ἔκ]κλησις γείνεται, πρότ[ε]ρον ἐμὲ | [ἐξετ]άσαι τὴν αἰτίαν·κτλ, 'So then if the appeal to Augustus is made I must first scrutinise the charge . . .' G.P. Carratelli, *PP* 30(1975) 102-04, has published the first nine lines of this letter; G.P. Burton, *ZPE* 21 (1976) 63-68, argues on the basis of those lines that Dio is correct in his claim (53.15.4) that proconsuls received instructions (ἐντολαί) from the emperor as early as Augustus. P.J. Sijpesteijn, *ZPE* 22 (1976) 107, holds that in the lines quoted above we should read [ἐπί]κλησις for [ἡ ἔκ]κλησις (cf. *SEG* 952).

The marginal sign in column 1 of the papyrus may represent χ(ε)ι(ρογραφία) or (-φον), a written note or handwritten report; the latter word occurs in the NT at Col. 2.14, where Paul employs a vivid metaphor. In law, a παραβόλιον (20) is a deposit made when an appeal is lodged (cf. LSJ, s.v., παράβολος, III). The noun ἀπελάτης (6) is very rare, only two examples being cited in LSJ; Lewis (1972:6) notes that this papyrus is the earliest attestation of the word in a legal text. For the sense of ῥᾳδιουργία (10) see Plut. *Cato Minor* 16. Civil cases are in view in *ll.*14-16.

13. A soldier's worries about family and debts

Provenance unknown   Turn of the Era
ed.pr. — R.A. Kraft and A. Tripolitis, *BJRL* 51 (1968) 151-54, no.4.

Ἡρακλᾶς Ὥρωι καὶ Ταχώνει, χαίρειν καὶ
ὑγειαίνειν. μὲ ἀγωνία περὶ ὑμῶν. ἐπὶ στρα-
τευόμεθα, ἐν τῶι πλοίωι πεπύκαμεν
ὀκτὼ ἡμέρας. θεῶν θελόντων, ἐν ταῖς τρι-
5   σὶ ἡμέραις ἐσόμεθα ἐν πλοίωι. τὸ παιδίν
ἐπειμβλέψον ὡς λύχνον, ἐπιδὰν ἀ-
γ]ωνιῶι περὶ ὑμῶν. ἐὰν ὁ τοῦ Ἀπόλλω-
ν]ος ἔλθη πρὸς ὑμᾶς περὶ τοῦ λοιποῦ, ὑπόδιξον αὐτῶι ὅτι τῆι ταχείστη ἔρχεται

10 Πτολλάτι τοῖς ἐμοῖς λόγοις. εἶπον ἐπίμ-

β]λεψα [   ] μειν λίαν ι ... ν ν θω αν

]ωι δοῦναι εἰς γνάφην περὶ

]ἐλαχείστων. οἶδα τοῦ γερδίου (δραχμαὶ) Δ

] (δραχμαὶ) Κ τοῦ ἄλλου γερδίου χάριν τοῦ

15]και ὑπόδιξον ὅτι τάχυ ὡς ἔρχομαι.

]ς σεβατοῦ, χοίαχ ῑγ

verso   ]καὶ ὥρωι τῶι υἱῶι

A reasonably well-preserved text with about a third of each of the last six lines missing. Read μὴ (2), ἡμῶν (2), ἐπεί (2), πεπλεύκαμεν (3), ἀγωνιῶ (6-7), ὑπόδειξον (8-9,15), ταχέως (15).
Bib. — SB 10799

Heraklas to Horos and Tachonis, greetings and good health. Don't worry about us. Since we've been on military duty we have been sailing in the boat for

5 **eight days. With the gods' will in three |days we shall be on shipboard. As for the child keep an eye on him as you would an oil lamp, since I am worried about you. If Apollo's son comes to you about what remains, indicate (pretend?) to**

10 **him that it is coming with haste |by (to?) Ptollas along with my accounts. I said that I kept an eye on . . . to give to the fuller concerning . . . least. I know about the weaver's 4 drachmai . . . 20 drachmai for the sake of the other weaver the**

15 **|. . . and indicate that I am coming quickly. Farewell — year of Caesar Augustus. Choiak 13 (= 9 December). *(verso)* . . . and to Horos his son.**

While absent on military service a man writes to his son and wife (?) expressing his anxiety for them and giving instructions about some financial matters (overdue debts, perhaps?). Whether his intentions towards his creditors are sincere or whether he wants the addressees to fob the latter off with promises of his speedy return depends on how the imperative ὑπόδειξον is understood at *ll.* 8-9, 15. The context is not sufficient for us to be certain. For the sense 'pretend' see LSJ, s.v., II,3. For this verb + dative of person + ὅτι in NT see Acts 20.35. Letters mentioning the writer's anxiety for his addressees or, conversely, telling them not to worry about him, are commonplace in the papyri.

The verb ἀγωνιάω does not occur in the NT but the noun form in *-ia* is used at Lk. 22.44. For λόγοι (10), 'financial accounts', note the metaphorical application at Phil. 4.17. The double compound ἐπεμβλέπω (6) is not found in the NT, although ἐμβλέπω is frequent in the gospels meaning 'fix one's gaze upon', while ἐπιβλέπω has the sense 'consider, care about,' at Lk. 1.48, 9.38; Jas. 2.3. 2 Pet. 1.19 provides an equivalent to the comparative phrase ὡς λύχνον (6). For θεῶν θελόντων, see **15**.

14. Corruption in the civil service?

Oxyrhynchos   Principate of Augustus
ed.pr. — V. Brown, *BICS* 17 (1970) 136-43 (pl.4)

> *Suneros.Chio suo.plur(imam).sal(utem).s(i).u(ales) b(ene).Theo adduxsit.ad.*
>   *me.Ohapim*
> *regium.mensularium.oxsyrychitem.qui quidem.mecum.est.locutus*
> *de.inprobitate.Epaphraes .itaque.nihil.ultra.loquor.quam.[[no]]*
> *ne patiarus.te.propter.illos.perire.crede.mihi.nimia.bonitas*
> 5 *pernicies.homin[i]bus est 'uel.maxsuma' .deinde.ipse.tibei.de.mostrabit*
> *qu[i]t.rei.sit.qum.illum ad te.uocareis.set.perseruera*
> *qui.de.tam pusilla.summa.tam.magnum.lucrum.facit*
> *dominum.occidere.uolt .deinde.ego.clamare.debeo.siquod.uideo*
> *deuom.atque.hominum.[[fidem.si.tu.[.].ista.non.cuibis]]*
> 10 *tuum.erit.uindicare.ne.alio.libeat.facere*
> (verso): *Chio.Caesaris*

A private letter — in idiomatic Latin epistolary style whose meaning remains obscure, but which is of palaeographical importance (see *ed.pr.*).
Bib. — *P.Oxy.* 3208

Syneros to his friend Chios, very many greetings. If you are well, fine. Theon brought along to me Ohapim, the public banker of Oxyrhynchos, who indeed spoke with me about the dishonesty of Epaphras. Therefore I say nothing more than, 'Do not allow your own ruin because of those fellows'. Believe me, too
5 **much kindness brings |calamity of the greatest kind upon men. Afterwards he himself will show you the significance of the matter, when you call him to you. But persevere. He who makes so large a profit from such a petty amount is willing to kill his master. Then I ought to shout out, if I read the situation aright,**
10 **"Gods and Men!" |It will fall to you to take revenge lest someone else may like to do it. (*verso*) To Chios, (slave) of Caesar.**

Specific details of the shady matter alluded to here are quite lost to us, but several people appear to have been involved. The writer offers various pieces of moral advice in the form of gnomic comments (4-5, 7-8); such clichés cannot be traced to any particular source and were no doubt in general currency. For similar sorts of statements in the NT, see especially 1 Cor. 15.33 (where Paul is quoting Menander). On the basis of epigraphical attestations of his name, Syneros may be of freedman status, while in view of the address on the verso Chios appears to be a slave (Brown, 140) who is a member of the *familia Caesaris,* the imperial household. The phrase *devom (= divum) atque hominum fidem* (9) — the last word was crossed out in error by the scribe — is a common exclamation. Rome's conquest of Egypt led to the breaking up of the state banking monopoly and its replacement by private banks. *Regius mensularius* is a translation of βασιλικός τραπεζίτης 'public banker'. The latter word occurs only once in the NT, at Mt. 25.27.

15. Personal news and greetings in a letter

Provenance unknown
ed.pr. — *P. Köln* I.56, pp. 168-174

Διοδώρα Οὐαλερίῳ Μαξίμῳ χαίρειν καὶ διὰ παντὸς ὑγιαίνειν.
γινώσκιν σε θέλω, ὅτι δεκαταῖ-
οι ἐπτακάμεν εἰς τὴν μητρόπο-
5   λιν[[ν]]· καὶ εὐθέως ἀνέβην πρὸς
τὴν ἀδελφήν σου· καὶ εἰθὺς
ἔγραψά σοι, ὅτι ἀπρόσκοπός ἰ-
μιν καὶ ἐσώθημεν τῶν θηῶν
θελόντων. ἀσπάζου Ἀμᾶν
10   καὶ Παυλῖναν καὶ Πόπλιν
καὶ Διόδωρον καὶ Γρανίαν
καὶ Τύχην· καὶ γ{α}ράψις μοι
[...]τε[.]ωκαν· καὶ ἠὰν πε-
[ραιώσ]ω τὸ μετήορον καὶ ὁμαι
15   [ἀπρόσ]κοπος, ταχὺ καταπλεύσω.
                    Φαῶφι α. ἔρωσ(ο).
(*verso*)   Διοδώ(ρας)
ἀπόδες Μαξίμῳ ἀπὸ

A private letter from Diodora to Valerius Maximus, presumably written by herself. She has arrived at her destination and gives him news that she has stood up to her journey, as well as signalling her plans.

Diodora to Valerius Maximus, greetings and continuous good health. I want you
5   **to know that we reached the metropolis after nine days, |and straightaway I**
went up to (see) your sister. And straightaway I am writing to you that I am all
10 **right, and we were kept safe, with the gods' will. Greet Amas, |Paulina, Publius,**
Diodoros, Granias, and Tyche. And write to me . . . If I settle the business in
15 **hand and I'm |all right, I will quickly sail down. 1 Phaophi (= 28/29**
September). Farewell.
(*verso*) Give this to Maximus from Diodoroa.

This letter is quite unaffected in its phraseology and contains numerous conventional turns of phrase (2, 3, 6-7, 8-9, 16). The use of nomen and cognomen for Valerius Maximus should show that he is a Roman citizen: is he a veteran or the descendant of one? The cognomen Paulina and the praenomen Publius need not imply Roman citizenship, such names having passed into Greek usage. Πόπλιν (10) =

Πόπλιον (cf. Acts 28.7-8) = Publius. The matter-of-fact familiarity of tone of the letter, the expectation of a reply, and the implication (in *l*.15) that Diodora lives in the same area as the addressee, suggest to the editor of this text that she may be Valerius' de facto wife (p.169); cf. R. Taubenschlag, *The Law of Greco-Roman Egypt in the Light of the Papyri* (Warsaw, 1955²; repr. Milan, 1972) 109.

The spelling is phonetic and inconsistent: e.g., the datives in *l*.1 and the infinitives in *ll*. 2-3. For the use of δεκαταῖος with a personal subject (3-4), C.J. Hemer draws my attention to τεταρταῖός ἐστιν (of Lazarus) at Jn. 11.39 (cf. MM, s.v.). In *l*.4 ἐπτάκαμεν = ἐφθάκαμεν. For φθάνω in this sense in the papyri see editor's note, ad loc.; another example occurs in the Ezana inscription (**94 bis**, below), *l*.32, and for the NT note Rom. 9.31. The verb in this sense of 'arrive' also appears in the LXX and is the predecessor of the modern demotic φτάνω (G.P. Shipp, *Modern Greek Evidence for the Ancient Greek Vocabulary* [Sydney, 1979] 555). Note the different lexical forms, εὐθέως|εὐθύς (5-6) in successive lines: little weight should be given to it, but one *may* be reminded of the redundant use of εὐθύς in Mk., where it seems to function as little other than a linking word, devoid of meaning. For ἀναβαίνω πρός + accus. of person, cf. Acts 15.2. Epistolary tenses occur: ἔγραψα (7), ἰμίν = ἤμην (7-8). In the NT ἀπρόσκοπος (*l*.7) has a moral force: 1 Cor. 10.32; Phil. 1.10; Acts 24.16. But in the papyri ἀ. εἰμί is an idiomatic way of saying, 'I'm all right'. The editor's note, ad loc., cites several papyrus examples of this use. At *l*.14 ὅμαι = ὧμαι; for parallels to this transition to the deponent inflection see B.G. Mandilaras, *The Verb in the Greek non-literary Papyri* (Athens, 1973) § 114. The genitive absolute at *ll*.8-9 is a common formula in papyrus letters; see editor's note for examples, and add *SB* 10799.4 (Turn of the Era; see **13**). For an example in a Christian inscription note *IG Aeg.* 9273.1-2 (374), τ]οῦ Παντ[οκ]ρ[άτ]ορος θεοῦ θελήσαντος καὶ|τοῦ Χριστοῦ αὐτοῦ, κτλ. One might compare *P.Laur.* 6 (97-117 AD), a transport contract which includes certain stipulations about sailing conditions to guarantee the safe arrival of the consignment, with a few escape-clauses, including ἀπὸ Διὸς βίας (10); see editor's note, ad loc.). At *l*.12 γαράψις (= γράψεις) is a future indicative with imperatival force: on this see Moulton/Howard/Turner, *A Grammar of NT Greek* III (Edinburgh, 1963), 86-87. The editor brackets the first alpha; but the insertion of a 'helping' vowel between two consonants is frequent in the papyri, and the process continues through into modern Greek. See F.T. Gignac, *A Grammar of the Greek Papyri of the Roman and Byzantine Periods* I (Milan, 1976), 311. At *l*.14 τὸ μετήορον (= μετέωρον) is a technical term, meaning something like 'unsettled matter, unfinished business'; other papyrus occurrences are mentioned in the editor's note.

The extended list of greetings at *ll*. 9-12 (which includes Greek, Roman, and local Egyptian names) has numerous parallels in the papyri, dated I-IV; see editor's note for examples, and add *BGU* 2349 (II), *P.Laur.* 20 (III¹), and *SB* 10840 (IV; cf.**84**) . The salutation passages in some NT epistles (e.g., Rom. 16.3-16) find their counterparts in these papyrus letters. *BGU* 2349 consists of the concluding section of a letter which includes greetings to a number of people, who do not all appear to be related to one another. In addition to the writer of the letter, another person has his greetings conveyed (cf. Rom. 16.22) to his mother 'and her children'. After the conclusion of the letter as such, there follows the enigmatic statement: 'This is the letter with one erasure at the beginning of the fifth line' (14-16). The reason for such concern that the contents of the letter not be altered is unclear (the fifth line of the letter is lost). By contrast, *P.Laur.* 20 is a complete letter consisting almost entirely of salutations, first to the writer Zosimos' brother and his family, then to Apas καὶ τοὺς ἡμῶν πάντας κατ' ὄνομα (5-6). This prepositional phrase in an epistolary greeting provides a further example to add to the two noted by MM, s.v. ὄνομα, 6. Two others, *P.Oxy.* 20(1952) 2276.28, and *P.Mich.* 8(1951) 5197, are quoted in **24**. In *P.Stras.* 637 (= **19**) the phrase occurs twice — see M. Nagel's list of other examples of the repetition of the formula in a letter (*P.Stras.* 637, p.57). In the NT the phrase occurs at 3 Jn. 15. Yet differences must not be glossed over between the NT salutation passages and these papyrus letters. Paul provides fuller comment on the individual greeted; he repeats the verb constantly (e.g., in Rom. 16), whereas in Diodora's letter there is one verb and a string of bald names linked by καί.

16. Deferential greetings to a patron

Provenance unknown   I/II
ed.pr. — J. R. Rea, *CPR* 19, pp. 45-47 (pl.18)

Ἑρμ.[*c. 15 letters*].[...
    καὶ ε[*c. 13 letters*] χ[α]ίρ[ειν
καὶ διὰ παν[τὸς ἐρρωμ]ένον
διαμένειν ὅλῳ [τῷ] σώματι
5   ἰς μακροὺς χρόνους, ἐπεὶ ἡ τύ-
χη σου ἐπέτρεψε ἡμῖν ἵνα σε
προσκυνήσωμεν καὶ ἀσπα-
σώμεθά σε. ὡς καὶ σὺ γὰρ ἡμῶν
ἐμνήσθης παρ' ἕκαστα κατ' ἐπισ-
10   τολήν, οὕτως κἀγὼ ἐνθάδε
τὸ προσκύνη[μ]ά σου ποιῶ παρὰ
τοῖς κυρίο[ις Διο]σκόροις καὶ
παρὰ τῷ κυρ[ίῳ Σ]εράπιδι καὶ
εὔχομαί σ[οι τ]ὴν σωτηρίαν
15   τοῦ παντὸς βίου καὶ τὴν ὀγίαν
τῶν τέκνων σου καὶ τοῦ παντὸς οἴκου σου. τὰ δὲ ὅλα ἔρρω-
σό μοι, ὁ πά[τ]ρων μου καὶ τροφεύς. ἄσπασαι τοὺς σοὺς πάν-
20   τες καὶ πάσας. ἀσπάζονταί σε
οἱ ἐνθάδε θεοὶ πάντες καὶ
πᾶσαι. (*vac.*) ἔρρωσο. Θὼθ ιϛ.
(*verso*) ....] (*vac.*) Σεραπίωνι τῷ κυρίῳ.

A virtually complete papyrus letter, possibly part of an archive of a certain Sarapion, who owned land in the Hermopolite nome (*P. Sarapion* ed. J. Schwartz [Cairo, 1961]).

Herm ... [to Sarapion] ... greetings, and that you may always remain in
5   good health in your whole person |for long years to come, since your good
genius allowed us to greet you with respect and salute you. For as you also make
10 mention of us on each occasion by letter |so I here make an act of worship for
you in the presence of the lords Dioskouroi and in the presence of the lord
15 Sarapis, and I pray for your safe-keeping |during your entire life and for the
health of your children and of all your household. Farewell in everything, I beg,
20 my patron and fosterer. Greet all your folk, men |and women. All the gods here,
male and female, greet you. Farewell. Thoth 16th. *(verso)* To Sarapion, the lord.

This letter entirely lacks circumstantial content. So taken up is it with fulsome
greeting of the addressee and his family and with prayers for their good health that
one may even wonder what gave rise to it at all. The recipient is called ὁ πάτ[ρ]ων μου
καὶ τροφεύς (18-19), which confirms the impression of the patron/client relationship
lying behind the letter. Neither of these terms occurs in the NT, although the latter
is used of God in Philo (see BAGD, s.v.). The writer speaks of ἡ τύ|χη σου (5-6), a
phrase which is used of officials in petitions in the papyri (see Rea's n.) Of most
import, perhaps, are the terms προσκυνέω (7) and προσκύνημα (11). For the verb in the
sense of worshipping God in the NT, note Mt. 4.10 (quoting LXX; = Lk. 4.8); Jn.
4.22-24; cf. Rev. 3.9, 9.20. No closer to the use in this papyrus is Cornelius' action
towards Peter, for the latter is there taken aback as though *proskynesis* is something
to offer gods, not men (Acts 10.25-26). The notion occurs in expressions of the
relationship between slaves and masters (e.g., Mt. 18.26), and so the presence of the
term in the not altogether dissimilar style of relationship existing between a client and
his patron is not surprising. One may be tempted to compare *ll.* 11-13 of the papyrus
with this last-mentioned NT passage, but in fact the formula employed is a variant
of a specialised one whereby the writer prays by the gods of his town for the safety
of the recipient. Since the Dioskouroi were Greek gods Rea suggests that the letter
may have originated in one of the three Greek cities of Egypt, Naukratis, Ptolemais,
or Alexandria, with the possibility favouring the last in view of the association with
Sarapis. On the *proskynema* formula, see G. Geraci, *Aeg.* 51 (1971) 3-211 (pp.197-
200 on π. and Christianity; cf. Naldini, p.12.). S.R. Pickering has pointed out to me
that *P.Oxy.* 14 (1920) 1775 (= Naldini no.66; IV) may possibly be a Christian use of
the formula; and he refers me to H.C. Youtie's publication of a Christian *proskynema*
in *ZPE* 28 (1978) 265-68.

Of other words in this letter note διαμένω (4), used absolutely in the NT at Lk. 1.22;
Heb. 1.11 (quoting LXX); 2 Pet. 3.4; μιμνήσκω + gen. of person (9), cf. Lk. 23.42;
1 Cor. 11.2; Heb. 2.6, 13.3; ἐπιστολή (9-10), frequent in NT in this sense; σωτηρία (14),
not in NT with this meaning of physical good health, but see **4**. The phrase ἰς (= εἰς)
μακροὺς χρόνους (5) is virtually synonymous with μακροχρόνιος at Eph. 6.3 (quoting
LXX). The words at *ll.*8 ff. raise the question whether any connection or comparison
is to be made with Paul's statements early in various letters that he remembers his
addressees in his prayers: Rom. 1.9; Eph. 1.16; Phil. 1.3; 1 Thes. 1.2; 2 Tim. 1.3;
Philem. 4; cf. 1 Thes. 3.6. Is the pagan *proskynema* some sort of equivalent to the
Jewish/Christian prayer for someone else?

17. An anxious letter

Edfu, Egypt   II
ed.pr. — R. S. Bagnall, *O. Florida* 17 (pl.9)

Σέντις Πρώκλῳ τῷ ἀδελ-
φῷ χαίρειν· καλῶς ἐπύ-
ησας, ἄδελφε, δοὺς Ἀγχούβι
τὰ δύο κολοφώνηα, καὶ γρά-
5   ψον μυ περὶ τοῦ ναύλου καὶ
εὐθέως συ πέμψω. οὐκ ἔπεμ-
ψά συ, ἄδελφε, κρέες ἵνα
μὴ ἀποτάξωμαί συ.
λοιπὸν ἐρωτῶ σε, κύριε,
10   δόξασόν με καὶ ἔρχου
μετὰ τοῦ Αἰθίοπες.
εὐφρανθρῶμεν [sic.].
ἔρρωσσο.

μὴ οὖν ἄλλως πυή-
15   σις ἀλλὰ ἢ φιλεῖς
με ἔρχου [[....]]
εὐφρανθῶμεν.

A vivid, if somewhat obscure, personal letter written on an ostrakon to a soldier
(?) from his wife (?). *Ll.* 14-17 are added at the left side at right angles to the rest
of the text.

Sentis to Proklos her brother, greetings. You did well, brother, giving the two
5   *kolophonia* **to Anchoubis. And write | to me about the fare, and I shall send it**
to you immediately. I did not send meat to you, brother, lest I 'bid you adieu'.
10   **Finally I ask you, sir, | respect me and come with the Ethiopian. Let us rejoice.**
15   **Farewell. So do not do otherwise, | but if you love me come . . . let us rejoice.**

The name Sentis is elsewhere attested only of males (Bagnall, 58), but φιλεῖς (15),
as well as κύριε (9) and the overall tone of the letter, suggest that the writer is a
woman, perhaps the wife of Proklos (ibid., 56). Letters in the papyri containing
ἀδελφός as an address between spouses are commonplace. 'Kolophonia' are liquid
measures used particularly of wine (Bagnall, ad loc.). For φιλεῖν, see **8.** The Ethiopian
here is almost certainly a slave: see **24.** There are a number of philological points of
contact with the NT in this brief letter. For λοιπόν (9) towards the end of a letter,
making what may be expected to be its last point or introducing its final section —
in this ostrakon *ll.* 14-17 are clearly a postscript — cf. 1 Thes. 4.1; 2 Thes. 3.1; 2 Cor.
13.11; Phil. 4.8. The verb εὐφραίνω, used absolutely (12,17), is common in the NT:

see BAGD, s.v., 2. The construction ἀποτάσσομαι with a personal object in the dative — συ (8) is to be understood as σοι — occurs at 2 Cor. 2.13; Mk. 6.46; Lk. 9.61; Acts 18.18. But the meaning required here is a little different. Sentis is saying that she did not want to cause Proklos' death: the verb, which normally means 'say farewell to, take leave of', appears here as a euphemism (very colloquial?). At *P.Oxy.* 2 (1899) 298.31 (I) it means 'get rid of, be done with'. Again, the construction δόξασόν με (10) is paralleled in the NT, but the sense here must be somewhat different. Above all, note Jn. 17.1, 4, 5, for which *PGM* 7.501ff. (addressed to Isis) is strikingly similar: δόξασόν με, ὡς ἐδόξασα τὸ ὄνομα τοῦ υἱοῦ σου Ὥρος (cited in BAGD, s.v.). Bagnall suggests that in this ostrakon the verb is to have a weaker sense than usual, 'show respect', although that meaning is unexampled.

How would Sentis have forwarded the money for Proklos' fare? *O.Florida* 15.5-7 (Edfu, II) provides a typical answer. In that ostrakon letter a father is writing to his son: ἐὰν |χρῆζεις χαλκοῦ ... γράψεις μοι καὶ πέμψω σοι |μετὰ οὗ ἐὰν εὕρω ἀνθρώπου ἀσφαλοῦς, 'if you need some money write to me and I will send it to you with any trusty person I can find'. (χαλκός here provides an example of the sense 'money, small change', attested in the NT at Mt. 10.9; Mk. 6.8, 12.41.) Earlier in the same letter (3-5), the father mentions having sent food to his son via Quintus the vet. (ἱπποιατροῦ). Presumably such a comment is included as a check that the goods did in fact reach his son. Such everyday statements will provide a background against which the Collection for the Jerusalem Church may be viewed (Acts 11.27-30), as well as such passages as Phil. 4.18.

18. Family terminology for social relationships?

Provenance unknown III/IV
ed.pr. — J. R. Rea, *CPR* 20, pp. 47-49 (pl. 19)

Χερήμων Εὐδαίμονι ἀδελφῷ `χ(αίρειν)΄.
καλῶς ποιήσις, ἄδελφαι, τέ-
λιαν τὴν εὐποιγίαν σου ἀπο-
δῖξαι καὶ πρὸς ὃ βλέπις. τὴν
5   ἀδελφὴν ἡμῶν, ἠὰν ἦν μό-
νη, πᾶν ποίησον πέμψε αὐτὴν
μετὰ τῆς μητρός σου, ἰ δὲ οὐ,
ἐν σοὶ γενέστω. καὶ πρὸς τὸ συν-
φέρων ἀντίγραψόν μοι. βίασε
10   δὲ τοῦ αὐτὴν πέμψε ἐν Ἀλεξανδρί-
ᾳ, ἠὰν δὲ ἴδῃς ὅτι ἀηδίαν ἔχι καὶ
οὐ δύνατε, ἀντιγράψατέ μοι
... τέλιάν σου τὴν εὐποιγίαν
ἀ[π]οδι[...]. [..........].

15   .....]..[
      .....]...[.].........[.
      ..].ησου..   . (vac.)
      ἀσπάζομέ σε καὶ τὴν σύνβιόν
      σου καὶ τοὺς σοὺς πάντας.
20   τὰ ἀντίγραφά μοι ταχὺ πέμψον
      παρὰ τὸν πατέρα σου.
(m.2) ἐρρῶσθαί σε εὔχομαι.
      (verso) ....[..].[..]....(vac.)....[(vac.)?]π(αρὰ) Χερήμονος.......

A personal letter on a sheet of papyrus broken across the middle, perhaps due to an original fold. Rea notes that the lacuna may thus be illusory, *l*.15 following directly after *l*.14. Phonetic spelling: ε for αι, ι for ει, αι for ε, η for ε, ω for o.

Chairemon to Eudaimon his brother, greetings. You will act rightly, brother,
5 **to exhibit as perfect your kindness and your goal. |If our sister is alone do all you can to send her with your mother. Otherwise, let her be in your hands. And**
10 **write back to me with regard to what is fitting. And try hard |to send her to Alexandria. But if you see that she is in difficulty and cannot come, write back**
15 **to me ... Exhibit as perfect your kindness ... |... I greet you and your wife and all yours. Send the copies to me quickly to your father's. (Second hand) I pray you are well.**
(verso) ... from Chairemon ...

The occurrence here of family terminology is what gives this letter its interest. 'The way in which Chairemon refers to "your mother", who is at Eudaemon's end of the correspondence, and to "your father", who is at his own end, rather than "our mother" and "our father", suggests that some, or even possibly all, of these terms of blood relationship are being used loosely to indicate emotional and social relationships' (Rea, p.47). These usages are common in the papyri and constitute a complicating factor in the interpretation of family relationship in such documents. Cf. **83, 84.** An epigraphical example of this occurs at *IMS* 125 *bis* (= *AE* 604), a funerary text from Moesia (II²), in which the term *fratris* (= *fratribus)* indicates that Chrysophoros and Primitiva, slaves of Adiutor are 'membres d'un collège' (*IMS,* p.140): *D(is) M(anibus)|Chrysophoro et Primitivae Adi|utoris [s]er(vis) [.....]|tus fratris b(ene) m(erentibus) p(osuit).* The names here are characteristic of people of humble status (*ed.pr.).*

The phrase καλῶς ποίησεις (2) is very common and is found in the NT with several constructions — absolutely, + dative, + participle (see BAGD, s.v., καλῶς). τέλειος used in a good sense of things (3) occurs at Jas. 1.17,25, and 1 Jn. 4.18; the noun it qualifies (εὐποιία, 3) appears only at Heb. 13.16. The intrusive -γ- is to be noted for this word in the papyrus (for the phenomenon, see F.T. Gignac, *A Grammar of the Greek Papyri of the Roman and Byzantine Periods,* I [Milan, 1976] 72). 1 Cor. 4.9 is the only occurrence of ἀποδείκνυμι (3-4); and πρὸς τὸ συμφέρον (8-9) is found at 1 Cor. 12.7 (cf. 1 Cor 7.35 [only some MSS]; Heb. 12.10, ἐπὶ τὸ σ.). Note οὐ for μή at *l*.7. The sense of βιάζω required here (9; see Rea's note) is not found in the NT. Another uncommon word occurring here is ἀηδία (11) which appears in the NT only at Lk. 23.12D, with the meaning 'enmity', i.e., unpleasantness. Rea suggests that 'illness' is a possible meaning (cf. H.C. Youtie, *Scriptiunculae* I [Amsterdam, 1973] 528). In contrast, ἀσπάζομαι is very common in the NT (e.g., Rom. 16 *passim)* — see **21**. So, too, ταχύ (20) is reasonably frequent with the sense required here (see BAGD, s.v., 2b, c). σύμβιος (18) is used by the Fathers of a spouse; while ἀντίγραφον (20) is also patristic, not occurring in the NT.

19. Social courtesies and obligations

Hermopolite nome   c.340
ed.pr. — M. Nagel, *P. Stras.* 637, pp. 54-57

```
                         ].ονω[
          ....].ατι προ[..]..[..]...[
          .[..] ἀδελφο[.] .τ[...]ναι τ....[...
          του καιροῦ καὶ ...ατρέχι[ν .].[....
    5     τος προσ... [.] εκ[.]νου ε[.]ιν[..
          μήσαντα τοῦ [..]η[..] ὑπὸ προ.[...
          του ἐν σπουδῇ κ...ου ὅ[π]ερ καὶ
          πρέπον ἐστίν. Ἑ γὰρ κατ' ἀπουσίαν
          γιγνόμεναι σπουδὲ διπλο[ῦ] τειμ[ίου
   10     τὴν χάριν ἀπονέμουσιν τῷ [ εὐ-
          εργετηθέντι, μά[λ]ιστα τοῖς [....
          ἀνδράσι ὧν ἑ προερέσις δ[ύ]ναταί
          εἰσιν ἀντ' ἀμίβεσθαι τ[ὰς] χάρι-
          τ[α]ς Προσαγόρευαι ὡς ἀπ' ἐμοῦ
   15     τ[ὸν] κύριόν μου πραιπόσιτον
          ἅ[μα] τοῖς αὐτοῦ πᾶσι κατ' ὄνομ[α,
          ἀπ' α]ὐ[το]ῦ μέχρις τοῦ ἀδεκίμου ἅμα τοῖς αὐτῶ(ν)
          πᾶσι κ]ατ' ὄνομα.τὰ λοιπ(ὰ) ὀπίσω.
          Σπούδασον δὲ καὶ βοήθησον, ἄδελφε,..[.......
   20     .πε.κιν μοι ἐρχόμενος ..ν[.........
          ἐπὶ πάνυ χρεία μοί ἐστιν ἀπειθι.[........
          νος καὶ λαβὶν παρὰ μὲν Παήσιος ἐπ[........
          ἄπερ οἶδας αὐτὸν χρεωστὶν μοι υφ[.........
          ἀπὸ Σερήνου καὶ Ἱωσήφιος τα[.]..[.........
   25     αὐτῷ Σερήνῳ εἰς τιμ(ὴν) τοῦ ὄνου ο.ο.[........
          Ὥρου Ἀμμωνιανοῦ ἐν Πρήκ(τει) τὴν τιμ(ὴν) τῶν α.[...
          σπαθίων ζ´ ὧν μοι χρεωστῖ ἢ ὅσα .[....
          ἕως παραγένωμαι εἰς τὴν Πρῆκ(τιν) φ[......
          μὴ ] ἀμελήσῃς. ἀεὶ παρείδῃ[ς] το.[..........
   30     ἀεὶ μὴ ὀκνήσαντα εἰς σέ ἐπ[ι............
                         πολλοῖ(ς χρόνοις
                         ἄδελφ[ε
```

Fragmentary section of a letter in a bad state of preservation, written on both sides of the papyrus sheet (*recto*, 1-18; *verso*, 19 *ad fin.*). The editor thinks two lines are lost from the top and several from the bottom. Date and provenance are derived from mention of Horos son of Ammonianos (26), and of the village of Prek(tis) (26,28), attested in other documents. Numerous confusions of *a/ε*; *ι* for *ει*.

(*ll.* 7ff.) . . . which also is fitting. The zealous exertions which arise in one's
10 **absence show gratitude of double worth | to the one who has been treated well, especially to the . . . men whose devotions are able to repay favours in return.**
15 **Greet as from me | my lord the *praepositus*, together with all his (family) by name, from him as far as the disqualified (?), together with all their (families)**
20 **by name. Continued on the back. Be zealous and help, brother . . . | . . . coming to me . . . since I have a great need to disobey . . . and to get from Paesis . . .**
25 **which you know he owes me as a debt . . . from Serenos and Joseph . . . | to Serenos himself for the value of the donkey . . . of Horos son of Ammonianos at Prek(tis) the value of the seven swords which he owes me or as much as . . .**
30 **Until I get to Prek(tis) . . . do not neglect. Always disregard the . . . | always, not hesitating to . . . to you . . .**

This business letter, whose writer and recipient are both unnamed in the extant lines, contains several discernible sections: a request for help, insofar as that is appropriate (1-8); a general comment on the friendship which is shown by the mutual exchange of help (8-14); greetings (14-18); specific requests for help (19-28); concluding advice and greeting (28-32).

The text contains numerous clichés belonging to the genre of letterwriting through which is revealed some idea of the continuing importance of *amicitia* in the late Roman world (cf. **85**). The general comment in *ll.* 8-14 exemplifies this. The sentiment is thoroughly different from the pattern of social attitudes reflected in the NT. Some words of special note as epistolographic clichés are ἀπονέμω (10, see Nagel's note; and cf. 1 Pet. 3.7 where the wording is ἀ. τιμήν + dat. person); εὐεργετέω (10-11, used absolutely in NT at Acts 10.38, though without the specific weight of meaning implied by this papyrus); and σπουδάζω (19, common in both NT and patristic letters — see BAGD, s.v., 2; for discussion of the verb in letters see H.A. Steen, *Cl & Med.* 1 [1938] 166-68). Of other words also found in the NT, note: σπουδή (9), but only in singular in NT, with sense of 'eagerness, zeal' (numerous references in BAGD, s.v., 2); τίμιος (9), 1 Pet. 1.19; 2 Pet. 1.4; Jas. 5.7; χάρις (10, 13-14), frequent in NT; ἀδόκιμος (17), 2 Cor. 13. 5-7, Tit. 1.16; cf. 1 Cor. 9.27. The sense in the papyrus cannot really be pejorative: the line seems to mean 'from the most important down to the least.' The line suggests to Nagel that the recipient of the letter must have belonged to the administrative office of the *praepositus pagi* mentioned (15). χρεία (21), common in NT; παραγίνομαι (28), common in NT (BAGD, s.v., 1); ἀμελέω (29), absolute at Mt. 22.5; cf. Heb. 2.3, 8.9; 1 Tim. 4.14; παροράω (29), a *v.l.* at Acts 17.30; ὀκνέω (30), Acts 9.38. While χρεωστέω (23) does not occur in the NT or patristic material, the noun χρεώστης is attested in Hermas (see BAGD). For προσαγορεύω (14), see **21**. For κατ' ὄνομα see **15**. In *l.*29 the idea of negligence is apparently repeated, although the syntax is not really certain. For the phrase τὰ λοιπ(ὰ) ὀπίσω (18), see *P. Tebt.* 1 (1902) 58.36-37 with edd. n., and 178.20.

20. A new letter from the Theophanes archive

Hermopolis Magna, Thebaid   IV
ed.pr. — B.R. Rees, *BJRL* 51 (1968) 164-83 (pl.)

Κυρίῳ μου ἀδελφῶι Νείλωι
Ἀνατ[όλ]ιος χαίρειν.
καὶ δ[ιὰ] τίνος ἦν εἰκός σοι γρά-
φειν [ὡς] διὰ τοῦ κυρίου μου
5   πάτ[ρω]νος Θεοφάνους εἰς Ἀλε-
ξαν[δρεί]αν ἀποδημοῦντος; πέ-
πεισό [μοι γ]ὰρ εἰ β[ούλ]η ὅτι ὁ [[μου]] πατέρ
μου [ἔτι τῆ]ς αὐτῆς προ[θ]έσεως
ἔχετ[αι ὥ]ς σε βουλόμενος ἥκειν.
10 ἐπε[ῖχε δὲ] αὐτὸν τὸ συμ[β]εβηκὸς
ἀνθρ[ώπι]νον τῇ ἀδελφ[ῇ] αὐτοῦ
τῇ πρ[εσβ]υτέρᾳ. μετὰ δὲ τὴν κηδί-
αν α[ὐτ]ῆς ἥξει ʽἐλεύσεταιʼ. προσαγόρευε
τὰς κυρίας μου ἀδελφὰς Νειλογεν[ί]αν
15 καὶ Κωμασίαν. προσαγόρευε πᾶν ὅτι μοι
φίλον.   ἐρρῶσθαί σε θεοῖς
                           πᾶσιν εὔχομαι
                           πανοικησίᾳ τῶν
                           ἱερέων τὸ ἀγλάϊσμα.

One of three letters written by Anatolios which belong to this archive. The margins of the papyrus are preserved, but there are some large holes in the papyrus where the folds were. There is a roughly made join of two papyrus sheets (called a *kollema)*. Spelling is very accurate: πατέρ (7) for -ήρ is the only error in all three of Anatolios' letters, according to Rees (176).

Bib. — *SB* 10803; E.A. Judge and S.R. Pickering, 'Papyrus Documentation of Church and Community in Egypt to the mid-Fourth Century', *JbAC* 20 (1977) 48, 53-54.

To my lord brother Neilos, Anatolios, greetings. And via whom was it (so)
5   **reasonable to write to you as via my lord |patron Theophanes who is on a**
journey to Alexandria? For believe me, if you would, that my father still keeps
10   **to the same intention of wanting to come to you. |But the calamity which is**
man's lot coming upon his elder sister held him back. But after her funeral he
15   **will come. Greet the ladies my sisters Neilogenia | and Konasia. Greet every(one)**
who is friendly to me. I pray to all the gods that you, the ornament of the
priests, are in good health with your entire household.

Over forty documents and letters are extant which address Theophanes directly or refer to him. He was a *scholasticus,* or jurist, who may have acted a a legal adviser in the fourth-century civil service in Egypt (Rees, 164). That he travelled widely is clear from this archive: about 320 he went to Syrian Antioch and much of the remaining letters and memoranda were written to or for him in connection with that trip (ibid., 173). The deference accorded him in these texts, including the one reprinted above, reveal him to have been of considerable standing: 'Clearly he occupied something akin to the position of a leader in the cultured, pagan circle to which he belonged' (ibid., 165). He had a close involvement with the cult of Hermes Trismegistos whose importance at Hermopolis Magna was considerable (ibid., 168). Theophanes will certainly have been aware of the considerable spread of Christianity in Egypt during IV[1] following the persecution initiated under Diocletian. 'In Theophanes we have an excellent example of the cultured Hellenist who learned to live with the Roman government but not with the Christian Church' (ibid., 168). On this subject see the series of essays in A. Momigliano (ed.) *The Conflict between Paganism and Christianity in the Fourth Century* (Oxford, 1963, repr. 1970); and E. R. Dodds, *Pagan and Christian in an Age of Anxiety* (Cambridge, 1965; repr. 1968).

The following philological points illustrating the NT may be mentioned: ἀποδημέω (6), Mk. 12.1 (= Mt. 21.33, Lk. 20.9), Mt. 25.14, 15; Lk. 15.13; πρόθεσις in the sense of 'plan, purpose, resolve' (8), 2 Tim. 3.10, Acts 27.13 (both of men), Rom. 8.28 (of God); ἐπέχω (9), Acts 19.22; τὸ συμβεβηκός τινι (10-11), Acts 3.10; ἀνθρώπινος (11) in the sense used here, 1 Cor. 10.13; cf. Acts 17.25 and 1 Cor. 2.13 where the word contrasts with divine creativity and divine wisdom respectively; for πρεσβυτέρα (12) of an older woman, note 1 Tim. 5.2, but note BAGD, s.v. πρεσβύτερος, where several references to Hermas are given in which the word is used of the personified Church; κηδία (12 and 13), the related verb κηδεύω at Mk 6.29 (*v.1.*); for the sentence in *ll.* 15-16, see **21**. πανοικησία (18), cf. πανοικεί at Acts 16.34.

Rees points to the ambivalent wording of some of the letters in this archive, which could be considered Christian were it not for a knowledge of their context which the rest of the collection provides. 'This difficulty of deciding whether a letter is pagan or Christian purely on the basis of its language and sentiments has often been remarked on in connection with papyri from the fourth century A.D.: the religious formulae of pagan and Christian letters are so similar that it is always dangerous to identify them firmly as one or the other without contextual support . . .' (179).

21. Recommending a client for protection

Provenance unknown   V
ed.pr. — J. R. Rea, *CPR* 23, pp. 51-53 (pls. 22 and 23)

τῷ δεσπότῃ μου ὡς ἀληθῶς τιμιοτάτῳ ἀδελφῷ
Γεροντίῳ Ἡλία Κτήσιππος χ(αίρειν).
ἐπιδὴ Μακά[ρ]ιος ὁ ἡμέτερος ναύτης ἐγόμοσεν
ὀλίγα βάκαν[α] ἐν Ὀξυρύγχον καταξιοσάτω

5 ἡ ⟨ὑ⟩μῶν ἀδελφωσύνη τοῦτον ποιῆσε πολῆσε αὐτὰ καλῆς τιμῆς οἴας αὐτὸς θέλι πολῆσε καὶ
ἀνεπηρήαστον αὐτῶν παρά τινος γενέσθαι
ἕως {.} ἂν ἀπαρτίσῃ τῷ πλοῖον, ἐμοὶ τὰ πολλὰ
χαριζώμενοι. καὶ γὰρ ὁ θεὸς οἶδεν ὅτι εἰ μὴ ἔ-
10 γραψα τῇ ὑμῶν ἀδελφοσύνη, χορὶς γραμμάτων λέγον ὑμῖν περὶ ἐμοῦ, οὐκ ἂν εἴχατε
ε[..]......παρά τινος ἐπερηασθῆνε. περὶ δὲ
..........] καταξιόσατε δηλῶσέ μοι, τὰ πλῖστά μοι
χαριζόμενοι. προσαγορεύει ὑμᾶς ὁ κύριός μου καὶ
15 ἀδελφὸς Φίλιππος. προσαγορεύω πάντας τοὺς φιλ-
οῦν{.}τας ὑμᾶς ἡδέος. ἐρρῶσθαι ὑμᾶς εὔχομαι πολλ.

· · · ·
(verso) τῷ δεσπότῃ μου ὡς ἀληθὸς φιλτάτῳ[......] (vac.)? .[

This letter may have been written at Oxyrhynchos (cf. *l.*4), but it is not likely to have been found there. In addition to the address (17), the back of the papyrus contains a draft of a financial account (= *CPR* 24) which bears no relation to this letter. The spelling is phonetic: read *o* for *ω*, *ω* for *o*, *ε* for *αι*, *αι* for *ε*, *η* for *ε*, *ε* for *η*, *ι* for *ει*. The end of the letter is lost but contained merely the conventional farewell statement.

To my master, my really most worthy brother Gerontios, son of Elias, Ktesippos sends greetings. Since Makarios our sailor has loaded a few cabbages
5 **at Oxyrhynchos, | let your brotherly kindness consider this man worthy to make a sale of them at a good price such as he himself wants to sell them for, and to be unmolested by anyone until he gets the boat ready — it's for me that you're**
10 **doing this big favour. For God knows that if I had not | written to your brotherly kindness and if without a letter he had spoken to you about me you would not have been able to allow him to be interfered with by anyone. And concerning . . . deign to inform me — a very big favour for me you'd be doing. My lord**
15 **and | brother Philip greets you. I greet with pleasure all those who love you. I pray you are very well . . .**
(verso) **To my master, my really most beloved . . .**

This letter of introduction is written by a patron on behalf of one of his clients; from the tone of *ll.* 1, 4-5, 9-11, 17, the recipient may well be a patron of the writer. The ephemeral subject which occasioned the letter underlines how pervasive the patron-client relationship continued to be in late antiquity. Such letters introducing the bearer to someone elsewhere are of a kind with letters of recommendation alluded to in the NT (Acts 18.27; 2 Cor. 3.1; Rom. 16.1; Col. 4.10) and used by Christians. In the NT the tone of the patron-client relationship is at its most noticeable in the letter to Philemon where, however, Paul is clearly not the formal *patronus* of the recipient. Paul plays on the notion of Philemon's indebtedness to himself as a way of securing what he wants. On recommendation in the Graeco-Roman world see P. Marshall, *Enmity and other Social Conventions in Paul's relations with the Corinthians* (Diss., Macquarie University, 1980), 141-202.

The verb γομόω (3) does not occur in the NT, but its related noun appears at Rev. 18.11-12. καταξιόω + infin. (4, 13) is found at Lk. 20.35, Acts 5.41, and in some MSS of Lk. 21.36. At 2 Thes. 1.5 the verb governs a genitive. The very rare ἀδελφοσύνη (5,10) is perhaps the most notable word in this letter. Rea cites two papyrus examples (*P.Med.* 2.87; *P.Apoll.* 60.16) and one epigraphical text (*MAMA* 5.91), and corrects errors in the entries of LSJ Suppl., s.v., and Index 9 to *WB* Suppl. (*Ehrentitel*). As with *P.Med.* 2.87, our new text uses the word as 'a polite way of referring to the addressee of a letter' (Rea, p.52). The other two attestations require the meaning 'fraternal sentiment'. In the latter sense the noun appears to be synonymous with one use of ἀδελφότης in the LXX and elsewhere, though not with that of the NT (BAGD, s.v., 2). The verb ἀπαρτίζω (8) is found in the LXX and patristic writing (but not in the NT), meaning 'complete, finish'. The sense required by this new letter is closely related but not identical. The construction χαρίζομαι τι τινι (8-9, 13-14) is frequent in the NT of God's favours to man. Whether the concept of the patron-client relationship of Roman social mores has been transferred by the NT writers, most notably Paul, to the divine/human level would need fuller investigation than can be offered here; but it may warrant some consideration. The use of 'polite' second plurals in a letter to one man (5,9,11,14) seems peculiar for this period. Rea offers two suggestions about *ll.* 9-12, and reading ἐ[ᾶσ]ε (= ἐᾶσαι) αὐτόν (12) he prefers the notion that 'if I had not written, his mere mention of my name would have led you to help him' (see ed.n.). For χωρίς + genitive (of a thing) (10) there are a few relevant NT examples: see BAGD, s.v., 2b, γ or δ. The word it governs also occurs with the same meaning at Acts 28.21. In this section of the letter Rea thinks λέγον (11) may be λέγον⟨τα⟩, agreeing with αὐτόν (12); or that perhaps it is an example of an idiomatic appositional phrase in the nominative (see ed.n.). J.A.L. Lee mentions to me in a note that it is more simply 'the common phenomenon of lack of concord in the participle, leading ultimately to the Modern Greek indeclinable form. Thus λέγον = λέγων, nom., not agreeing with anything in particular.' The NT meaning, 'designate', does not apply to προσαγορεύω here (14, 15), though 'greet' is a very common sense in the papyri (see, e.g., *P.Stras.* 637.14; = **19**). The regular NT equivalent is ἀσπάζομαι (e.g. Rom. 16, *passim*). The participle in *ll.* 15-16 provides a good parallel to Tit. 3.15, ἄσπασαι τοὺς φιλοῦντας ἡμᾶς ἐν πίστει. BAGD, s.v. φιλέω, 1, alludes to U. Wilcken, *APF* 6 (1920) 379, a discussion of *P.Ryl.* 2 (1915) 235.5 τοὺς φιλοῦντας ἡμᾶς κα[τ' ὄ]νομα, which provides a couple of other examples of the phrase; *SB* 3 (1926) 7253.19-20 is also quoted (= J.G. Winter, *JEA* 13 [1927] 73-74, no. 7 [pl. 26]). Note also *SB* 10803. 15-16 (= **20**), προσαγόρευε πᾶν ὅτι μοι φιλόν.

22. 'The beginning and the end' (Rev. 22.13)

P. Köln 6 consists of portions of seven lines of a poem in hexameters which greets various deities, among them Ouranos and Poseidon. The authorship is unknown, as is the provenance. *Ed. pr.* — L. Koenen and J. Kramer, *ZPE* 4(1969) 19-21 (pl. 3d). The conjunction of terms in *l.4* ...χαῖρ'] ἀρχή, χαῖρε τελευτή,|..., occurs in various Greek poetic and magical texts, particularly those linked with Orphic religion.

Koenen/Kramer (20) quote several passages of which one may note particularly the Orphic Hymns to Ouranos (*ll*.1-5) and to Apollo (*ll*.1f.). *PGM* IV.2786ff., part of a magical hymn to Selene, is also to be noted. Other references are included in the editor's note to *P.Köln* 6 (p.25); cf. BAGD, s.v. ἀρχή, ld. In the NT, at Rev. 22.13 (cf. 1.8 [a *v.l.*], 21.6) Christ speaks of himself as τὸ Ἄλφα καὶ τὸ Ὦ, ὁ πρῶτος καὶ ὁ ἔσχατος, ἡ ἀρχὴ καὶ τὸ τέλος. The second of these phrases is a quotation from Is. 44.6 (= 48.12); the first and third reflect the Hellenic milieu in which Rev. was written. For the author has referred to the Greek alphabet in order to make his first point; while the third phrase echoes — unintentionally? — a way of referring to Greek deities. The quasi-philosophical force of the phrase should not be lost from sight in the NT passages. MM lack discussion of the phrase in either of the entries ἀρχή, τέλος. P.W. van der Horst has drawn my attention to W.C. van Unnik, *Het Godspredicaat 'het begin en het einde' in Flavius Josephus en in de Apocalyps van Johannes (Med. van de Kon. Ned. Ak. van Wet., Afd. Lett.,* N.R. 39.1; Amsterdam, 1976) — *non vidi.*

The letters ΑΩ (cf. F. Cabrol, *DACL*, I.1 [1907] cols. 1-25; E. Lohmeyer, *RAC* 1 [1950] 1-4) are used in various magical texts. D. Wortmann, *Bonn. Jahrb.* 168 (1968) 106, no.9, publishes the following Christian amulet on papyrus (VI; provenance unknown).

<pre>
      †   †   †
      A   Ω
      Ω   A
      A   Ω
      Ω   A
      A   Ω
      Ω   A
      A   Ω
  † Ἰ(ησοῦ)ς   Χ(ριστό)ς †
  † βοήθεια   †
</pre>

The same scholar, in *Bonn.Jahrb.*175(1975) 74, no.13, published a carved gemstone with ΑΩ on its reverse side. See his notes to these two texts for further examples. The ΑΩ sign occurs occasionally on Christian epitaphs of Byzantine date, e.g., *IGLR* 88 (Tomis, V/VI).

The platonising Fathers took a very different direction in their use of a passage like Rev. 22.13. Commenting on Ps. 18.2 Clement of Alexandria says that 'the sensible types (τύποι) are the sounds (στοιχεῖα) we pronounce. Hence the LORD himself is called "the Alpha and the Omega, the beginning and the end" ' (*Strom.* 6.141.6-7 GCS [= Migne, *PG* 6.16]). Such an interpretation may owe much to Philo, who was in turn not only synthesising Platonism with Judaism, but incorporated some Orphic material.

23. Epitaph for a much-travelled Christian missionary?

Lyon   III/IV
ed.pr — J. Pouilloux, *JSav* (1975) 58-75 (ph., 59)

Col.1 εἰ γνῶναι ποθέεις ὅστις βροτὸς ἐνθάδε κεῖται,
οὐδὲν σειγήσει τάδε γράμματα. πάντα δὲ λέξει·
Εὐτέκνιος ἐπικλήν, Ἰουλιανὸς τοὔνομα τῷδε,
Λαοδίκια πατρίς, Συρίης περίβλεπτον ἄγαλμα·
5 ἔντιμος πατρόθεν, μήτηρ·δ' ἔχε δόξαν ὁμοίην,
χρηστὸς καὶ δίκαιος, πᾶσιν πεφιλημένος ἀνήρ,
οὗ Κελτοῖς λαλέοντος ἀπὸ γλώσσης ῥέε πειθώ·
ποικίλα μὲν περιῆλθεν ἔθνη, πολλοὺς δέ ⟨τε⟩ δήμους
ἔγνω καὶ ψυχῆς ἀρετὴν ἤσκησεν ἐ⟨ν⟩ αὐτοῖς·
10 κύμασιν καὶ πελάγει συνεχῶς ἐπέδωκεν ἑαυτόν,
δῶρα τὰ πάντα φέρων εἰς Κελτοὺς καὶ Δύσεως γῆν
[ὅ]σσα θεὸς προσέταξε φέρειν χθόνα πάνφορον Ἠοῦς·
[τοὔνε]κα τὸν φιλέ[ε]σκε βροτὸν τριπλὰ φῦλα τὰ Κελτῶν.

Col.2 ἤλασεν εἰς ΒΑΘ
15 ἀντὶ τρόπων Α.
τῷ πάντων ΚΡ
ἐν δόξῃ ΚΑΤΕ
ὑεῖ ΠΑΝΜΑΚ
καὶ πᾶσιν ΤΟ
20 τοὔνεκα ΤΟ
υἱὸς Η.ΕΚ
ΑΙΤΗΤΟΣΙ
ψυχῆς ΤΕ
δοίη ΤΕΘ
....
....

One of the numerous Roman and palaeo-Christian inscriptions found in excavations at the Church of Saint-Just; the building remains date IV-XV. This stele, consisting of two columns of text — 13 lines each, though the last two of col. 2 have been erased — is broken on the right side, rendering unintelligible the few words which remain of col. 2. Size: .74m high, .55m deep, 1.47-1.29m wide (originally c.2.40m.).

Bib. — Pouilloux's publication is preceded by J-F. Reynard (47-56) and A. Audin (56-58), who provide details about the place of discovery and the stele itself. M. Guarducci, *MEFR* 88 (1976) 843-52 (photo); *C.P. Jones, *AJP* 99 (1978) 336-53; *SEG* 1214; *BE* 799; (1977) 599 *bis;* (1979) 663.

Col.1. If you desire to know what mortal lies here, this writing will not be silent, but will tell all. Euteknios is his surname, Julianos his name; Laodicea his city,
5 **Syria's remarkable ornament. |His father's family was held in esteem, and his mother had a similar reputation. He was good and just, a man beloved by all. When he spoke to Kelts, persuasion flowed from his tongue. He went about among diverse nations, and knew many peoples; and he practised a virtuous life**
10 **among them. |He gave himself continually to the waves and to the sea, carrying to the Kelts and to the land of the West all gifts which God instructed the bountiful East to bear. For this reason the threefold tribes of the Kelts loved the man.**

Very divergent interpretations have been attached to this inscription in the couple of years since it has become known. Pouilloux suggested (72-74) that Julianos was an itinerant philosopher or teacher, possibly a Christian missionary. Guarducci urged much more definitely that Christianity was in view in this epitaph, though not a little of her article was devoted to restorations of incomplete words in col.2 which bolstered her hypothesis (*ll.*14, 18, 21). On this view, a Christian from Syria brought the Gospel to the western city of Lyon, or more generally to those Kelts who inhabited the *Tres Galliae,* Lugdunensis, Belgica, and Aquitania. By dint of much travel, persuasiveness and example of life he won a lasting memorial from those to whom he came. In contrast to this, Jones — who wrote without knowledge of Guarducci's article, though he was able to add brief discussion of it in a postscript — proposed a number of new readings and punctuations in col.1 (especially 4, 6, 9, and the punctuation at 13), several of which Pouilloux has confirmed (Jones, 337, n.4; cf. *BE* [1977] 599 *bis*). Jones argues that the final four verses of col. 1 (10-13) reveal Julianos to be simply a trader (on eastern traders in Gaul see Pouilloux, 65, n.19). 'Though such men might buy or sell wherever they put in, they tended to move on an axis between two cities or regions . . .' (Jones, 344), i.e., Lyon and Laodicea in this case. Itinerant teachers would move about on land, making contact with people from village to village, town to town. To be constantly at sea is what we should expect from a merchant, not from a philosopher/teacher. Jones' general point is borne out well by the NT situation. Not merely do the gospels portray Jesus constantly on the move in his preaching ministry, but especially the great mobility of Paul illustrates that sea travel was merely a means to prosecute his land-based strategy more efficiently.

Pouilloux showed very clearly how conventional Homeric formulae find expression in modified form throughout this hexameter verse epitaph. But the heightened tone of several of the verses '. . . is not out of place for a mundane profession' (Jones, 347). Whereas such words as χρηστός (6), πειθώ (7), and ἔθνη ... δήμους (8) could be interpreted as semicryptic indications of a link with Christianity (see Pouilloux, 73-74), there is no compelling need to understand the terms in that way. Again, whereas Pouilloux (73, followed by Guarducci, 834) took θεός as subject of φιλέεσκε (13), to show that Julianos' deity is a god of love, by a change of punctuation necessitated by the *vacat* at the end of col.1, Jones has argued forcibly that θεός cannot be the subject of that verb. Before leaving aside the wording of the inscription one may note in passing the presence of λαλεῖν (7) as a general word for 'speak': J.A.L. Lee points out to me that the writer has not been able to avoid the anachronism of a Koine usage in the midst of extremely archaic Homeric language. For Julianos' double name, cf. **55**, IIA.

The date of the text has not been settled: post 180 (Guarducci, 852); II²/III *init.* (Pouilloux, 60,61); III or IV (Jones, 349-50). Jones' conclusion is very cautious: while it cannot be proved that Julianos was not a Christian, nothing in the inscription lends weight to such a conclusion, and thus 'it may not be imprudent to incline towards a pagan interpretation' (353).

24. The distribution of a deceased man's slaves

A private agreement between three heirs of Tiberius Julius Theon sets out the slaves to be allocated to each man. *P.Oxy.* 3197 (dated 20/10/111) is a fairly complete text, twenty-two lines long, edited by J.D. Thomas (pp.169-74). This very wealthy family of Roman citizens held numerous official posts in their city of Alexandria. This papyrus shows that they owned property in several districts (nomes) of Egypt. The text is not included in *P.Theon,* having come too late to the attention of the editor of that collection of papyri dealing with this family (*P.Theon,* p.1). A few observations are offered below about the division of the estate and about the slaves mentioned in this papyrus.

Each of the parties appears to be receiving fifteen male slaves, in addition to ones already owned. There certainly will have been female slaves belonging to the estate as well. 'We shall hardly be in error, I think, if we suppose [the deceased] to have owned at least a hundred slaves. This figure is astonishingly high for Roman Egypt' (Thomas, p.170). The slaves are distinguished by metronymic, job description, or whereabouts. Occupations mentioned include a γραμματεύς, two προχειροφόροι (amanuenses), five νωτάριοι (short-hand writers?), μάγ(ε)ιρος (cook), an ἠπητής (repairer; or cobbler?), and a κουρεύς (barber). The number of slaves with writing skills is indicative of the administrative load which such an estate faced in Roman Egypt. In the NT was Tertius, Paul's amanuensis (Rom. 16.22), a slave?

Two of the servile names to occur here are Demas (cf. **51**) and Epaphrys; another is Abaskantos *(bis)* closely akin to which is 'Abaskantion the Ethiopian' (*l.*13). Abaskantos was the name of a secretary of Domitian (*CAH* XI [1936] 30). As an epithet, 'may he be untouched by the evil eye', it is used most commonly of children. In *P.Oxy.* 20 (1952) 2276.28 (III²; = Naldini, no.18), the writer says ἀσπάζομαι κατ' ὄνομα τὰ ἀβάσκ[αν]τά| [σο]υ παιδία... A similar phrase (μετὰ τῶν ἀ. π.) occurs at *PSI* 7(1925) 825.21-22 (provenance unknown, IV¹; = Naldini, no.44), and again (τὰ ἀ. σου τέκνα) at *PSI* 8(1927) 972.4 (Oxyrhynchos?, IV; = Naldini no.64 = *SB* 10841 = **85** in this review). At *P.Mich.* 8(1951) 519.3-7 (Karanis, IV; = Naldini 67) the writer of the letter says προσ|αγορεύω καὶ τῆι μητρεί μου Θερμού|τεις καὶ [τ]οῦ (sic) ἀβ[άσκ]αντάν σου οἴ|κου κατὰ ὄν[ομ]α. Of these four letters, *PSI* 825 may not be Christian, despite Naldini's inclusion of it in his collection. Naldini comments on the word at p.279. A Latin text from Nomentum (modern Mentana) in Italy includes . . .*Ab]ascantus,* which from the fragmentary context may be the name of a child (*AE* 119). In two letters (*O.Florida* 15, 18) the writer prays that the recipient is in good health μετὰ τοῦ ἀβασκάντου σου ἵππου. The phrase (partly restored) also occurs at *O.Amst.* 18. For a more accurate translation of the word as a 'benign wish' in such a context, H.C. Youtie, *ZPE* 36 (1979) 73-76, suggests 'your horse which I pray may be preserved from the evil eye'. For further discussion of the word see R.S. Bagnall's note to *O.Florida* 15. 2-3 (pp. 54-55), and E.P. Gibson, *BASP* 12 (1975) 153-54. *O.Florida* 17.11 mentions an Ethiopian, probably a slave (cf. Bagnall's note, *ad loc.;* q.v. **17** above). More generally, F.M. Snowden, *Blacks in Antiquity. Ethiopians in the Greco-Roman Experience* (Cambridg, Mass., 1971), especially 184-186. Snowden includes brief discussion (206, with the notes) of the Ethiopian eunuch who figures in the incident in Acts 8.26-40.

By analogy with other texts, κυρι]εύειν is restored at *l.*17; a genitive follows. Land-leases from Oxyrhynchos contain the distinctive clause that the lessor shall have control (κυριεύειν) of the crop until he receives the rent (e.g. *BGU* 2340.14 [clearly III] — see editor's note, ad loc.; *P.Coll.Youtie* 68.24-25 [**266**]). This verb, attested also at *P.Coll.Youtie* 83.14 (12/12/353), occurs occasionally in the NT, though the construction varies. For κ. + genitive in a sense not dissimilar to the use in this *P.Oxy.* text, note Lk. 22.25. The meaning of the verb has been discussed recently by K.W. Clark in J. K. Elliott (ed.), *Studies in New Testament Language and Text* (Leiden, 1976), 100-05.

25. 'A Pure Bride' (2 Cor. 11.2)

A woman and her mother are each described as ἱερὰ παρθένος in *P.Oxy.* 3177.2-3 (mid III). The title 'refers to female attendants of the deity, but it is infrequently attested in Greco-Roman Egypt' (ed.n. ad loc.). The only other papyrus text to use the phrase is *P.Merton* 2.73.1 (Oxyrhynchos, 163/64), in which a declaration is made of the sources of income of Taophryonis, ἱερᾶς παρθ[ένου]. A Ptolemaic inscription from Kanopos in Egypt, *OGIS* 56.66-68 (239/38), lays down that Berenike is to be hymned by chosen sacred virgins, ὑμνεῖσθαι δ' αὐτὴν καὶ ὑπὸ τῶν ἐπιλεγομένων ἱερῶν παρθένων. This function of sacred *parthenoi,* viz., *hymnodoi,* is attested from Asia Minor: W.M. Ramsay, *ABSA* 18 (1911/12) 44-45, mentions that at Klaros in Ionia such women provided a chorus to sing in honour of Apollo on certain occasions (see below). Ramsay, ibid., 58, publishes a text from Lykaonia which speaks of a παρθένος ... ἱέρεια τῆς θεοῦ (viz., Ma). The duty of serving as a sacred *parthenos* is said by him to have been an hereditary one within certain priestly families in 'the late pagan revival,' which is paralleled by the *P.Oxy.* text above. In Greece proper, a regulation concerning the mysteries (Andania in Messenia, 91 BC) includes the words αἱ παρθένοι αἱ ἱεραί (C. Michel, *Recueil d'inscriptions grecques* [Paris, 1900; repr. Hildesheim, 1976] 694.29).

These phrases come close, but do not provide an exact parallel, to Paul's description of the Church in 2 Cor. 11.2 as the παρθένον ἁγνήν which he had betrothed to Christ. Sacred virgins were commonly thought of in various cults as the brides of the god they served. But another idea may well be present here as well. Marriage contracts occasionally specify that the new wife must not have sexual relations with other men. In these documents παρθένος is not used, since virginity is not always a pre-requisite for the marriage. But whole clauses spell out the chastity requirement incumbent on the woman, e.g., *BGU* 4 (1912) 1050.22-23 (Alexandria, principate of Augustus), where a woman is enjoined μηδ' ἄλλῳ ἀνδρὶ | συνεῖναι, under pain of loss of her dowry. The same formula occurs also at *BGU* 4.1051.31, 1052.29, 1098.38, 1101.17 (all from Alexandria, principate of Augustus); and *P.Tebt.* 1 (1902) 104.28-29 (92 BC). The only marriage contract noticed among the 1976 publications, *SB* 10924 (Theadelphia, 14/6/114; first published by G. Kiessling, *Proc. XII International Congress of Papyrology* [Toronto, 1970] 243-45), lacks this 'fidelity' clause, probably merely because the papyrus breaks off before that formula is reached. On marriage contracts see the useful bibliography in Kiessling, 244, n.3. In 2 Cor. 11. 2ff. Paul raises the possibility that his addressees may cease to be faithful to Christ. The image of a faithful wife is not drawn out as explicitly as in such OT books as Hosea. While we may thus focus upon the two ideas which may have been behind the choice of words in 2 Cor. 11.2, Paul's statement remains very bold; we have no analogy to a group of people being regarded collectively as a παρθένος. In the Fathers ἁγνή, not ἱερά, is quite often used with παρθένος (Lampe, s.v., παρθένος, C.1-2); ἱερός is an epithet of other groups of people, including apostles and clergy (ibid., s.v., ἱερός).

Since *hymnodoi* have been mentioned above, it is relevant to refer here to a number of recently-published inscriptions. The *mystai* of a cult of Dionysos at Ephesos make a dedication to Hadrian on an altar (119-29); several officials are named, including priest, hierophant, *epimeletes* (superintendent), *mystagogos,* and *hymnodos* (D. Knibbe, *JÖAI* 50 [Beiblatt, 1972-75] 75-77, no. 6 [photo]; cf. *SEG* 1272). A number of *hymnodoi* have been noticed in *BE* over the years: from Lindos on Rhodes, (1942)

113; Daphne in Attika, (1954) 102; Ephesos, (1956) 255; Istros, (1955) 163a, (1956) 190, (1962) 240. Related is a Latin epitaph from Rome (end II-III; *AE* 13): M. Aurelius Secundinus is a *(h)ymno(l)eg(us) M(atris) D(eum) Mag(nae) Idaeae Palatin(a)e*. For other examples from Rome, Note *CIL* 6.9475, 17288, 32444 (with the note). *AE,* n. ad loc., provides other attestations. Closely akin to these are two inscriptions from Klaros in Ionia, set up by towns which sent embassies to consult the oracle of Apollo (L. Robert, *Stud.Clas.* 16 [1974] 74-80 [pl.6]; cf. *SEG* 1289). These delegations were sent from Perinthos and Bargasa early in the second century, before 115. In the first, nine men were sent in accordance with an oracle, ὑμνήσαντες τὸν θεόν (*SEG* 1288.8-9; cf. 1289. 7-8, παῖ[δε]ς οἱ ὑμνήσαντες τοὺς θεούς). The expression ὑ. τὸν θεόν provides a useful analogy to Acts 16.25. So too at Heb. 2.12 — a quotation from Ps. 22 — where σε stands for τὸν θεόν. Presumably the intransitive use of the verb at Mk. 14.26 (= Mt. 26.30) is the equivalent of the transitive in the Acts passage. Pliny's famous letter about the Christians in Bithynia reports the claim *carmenque Christo quasi deo dicere* (10.96.7).

25 *bis.* πρώτη γυναι|κῶν

— *I. Assos* 16.3-4. This dedication is dated prior to 2 BC during Augustus' principate. Lollia Antiochis set up a bath in honour of Aphrodite Julia (i.e. the daughter of Augustus) and for the demos. The phrase accorded to her, 'first of women', appears to be an honorific title. Merkelbach's note to this text on p.41 refers to other examples. Is the phrase used of women at Thessalonike in Acts 17.4 also a title, or merely a descriptive way of referring to leading women?

26. A state schoolteacher makes a salary bid

Oxyrhynchos   253-60
ed. pr. — P. J. Parsons, *P.Coll.Youtie* 66, pp.409-46 (pl.21-22)

A (*Recto* col. i)

[τ]οῖς [γῆς κ]αὶ θαλάτ[τ]ης δε[σπό]ται[ς] αὐτ[οκ]ράτ[ορσι]
[κ]αίσα[ρσι Πο]υπ[λίωι Λι]κιν[νίωι] Οὐα[λερια]νῶι
[κ]αὶ Π[ουπλίωι] Λ[ικιννί]ωι Οὐ[αλεριανῶι Γα]λλιη[νῶι]
εὐσε[βέσι ε]ὐ[τυχέ]σι σεβ[αστοῖ]ς
5 πα[ρ]ὰ Λολ[λ]ιανοῦ τοῦ κ[α]ὶ Ὁμοί[ο]υ δημοσίου [γρ]αμ-
ματικοῦ τῆς Ὀξυρυγχειτῶν πόλεως. ἡ [ο]ὐράνι-
ος ὑμῶν μεγαλοφροσύνη ἡ᾽ ἐπιλάμψασα τῆι ὑμε-
τέραι οἰκουμένηι καὶ ἡ πρὸς τὰς Μούσας [[καὶ παι]]
[[   ]] [οἰ]κείωσις – – παιδεία γὰρ ὑμεῖν σύνεδρος – –

10   ...[.]ελπιστιαν .[ ]... ἀξίωσιν ἀνεν[ε]γκεῖν
      ὑμεῖν δικαίαν τε καὶ νόμιμον, ἔστιν δὲ αὕτη·
      οἱ θεοὶ πρόγονοι ὑμῶν ὥρισαν κατὰ μέγεθος τῶν
      πόλεων καὶ ποσότητα δημοσίων γραμματικ[ῶ]ν,
      προστάξαντες καὶ συντάξεις αὐτοῖς δίδοσθαι
15   ὅπως εἴη [[±17   ]] ἀνεμπόδιστος
      ἡ περὶ τοὺς παῖδας ἐπιμέλεια.

B (*Recto* col. ii)
(*ll.* 17-22 omitted as too fragmentary)

κ(αὶ) παιδ .[.]ασ[[.]] ὁ ἀπ[α]ραίτ[ητ]ος δεσμὸς εἴργει, ἐπι[στέλλω] σοι, ἄδελφ[ε ...
    ...]ε, ταύτ(ην) τρίτ(ην) ἐπιστολ(ήν), [ἵ]ν[α]
με συνε[χ]ῶς εὐφραίνῃς π[ερὶ τ(ῆς) σ]ωτηρίας σου [[ἐπιστελλ]] ʽἀεὶ γράφʼων·
    εὐπορήσει[ς δὲ ῥα]δίως τ(ῶν) εἰς Ἀλεξάνδρειαν
25 ἀ(πὸ) τοῦ κομιτάτου εἰσϊόν[των] ἐὰν Ἀμμωνιανῷ τῷ ὀπτίωνι τ[(ῶν) βενε]φικιαρίων
    πέμ[[ψ]]ʹπʹῃς ἑταί-
ρωι μου ὄντι εἰς τὰ μάλ[ισ]τα ([[ὃς διαπέμψεταί μοι ἐνθάδε· κ(αὶ) γ(ὰρ) κ(αὶ)]] ʽἔστιν
    δὲ ὁ ἀνὴρ [.]ω ͺτος συγγενικὸς ὢν τοῦ
διασημοτάτου Θεοδώρου) ἅμα δὲ καὶ ἀξίωσίν τινα [.] προσεοικ`υῖαν ὁμ[ο]ίωι
    χαρίσασθ(αι) ἐπέστειλα ἵνα
μοι αὖ .[.]] κ(ατα)πράξῃ εἰς ἐφόδια τοῖς παιδίοις [[καὶ ...]τροφῶν, `ἣν [...]μώνιος
διὰ τοῦ ἀδελφοῦ αὐτοῦ Ἡρακλάμμων[ος τοῦ] καγκανικλαρίου [.] τύπον
    ἔπεμψεν, ὧι καὶ κοινώσει πρότερ(ον) εἰ προφθάνει αὐτὸ διηνυκώ[ς], ἵνα μ[ὴ]
    δὶς περὶ τοῦ αὐτοῦ ἡ αἴτ[ησ]ις γίν[ηται]·ʼ [[φ]]ψηφισθεὶς γ(ὰρ) ἐνταῦθα ὑπὸ
    τ(ῆς) βουλ[(ῆ)
δημόσιος γραμματικὸς τὴν σύνταξιν τ(ὴν) εἰωθυῖαν οὐ πάνυ λαμβάνω, ἀλ(λ)' εἰ τύχοι
    ποτὲ ἐν ὄξεσιν ἀν-
30 τὶ οἴνων καὶ σίτοις σητ[ο]κόποις [[δοκῶ τι ἄρνυσθαι]] ʽ[[.]] ὡς κ(αὶ) αὐτὸς ἐπίστασαι
    τὰ παρ' ἡμῖν πράγματα.ʼ ἔσται [ο]ὖν σοι [.]... δυναμένωι κἀμοί τι συμ-
βαλέσθ(αι) [[ἵνα]] κῆπόν τ[ιν]α τῶν ἐνταῦθα [[μοι]] κ(ατα)πράξ[[[η]ι]]ʽασθ(αι)ʼ, ὃν
    ἐτυγχα[ν ...]δρομευς ʽτιςʼ πρότερον ᾐτη[μέ-]
νος ἀντὶ τῶν σ(υν)τάξεων [] .[] συγχωρηθέ[ντα], οὗ κ(αὶ) τ(ὴν) αἴτησι[ν] κ(αὶ) τ(ὴν)
    σ(υγ)χώρ[ησίν] σοι ἀπέστειλα κ(αὶ) τὸν τύπον
τῆς ἡμῶν ἀξιώσεω[ς ἵ]να ἤτ(οι) κοινωσάμενος το .[.]ʼ ταῦτα ἢ αὐτὸς [δ]ιακρίνας
    το(ῦτό) μοι χαρίσῃ. ἔχεις
δὲ κ(αὶ) τὴ[ν] ποσότητα τ(ῆς) σ(υν)τάξεως διὰ τ(ῆς) αἰτήσεως ὅτ(ι) φ εἰσιν ἀττικ(αί),
    κ(αὶ) τὸν φόρο(ν) τοῦ κήπου ὅτ(ι) [[εἰσιν]] ἐν χ ἀττικ(αῖς),
35 κ(αὶ) τὸν ἐμὸν χρηματισμὸν ὅτ(ι) Λολλιανὸς ὁ καὶ Ὅμοιος Ἀπόλλωνι... . σὺ γ(ὰρ)
    κ(αὶ) τοὺς ὑπάτους εἴσει
κ(αὶ) ἁπλῶς τὸ σ(υμ)φέρον ἡγήσει ὡς ὑπὲρ σχολαστικοῦ καὶ φίλου [[δ]]καὶ δ[εο]μένου
    σκοπῶν· ἔσται δὲ καὶ ἡ ἀν-
τιγραφὴ ἀ[ν]αμφίβολος πρὸς τὸ μὴ ὑ(πὸ) κακοηθίας .[.].[ἀ]νασκευασθῆναι.
    (Parenthesis, *ll.* 37-39, omitted; bracketed by the writer)

C (*Verso* cols. i-ii)
(Lines marked (a) are superscript)

40 [τοῖς γῆς καὶ θαλάττης καὶ παντὸς ἀνθρώπων ἔ]θν[ο]υ[ς αὐ]τοκ[ρά-]
[τορσι καίσαρσι Πουπλίωι Λικιννίωι Οὐ]α[λε]ριανῶι κ[αὶ]
[Πουπλίωι Λικιννίωι Οὐ]α[λεριανῶι Γαλλιη]νῶι εὐσεβέσ[ιν]
[εὐτυ]χέ[σι σεβαστ]οῖς

(*m.2*) [παρὰ] Λολλιαν[οῦ] τ[οῦ καὶ] Ὁμοίου.

45 (*m.1*) [ἡ οὐρ]άνιος ὑμ[ῶν] μεγαλοφροσύ[ν]η, μέγιστοι [αὐ]τοκράτορες,
τ[ὴ]ν αὑτῆς φιλανθρωπίαν ἐκτείνασα ἐπὶ πᾶσαν ὑμῶν
τ[ὴν ο]ἰκ[ου]μένην καὶ ἐφ' ἅπαντα τ[ό]πον ἐκπέμψασα
κἀμὲ εἰ[ς] εὐελπιστίαν ἤγαγεν ἀξίωσιν ἀνενεγκεῖν
τῆι ι θείαι ὑμῶν [τ]ύχηι, ἐχομένην καὶ λόγ[ο]υ καὶ νόμου.

50 ἔστιν δὲ [αὕτη]· ο[ἱ] θεοὶ πρόγονοι ὑμ[ῶ]ν οἱ κατὰ χρόνους
βασιλεύσαντες ἐν ἀρετῆι καὶ πα[ι]δείαι ἐπι[λάμ]ψαντες
τῆι αὑ[τῶν] οἰκουμένηι ὥρισαν κατὰ [μέγ]εθος τῶν π[ό]-
λεων [καὶ ποσό]τητα δημοσίων γραμ[ματικ]ῶν πρ[οσ]τά-
ξαντε[ς.....

(col. i, *ll.* 54,54a and col. ii, *ll.* 55a-57 omitted as too fragmentary)

59 ὥδη επε...[] δύνασθαι τῶν παίδων ἀσχολούμενον ἀ-
60 εἰ [τ]ῆ αἰτήσει προσλειπαρεῖν) ἀνάγκην ἔσχ[ο]ν τὴν ἱκε-
61a [[μὲν προσφέρω ὑμ[[ει]]ῶν τοῖς ἴχ[ν]εσι, θειότατοι αὐτοκράτορες
61 τηρίαν ταύτην τοῖς ἴχνεσιν ὑμῶν προσενεγκεῖν) ἄλυ-
62a μὲν
62 πον τῶι τῆς πόλεως λόγωι κατὰ τὸ δικαιότατον δέ μοι λυσιτε-
63a ε
63 λοῦσαν, ὥστε κῆπον τῆς πόλεως ἔνδον τ[ι]χῶν ὄντα κα-
64a ε   οὖσι
64 λούμενον παράδισον Δικτύνου σὺν τοῖς [[ἄλλοις]] φυτοῖς καὶ
65a ε
65 [τ]ῷ πρὸς ἀρδείαν ὕδ[α]τι, φέροντα [ἐ]ν μισθώσ[ι] χ̅ ἀτ'τικάς,
δοθῆναί μοι κ[ελεῦ]σαι τὴν μεγίστην ὑ[μ]ῶν τύ[χην],
[ἵ]να αὐτόθεν ἔχων τὰ πρὸς χρείαν πρόσφορα τῆ
68 [τ]ῶν παίδων διδασκαλία προσευκαιρεῖν δύνω[μ]αι και

(*ll.* 69a-70 omitted as too fragmentary)

A short roll, 19.2 x 55.6 cm., containing on the front (along the fibres) a partial draft of a petition to Valerian and Gallienus (A), and a draft of a letter about it to a friend at court (B), and on the back (across the fibres) a second, fuller draft of the same petition (C), all in different hands. Parsons conjectures that B, a small neat hand of the type used for commentaries, with frequent abbreviations, may be that of the petitioner, the schoolteacher Lollianos, himself, while A, a sub-literary script, could be his attempt at more formal writing, and C, a large, clear cursive, may have been written at his dictation. The roll, which was folded or flattened, and thus now has many gaps, was presumably his own file copy. The 'vocabulary is determinedly choice and the syntax carefully elaborate; the grammarian shows in touches like the learned final optative' (Parsons, p.411).

Bib. — *P.Oxy.* 47 (1980) 3366.

A To the masters of land and sea, the commanders Caesars Publius Licinius
Valerianus and Publius Licinius Valerianus Gallienus, pious, fortunate, august,
|from Lollianos also called Homoios, public grammar-school teacher of the city
of Oxyrhynchos. Your celestial high-mindedness which has enlightened your
(whole inhabited) world and your familiarity with the Muses — for education
is enthroned beside you — |[encourages me] to bring you a just and lawful
petition, and it is this: — The gods your forebears determined a quota of public
grammar-school teachers according to the size of the cities, prescribing also
contributions to be paid to them |so that the responsibility for (school-) boys
should not be obstructed [. . .].

B [6 lines too damaged to translate] I send you, [. . .] brother, this third letter,
so that you can continually give me joy by always writing about your good
health. You will easily have good access to those arriving in Alexandria |from
the court if you make contact with Ammonianos, the *optio* of the *beneficiarii,*
who is particularly close to me: {he will send word on to me here; and indeed}
the man is [. . .], being a relative of the most distinguished Theodoros. I also
enclose a petition likely to be conceded to such a one, so that you can secure
. . . for the expenses of my children. Ammonios (?) has sent the text of it
through his brother Heraklammon, the *canaliclarius,* and you should consult
with him first in case he has already won the point, so that a petition is not
lodged twice on the same thing. Having been elected public grammar-school
teacher here by the council, I am not receiving the normal contribution at all,
but if I am lucky (I get it) in vinegar instead |of wine and in weevilly grain, as
you yourself know is the case with us. You will therefore be able in your position
to give me some help, by getting me one of the orchards here, which one of my
predecessors (?) earlier had had allocated to himself on request in place of the
contributions. I have sent you the request and the allocation, along with the text
of our petition, so that you can do me this favour either in partnership with [. . .]
or by yourself. You have also the quota for the contribution included in the
petition, namely 500 attics (sc.*denarii),* and the payment for the orchard, namely
600 attics, |and my correct designation, namely Lollianos also called Homoios
son of Apolloni . . . You will also know (the names of) the consuls and in short
you will take the right initiative, watching on behalf of a scholar, a friend and
a man in need. And the rescript too will (have to) be ambiguous so that it cannot
be overturned through malice [2½ lines omitted; they were bracketed by the
writer and partly added above *l.*28].

C To the commanders of earth and sea and of every race of men, the Caesars
Publius Licinius Valerianus and Publius Licinius Valerianus Gallienus, pious,
fortunate, august, from Lollianos also called Homoios. |Your celestial high-
mindedness, greatest commanders, having extended its philanthropy over all
your (inhabited) world and sent it out over every place, has led me too to the
good hope of presenting a petition to your divine fortune, (a petition) related
to both reason and lawfulness, |and it is this:— The gods your forebears who
reigned from time to time and enlightened their (whole inhabited) world through
morality and education, determined a quota of public grammar-school teachers
according to the size of the cities, prescribing [5 lines too damaged to translate]
even the necessities of life, since, being kept busy by the children I was not able

60 |always to be persistent in petitioning, and was compelled to bring this plea
    before your footprints, most divine commanders, (a plea) that on the one hand
    is harmless to the city's accounts but on the other is profitable to me in a most
    just way, namely that the orchard of the city, being within (the) walls, called the
65 garden of Diktynos, with the plants there, and |the water for irrigation, yielding
    in rentals 600 attics, your greatest fortune should order to be given to me, so
    that having from it the income I need, I may be able to devote my best time to
    the teaching of the boys and [2 lines too damaged to translate].

This is the first case of a state schoolteacher attested in Egypt, though as Lollianos
claims, it was a long-established imperial policy to encourage the cities to establish
them. Parsons (441-46) reviews the evidence for the policy, relating mostly to II and
later, and concludes that Lollianos is probably overstating the position if he is
implying that there was an obligatory number to be appointed. A.H.M. Jones, *The
Greek City from Alexander to Justinian* (Oxford, 1940), 220-26, contrasts the
apparent decline of interest in the public provision of primary education in the first
three centuries with the public attention paid to higher (ephebic) education. Grammar,
rhetoric and philosophy all benefited from this. On the hellenistic institution of
grammar schools, see H.I. Marrou, *Histoire de l'Education dans l'Antiquité* (Paris,
1955³), 223-43, and M.P. Nilsson, *Die hellenistische Schule* (Munich, 1955).

The papyri provide two particular kinds of evidence on basic education in Greek:
school exercises, catalogued in R.A. Pack, *The Greek and Latin Literary Texts from
Greco-Roman Egypt* (Ann Arbor, 1967²), nos. 2642-2751, and the frequent reference
in documents to the illiteracy of the person signing them. Recent discussions of these
matters (not all seen by me) include:— R. P. Duncan-Jones, *Chiron* 7 (1977) 333-53;
D. Bonneau, *Recueils de la Societé Jean Bodin* 39 (1975) 101-15; P. Schmitter, *AJP*
96 (1975) 276-89, M. Hamdi Ibrahim, Ἡ ἑλληνορωμαϊκὴ παιδεία ἐν Αἰγύπτῳ (Athens,
1972): P. J. Sijpesteijn, *Hermeneus* 42 (1971) 251-55; H. C. Youtie, *ZPE* 17 (1975)
201-21, 19 (1975) 101-08; id., *Akten des XIII. Internationalen Papyrologenkongresses*
(Munich, 1974), 481-87; id. *HSCP* 75 (1971) 161-76; id., *GRBS* 12 (1971) 239-61.
Some of these studies by Youtie, with others on the subject, are collected in his
Scriptiunculae II (Amsterdam, 1973).

In NT and later times there was no particular interest in literacy amongst the
churches, in spite of the fundamental importance of it to their work, and of the fact
that the preaching raised vernacular languages, such as Coptic, for the first time to
a generally accessible literary expression. Julian's attempt in mid-IV to compel the
churches to provide their own education based on Scripture provoked a crisis and
discloses the cultural reality. They were in fact dependent upon the hellenic
educational system to maintain their place in the common culture, while the scriptural
catechesis was essentially incompatible with formal education, and addressed to other
objectives altogether. See E. A. Judge, *Journal of Christian Education* 9 (1966) 32-45,
JbAC 15 (1972) 19-36, and *The Conversion of Rome: Ancient Sources of Modern
Social Tensions* (North Ryde [NSW], 1980).

The first draft (A) of Lollianos' petition was left incomplete, while the second (C)
incorporated the substance of the request as elaborated in the meantime in the letter
(B) to his friend at court. There are interesting differences between the two draft
preambles to the petition. The image of the ruler irradiating the world with education

is transferred from Valerian and Gallienus themselves in A to their predecessors in C. Perhaps Lollianos decided it was more subtle to tempt the present Caesars with the prospect of winning their predecessors' reputation rather than accord it to them by way of flattery in advance. The documentary record offers several sets of texts illustrating redactional processes which may be of use in NT criticism. For other examples see the epigraphic copy from Lyons of the speech of Claudius in 48 on the admission of Gallo-Romans to the Senate, E.M. Smallwood, *Documents illustrating the Principates of Gaius, Claudius and Nero* (Cambridge, 1967), no.369, trans. A.C. Johnson, *Ancient Roman Statutes* (Austin, 1961), no.175, compared with the version of Tacitus, *Annals* 11.24, on which see K. Wellesley, *G & R* 1 (1954) 13-33; and *P. Fouad* 21 compared with *P. Yale* inv. 1528 (both reproduced in Smallwood, 297), two rival contemporary versions of a mutiny in the Roman army in Egypt, on which see A. Segré, *JRS* 30 (1940) 153-154, and W. L. Westermann, *CP* 35 (1941) 21-29. The drafts of Lollianos also illustrate the complex process of correction, bracketing and supplementation by which a careful writer made up his mind about the wording of an important document.

Several NT *hapax legomena* are illustrated by this papyrus. διανύω (*l*.28) supplies a documentary parallel for Acts 21.7 : none was cited in MM, though BAGD refer to *P.Oxy.* 12 (1916) 1469.4, of 298, and others are noted in *Spoglio*. σητόκοπος (*l*.30) is now (for the first time?) attested outside the handful of late literary sources cited in LSJ. Its equivalent, σητόβρωτος (Jas. 5.2), has in the meantime also attained documentary illustration from *P.Fam. Tebt.* (1950), 15.3, 24.66 (II, of motheaten files). The occurrence of the noun χρηματισμός (*l*.35), corresponding with the passive sense of the verb ('I am officially addressed in such-and-such a style'), provides the occasion to mention that MM surely misconstrue the papyrological instances they cite on the noun when it corresponds with the active sense ('I pronouce'), in translating them as 'report' : the term refers in the documents rather to a magistrate's rescript or decision, which lends an appropriate colour to its use in Rom. 11.4 of God's 'response'. κακοήθεια (*l*.37) provides a parallel with Rom. 1.29 closer in time than that cited by MM.

The old question of the status of two documents in Acts is sharply illuminated by the double use of τύπος in the letter of Lollianos (*ll*.28,32). Since he applies the term both to the copy of his petition sent through Keraklammon and to the one now being sent to the unidentified friend at court, and since he has adopted this double approach as a fail-safe technique, it seems to me inescapable that two identical texts were sent (though Parsons wonders whether the second copy may have been an outline only). In Acts 23.25, however, τύπος seems now often to be taken to imply a rhetorical approximation. The letter of Claudius Lysias is thus put on a par with the speeches in Acts. But may the treatment of speeches by the ancient historians not have been different from that of letters, the one genre providing the vehicle for the historian's presentation of the leading ideas expressed upon an occasion, while the other provided what we should now call documentation? This would correspond with a difference in the originals themselves : written speeches will often have arisen only as retrospective stocktaking by their authors, their text remaining within their own discretion, while letters passed at once into the possession of their recipients and would be preserved by them as proof of the point they documented. The value of copies of letters would lie precisely in their being made verbatim. The word τύπος, anyway, ought always to refer to replication in some form or other (e.g. a seal impression, an image, an archetype, an outline, a set form — for the diversity of particular uses see LSJ), and one should not expect it to mean 'roughly as follows'. Certainly the τύποι ἐπιστολικοί of Demetrius are standard models for letters on various occasions, but that is hardly what we have in Acts 23.26-30. The letter of Lysias is highly individualistic and appropriate to its occasion, as is that of Philopater in 3 Macc. 3.12-29, where the τύπος of it is also said to be given (30). *TDNT* (Goppelt, p.248) rightly states that this must mean the 'text' of the letter. The term surely prevents us treating the letters on the same basis as the speeches. We must ask both with regard to the letter of Lysias and to that which transmitted the decision of the Jerusalem council (Acts 15.23-29) whether the author of Acts did not mean his readers to take them as the direct citation of transcripts available to him.

(E. A. JUDGE)

27. A guarantee of continuing service by the shopkeepers

Herakleopolis   late V
ed. pr. — J.R. Rea, *CPR* 17, pp. 40-43 (pl. 16)

> *c. 30 letters*   ]..[.]....[...].[..
> *c. 27 letters*   π]όλεως χ(αίρειν). ὁμολογῶ
> ἑκουσίως καὶ αὐθαιρέτως ἐπομνύ]μενος θεὸν παντο-
> κράτορα καὶ τὴν θείαν εὐσέβιαν τῆς καλλινίκου κορυφῆς
> 5 ἐγγυᾶσθαι καὶ ἀναδέχεσθαι μονῆς καὶ ἐμφανίας τὸ
> σύστημα τῶν καπήλων Ἡρακλέους πόλεως παρα-
> μένοντας καὶ ἐξυπηρετουμένους τῇ ἀφθονίᾳ τῆς πόλεως
> κτλ.

Part of a fragmentary deed of surety; the entire extant text contains 14 lines, with part of a further line on the back of the papyrus.

**(*l.*2) I agree of my own free will, and voluntarily, swearing my oath by God
5 Almighty and by the divine piety of his gloriously triumphant Highness, | to give
surety and pledge for the continuing presence of the guild of shopkeepers of
Herakleopolis, that they remain and assist to the utmost the abundance of the
city, etc.**

This papyrus gives us a useful minor example of the increasing regimentation imposed from above upon a society well into the process of decay. As not uncommonly for suppliers of specific commodities, an individual goes surety for the town's corporation of shopkeepers. Whether he was the president of the guild is impossible to determine. Rea argues with some force that καλλίνικος κορυφή (4) alludes to the emperor, not to Christ, as is supposed by E. Seidl, *Der Eid im röm.-ägypt.*

Provinzialrecht (Munich, 1935); see n., *ad loc.* The clearest parallel to our text is Theodoretus *ep.* 119 where the same two words are used with reference to Theodosius II (see Lampe, s.v. κορυφή; passage cited more fully by Rea). This papyrus, then, contains a standard early Byzantine oath by the Emperor. However, the noun does appear to be used of Christ in oaths of later date (see Rea's n.). The phrase θεὸς παντοκράτωρ (3-4) occurs in the NT of the Christian God only at 2 Cor. 6.18 outside the book of Revelation (nine times there). With the single exception of Acts 3.12, εὐσέβεια is confined to the Pastorals and 2 Peter. Given the date of the text the guarantor may have been a Christian, notwithstanding the oath by the emperor being more likely. παραμένω (6-7) in the sense of 'continuing in one's occupation', occurs in the NT at Heb. 7.23. The compound ἐξυπηρετέω (7) does not appear in the NT, although for the simple verb + dative of thing cf. Acts 20.30 (LSJ cites another couple of examples). The simple verb appears in participial form at *BGU* 2252.8-9 (Kynopolis, 16/2/330), a nomination for a liturgy in which the proposers recommend as suitable a man who is 'blamelessly serving the public good', ἀμέμπ[τως] ὑπηρετούμενον | τῇ δημο[σίᾳ] χρείᾳ. The noun is found three times in 1976 texts: *BGU* 2247.21, 2249.17, and *SB* 10792. On *hyperetes* in general see H. Kupizewski and J.Modrzejewski, *JJP* 11-12 (1957-58) 141-66. The noun ἀφθονία (7) is a *v.l.* at Tit. 2.7.

28. Census returns and registers

The term ἀπογραφή /-φομαι occurs in a series of texts dealing with census matters: *BGU* 2221-8 (160/61-203 AD). Some of these are census returns wherein a person registers himself and his family and makes a statement of property owned. Nos. 2227-8 are extracts from a census register.

No. 2223 is a typical return (August 24-29, 175):

—— —— —— —— —— —— —— —— —— ——

παρὰ Σαραπίωνος διὰ ...[± 7]
νίωνος· ὑπάρχει τῇ φροντιζο-
μένῃ ὑπ' ἐμοῦ Ἰσιδώρᾳ τῇ καὶ
Ἁρποκρατιαίνῃ θυγατρὶ Γαίου Ἰου-
5 λίου Γ[..]λλ.ου ἀστῇ, μεθ' ἃ ἀπεγρα-
ψάμην [δι'] ἑτέρου ὑπομν[ή]μ[α-]
τος α.[.].ς ἀπογρ(άφομαι) ἥμισυ [[...]]
οἰκίας καὶ τρίτον μέρες αμ[..]
πέμπτον μέρος ψειλῶν τόπων
10 καὶ ἥ[μισυ] τρίτον μέρος ἑτέρας οἰκίας, πάντα ἐπ' ἀμφόδ(ου) Σεκνε-
πτυν[εί]ου, ἐν οἷς {ου} οὐδεὶς [ἀπογράφεται·]
(ἔτους) ιε Αὐρη[λ]ίου Ἀντωνείν(ου) Καίσαρος
τοῦ κυρί[ου Μ]εσορὴ ἐπαγομένων.

From Sarapion through N., son of -nion. There belongs to my ward Isidora also
5 **called Harpokratiane, daughter of Gaius Julius |G-, a citizen of Alexandria, after the things which I declared via another memorandum, . . . I declare a half-share of a house, and a third-share of . . ., a fifth share of a vacant block of**

10 land, |and a ⅚ share of another house. They are all located in the Sekneptynion
quarter, and no-one is registered in them. Year 15 of Aurelius Antoninus Caesar
the lord, Mesore on the -th intercalary day.

No. 2228 is a typical extract from a Register (175-88):

ἐκ β[ιβλ(ιοθήκης)] δη(μοσίων) λόγων ἐξ εἰκο(νισμοῦ)
ιδ [(ἔτους) ἐν κ]ώ(μῃ) Σοκνο(παίου) Νήσο(υ)
κ[ολ(λήματος) ..] —

δ⁻ φυλ(ῆς) μέρος Πατοξ.κης
5   οἰκ(ίαι) β⁻ κ[αὶ] αὐλ(ὴ) καὶ αἴθ(ριον)
συνεχ(εῖς) ἀλλήλ(αις)
Στοτοῆτις Ἀγχώφεως τοῦ
Στοτοήτεως μητ(ρὸς) Τεσενούφεως
τῆς Ὀννώφρεως (ἐτῶν) κς
10   ἄση(μος) ιγ (ἔτει)(ἐτῶν) κε ε( ) (ἐτῶν) κδ
οὐλ(ὴ) μετώ[(πῳ)] ἐκ δεξιῶν

(Text continues *ll.* 12-16, but very fragmentary)

**From the archive of public records from the register which contains census
details of the 14th year in the village of Soknopaiou Nesos, column —. Fourth
5 tribe, division of Patoike (?): |two houses, a hall and a courtyard adjacent to
one another. Stotoetis, son of Anchophis and grandson of Stotoetis, whose
10 mother is Tesenuphis, daughter of Onnophris, aged 26, |without distinguishing
mark. In the 13th year aged 25 . . . aged 24, with a scar on the right side of his
forehead . . .**

Texts like these help us to fill out, at least in part, what documents would have been
involved for those registering in the census mentioned in Lk. 2.1 ff. On the census in
Roman Egypt see S.L. Wallace, *Taxation in Egypt from Augustus to Diocletian*
(Princeton, 1938), 96-115. Concerning Lk. 2.1 ff. and the problem of dating the
Nativity see J. Thorley, *G & R* 28 (1981) 81-89. R. Syme, *Akten des VI. Internat.
Kongresses für gr. und lat. Epigraphik, München, 1972* (Munich, 1973), 585-601 (cf.
J. Reynolds, *JRS* 66 [1976] 185,195), discusses the impossibility of deducing a date
for the Nativity in his treatment of a damaged inscription, *CIL XIV. 3613* (= *ILS*
918). Frequently attributed to P. Sulpicius Quirinius, Syme argues that the text refers
to L. Calpurnius Piso.

29. Customs administration

Toll receipts appear in plenty in the papyri. For examples in *BGU* see nos. 2304-25
(I-III). Nos. 2326-27 are also relevant, being extracts from a register of a customs
house. On customs-duties generally, see S.L. Wallace, *Taxation in Egypt from
Augustus to Diocletian* (Princeton, 1938), 255-76. For discussion of such texts see N.
Clausen, *Aeg.* 9 (1928) 240-77; E.M. Husselman, *TAPA* 82 (1951) 164-7; Z.
Borkowski, *JJP* 16/17 (1971) 131-9. No.2305 is typical (20/11/51):

Δι[ο]γένη(ς) ὁ πρὸ(ς) τῆ πύλ(η) Σο[κ(νοπαίου)] λι(μένος) Μέ(μφεως)
ἐρημ[ο](φύλαξι)· παρέσ(χε) Δίδυμος ἐλαίο(υ) ὄνο(ν)
ἕνα μετ(ρητὰς) δύ[ο] (γίνονται) μετ(ρηταὶ) β [(ἔτους)] ια Τιβερίου
[Κ]λαυδίο(υ) Καί[σ]αρος Σεβα[σ]τοῦ Γερμα[ν(ικοῦ)]
5   Αὐτοκράτορος μη(νὸς) Νέου [Σεβασ]τοῦ
      τρίτι καὶ εἰκάδι

   Diogenes, superintendent of the customs house at Soknopaiou Nesos for the Memphis harbour-tax, to the desert-guards. Didymos presented one donkey load — = two measures — of oil, total two measures. Year 11 of Tiberius Claudius
5   **Caesar Augustus Germanicus |Imperator on the 23rd of the month New Augustus.**

Texts such as this offer general background material to Mt. 9.9 f. (and parallels). For a good general survey of τελωναί in Egypt and Palestine, see H.C. Youtie, 'Publicans and Sinners', *ZPE* 1 (1967) 1-20 (repr. in *Scriptiunculae* I [Amsterdam, 1973], 554-78 [brief notes added]).

30. **Milestones from the Egnatian Way**

   In addition to Strabo, our main literary source for this major road linking Italy with Greece, a number of milestones have been recovered which provide detailed measurements of distance between cities on the route. P. Collart has provided a very useful survey of our information on the sixteen known milestones in *BCH* 100 (1976) 177-200 (cf. *SEG* 1883; *BE* [1977] 14). The earliest and single most important of these was discovered not far from Thessalonike and published only recently by C. Romiopoulou, *BCH* 98 (1974) 813-16 (pl., fig.1); cf. *AE* [1976] 643; *BE* 456). This bilingual inscription was set up by Cn. Egnatius C.f., the proconsul of Macedonia who built it, and thus confirms finally that the road took its name from him. The road must have been constructed in the years between Rome's annexation of Macedon in 146 and c.120 BC (Collart, 181). After this milestone, the earliest extant date from Trajan's time: during his reign the road — whose upkeep had been neglected because of the long years of civil war during the late Republic — was repaired in preparation for the emperor's Parthian campaign (Collart, 193-94). As a result of great instability in the Roman Empire, the Via Egnatia ceased to be much used from the early fifth century, thus bringing to a close some five and a half centuries of use as a Roman road (Collart, 197).

   G. Daux, *JSav* (1977) 145-61 (cf. *SEG* 771-773; *BE* [1978] 291) republishes the milestone listed as no. 4 in Collart's chronological inventory (pp. 197-200). Note also N.G.L. Hammond, 'The Western Part of the Via Egnatia', *JRS* 64(1974) 185-94.

   Although the Via Egnatia is not specifically mentioned in the NT it is certain that Paul followed it for some sections of his journeyings. Detailed study of the route of this road and the towns on its course may prove fruitful for NT scholars trying to recover the reason(s) why Paul stopped at certain cities, to account for the route he chose, and to speculate about other cities which he may have visited but which are not recorded in Acts' selective account.

31. The Areopagos at Athens in the Roman period

The status of the Areopagos in the Roman period is discussed by D.J. Geagan, 'Ordo Areopagitarum Atheniensium', in *PHOROS. Tribute to Benjamin Dean Meritt,* edd. D.W. Bradeen and M.F. McGregor (New York, 1974), 51-56 (cf. *BE* 205). Even though the *boule* continued to exist, the Areopagos returned to prominence — perhaps from the time of Sulla — and came to resemble a municipal or colonial senate. Its diverse functions — judicial, financial, foreign relations, determination of citizen status — make plain that it was the governing body of the *polis.* While little is known about qualification for membership of the Areopagos, one based on birth was being applied by the time of Marcus Aurelius. The size of this body (c.100 members) was considerably smaller than that of the *boule.* A fragmentary ephebic catalogue from Athens (*IG* II² 1723), republished in 1976 (cf. *SEG* 166) and dated 61/62 (?), includes mention of the herald of the Areopagos (*l.*16). For comments on this official, see Geagan, 53-54, 55-56. In Acts 17.34 the adherents of Paul's message include one Areopagite; and Haenchen implies (Comm., ad 17.34) that Luke may have inferred that Paul preached before the Areopagos because of this particular convert. But Geagan, *The Athenian Constitution after Sulla (Hesperia Suppl.* 12; Princeton, 1967), 50, holds that 'the account of Paul's speech before the Areopagus illustrates its surveillance over the introduction of foreign divinities'. On Areopagites, see ibid., index, p.218, s.v.

32. Asiarchs

M. Rossner, *Stud. Class.* 16 (1974) 101-42 (cf. *SEG* 1684), examines the terms Ἀσιάρχης and Ἀρχιερεὺς τῆς Ἀσίας. Against such discussions as D. Magie, *Roman Rule in Asia Minor* I (Princeton, 1950), 449-50, she argues that the terms designate the same function. Some people are accorded both titles, although never in the same text. Her epigraphically-based prosopography of holders of the titles, as well as her collection of the less frequent references in literary and legal texts — Acts 19.30-31 is one of the earliest — allows her discussion to supersede L. R. Taylor's in Jackson/ Lake, *The Beginnings of Christianity* V (London, 1933), 256-62. Magie, II, 1298-1301, provides a useful survey of different opinions about this question.

B. MINOR PHILOLOGICAL NOTES

33. ἀρ(ρ)αβών

— 'down payment', *BGU* 2243.13 (168), *SB* 10801.5 (III). Two more examples of the word to illustrate MM's useful entry. On this type of payment see F. Pringsheim, *The Greek Law of Sale* (Weimar, 1950) 333-429. The metaphorical use of the word found in the NT is still unparalleled in non-literary texts. BAGD, s.v., refers to two literary parallels, but of these the first (Arist. *Pol.* I.11, less confusingly 1259a12) is clearly a literal, not a figurative use; while the second, Stob. 4.418.13H is more revealingly referred to as Antiphanes 123.6 (Kock, *CAF*) — thus LSJ. For this use can thus be shown to be present in IV BC.

34. διαταγή

— 'allotment' (?), *BGU* 2347.5 (c. 250). The term frequently appears in texts dealing with orders for wine, and for other commodities (see ed.n.). In such contexts the sense is not certain; it does not appear to mean 'ordinance, direction', which is the NT use. This example may serve to supplement MM's entry; but it does not help the elucidation of the unusual phrase at Acts 7.53. There, instrumental εἰς causes no difficulty: the awkwardness is occasioned by the very elliptical διαταγὰς ἀγγέλων.

35. δικαιοκρισία

— *CPR* 12.17 (Arsinoite, 5/7/351), almost at the end of a papyrus record of official correspondence. This section of the text is the beginning of a copy of a petition to a governor. The sentence begins, ἡ σὴ δικαιοκρισία, ἡγεμών ... For this noun in the NT note Rom. 2.5; it appears as a *v.l.* at 2 Thes. 1.5. A further example to add to the three papyrus instances given in MM.

36. σχῆμα δικαιοσύνης

— *I. Kyme* 47 (III/II BC). An elegiac couplet provides the epitaph for Dionysios ... ὃς μέγα πᾶσιν |ἔσχεν ἐν ἀνθρώποις |σχῆμα δικαιοσύνης, 'who possessed in a great degree a righteous bearing among all people.' σχῆμα in the NT is used of 'external appearance' (1 Cor. 7.31, Phil. 2.8). While the phrase in this epitaph appears to be unparalleled, ὁδὸς δικαιοσύνης at Mt. 21.32 and 2 Pet. 2.21 offer a parallel formation; and the phrase in Mt. may even not be too far removed in meaning.

A statue of Dikaiosyne is mentioned in a temple inventory, *BGU* 2217, col.2, *l.*13 (Soknopaiu Nesos, after 161).

37. εὐχαριστία

— *I. Assos* 7.22 (c.100 BC). This honorific decree by a state (whose name is lost) expresses gratitude to the people of Assos. The state will send ambassadors to Assos to deliver the decree so that the people of Assos may know 'both the goodness of the men and the gratitude of the demos', τήν τε τῶν ἀνδρ[ῶν] καλοκἀγαθίαν καὶ τὴν |τοῦ δήμου εὐχαριστίαν ...The wording is perfectly usual for such texts: other examples in *I. Assos* include 8.24 ff., 11.7 ff., 11A.24 ff. For this sense of the word in the NT see Acts 24.3. The related verb, very common in the NT, is found in another Hellenistic honorific decree, *ISE* 77.14 (Delphi, 256/5 ?).

38. θλίψις

— used metaphorically in an honorific inscription from Arsinoë (Tokra) in Kyrenaike (*SEG* 1817). J. M. Reynolds first published the text — *Arch.Class.* 25/26 (1973/74) 622-30 (pl.97-98); cf. *BE* (1977) 594; L. Moretti, *RFIC* 104 (1976) 385-98; *BE* (1978) 561. This long text, of some eighty lines, praises Aleximachos for his service to the city. *Ll.* 37-39, θεωρῶν καὶ ἐν τούτοις | τὰν τῶν ἰδίων συνπολιτᾶν θλίψιν | διὰ τὰν τῶ καιρῶ περίστασιν..., 'seeing in these events the distress of his own fellow-citizens because of the crisis of the occasion . . .' Reynolds (628) dates the inscription II/i BC though allows the possibility of a later date. This example serves to illustrate the NT usage well, and provides further support for the entry on this not very common word in MM. The related verb occurs in a literal sense in the Ezana inscription (**94 bis**, below), *ll.*26-27.

39. λευκός

— used of favourable votes: *SEG* 1817.80, λευκαί (sc. ψῆφοι) ρθ', '109 votes in favour'. J.M. Reynolds, who published this inscription (see **38**), cites three other honorific examples (p.267): *SEG* 9 (1944) 354.25, from a village near Kyrene; *SEG* 16 (1959) 931.21, λευκαὶ πᾶσαι, 'unanimous favourable vote', a decree of the Jewish *politeuma* at Berenike (Benghazi); and C. Vatin, *BCH* 86 (1962) pp. 57-63, *l.*26 of the inscription (II, Gazoros in Macedon), ἐγένοντο πᾶσαι λευκαί. Commentators on Rev. 2.17, δώσω αὐτῷ ψῆφον λευκήν, have not reached a consensus on its meaning; some (e.g. R.H. Charles, H.B. Swete) mention the possibility that the allusion is to a voting context, understood metaphorically. But none, so far as I am aware, has drawn upon the epigraphical evidence which may add some support to this approach. For the phrase in a literary source not so far in time from Rev., note Lucian, *Harm.* 3. These references supplement MM's entry, where Rev. 2.17 is mentioned as unparalleled. The fullest treatment of the diverse interpretations of this verse is contained in C. J. Hemer, *A Study of the Letters to the Seven Churches of Asia, with Special Reference to their Local Background* (Diss. Manchester, 1969).

40. μέτοχοι

— 'business partners'. The financial administration of Egypt is constantly brought before us in the papyri, with a multitude of snippets of information which cumulatively help us to form some idea of the massive bureaucracy involved. Excluding texts where the word is restored, however confidently, some 40 texts published in 1976 contain the word μέτοχος, usually in the plural. Most of these are in *BGU* and *O.ROM.* The documents are largely receipts for the payment of various taxes and fees. The form of these normally brief documents varies, but usually one or two men are named, καὶ μέτοχοι, and their area of responsibility (e.g., overseers of the tax on weavers, *O.ROM* 143; overseers of the tax of the granary of the temples, *O.ROM* 131; chaff-collectors, *O.ROM* 224; dyke-supervisors, *O.ROM* 230; state bankers *BGU* 2270; inspectors of the sale of wool cardings, *BGU* 2295; collectors of tax in money form [i.e., as opposed to 'in kind'], *SB* 10960; inspectors of the sale of holy objects, *SB* 10985-87). These texts are mostly dated II. *CPJ* III. 462c has a brief note on μέτοχοι.

The word is sufficiently loose to refer to something less formal than a legally-arranged business partnership. 'Two small family fishing businesses might co-operate regularly *or* occasionally with each other, and in their acts of co-operation refer to one another as μέτοχοι' (K.L. McKay in a note to me).

These texts point up in unremarkable fashion the sense of μέτοχος which lies behind Lk. 5.7. When the haul of fish is too large for Peter's boat to manage, they get help from their partners in the other boat. A little later, in v.10, κοινωνοί is to be understood as a synonym for μέτοχοι. At Heb. 3.14 the relationship between Christ and the addressees of the letter is conceived of in the binding terms of a (business) partnership; but the metaphorical use of μέτοχοι here makes the force of the word somewhat less specific. For the privative form in quite another context, see *l*.21 of the text in **6**.

To revert to fishing-cooperatives, *P.Laur.*1 (Arsinoite nome, 192/3?) is a copy of a petition to a prefect which an individual brings forward on behalf of [τῶν] λοιπῶν ἁλιέων κώμης (4). See ed. n. on *ll*.2-4 for bibliographical references to guilds of fishermen in Egypt. On commercial fishing in first-century Palestine, with reference to μέτοχοι see W.H. Wuellner, *The Meaning of 'Fishers of men'* (Philadelphia, 1967) 26-63, especially 37-38, 51-52. An epitaph from Joppa, *CIJ* II.945 (II), refers to an association of fishermen which may well be less than a guild and more like the situation alluded to in Lk. 5 (see Frey's note, ad loc.): Παριγορίου καὶ Κύρας τῆς ⟨τῆς⟩ ἐς τὸν βόλον συνγενικῆς τοῦ Λυσᾶ Εἰοπιτῶν, '(Tomb) of Paregorios and of Kyra, belonging to the fishing association of Lysas, from Joppa.' Neither βόλος nor συγγενική is attested in LSJ or LSJ Suppl. in the sense required of each here.

41. νάρδος

A medical recipe *(P.Coll.Youtie* 4; pl.3a) which the ed., T.T. Renner, dates III includes mention of ν]άρδος Κελτική (4). Renner (p.64) offers other references. MM, s.v., note several other papyrus examples. For other varieties of nard, see LSJ, s.v. Pliny, *HN* 21.134, lists various medicinal uses of Gallic nard; at 14.107 he says that this variety of Syrian nard may be included to make an aromatic wine. At 12.42-46 he provides his fullest discussion of the qualities and prices of the various kinds of the perfume: the cost is 100 denarii to the (Roman) pound. In the incident recounted in Jn. 12.3ff. (cf. Mk. 14.3-5) it is claimed that a similar weight would fetch 300 denarii. Apart from differences of quality and type — and Pliny's statement is a general one: more specific prices follow in sect. 44-45 — this large difference in price may be due to geographical and trade factors. Prices of luxury goods could fluctuate wildly. Or again the amount in Jn. may be exaggerated to make the woman's generosity appear greater, and Judas look worse.

42. οἶνος ... ὄξος

— 'wine ... vinegar', *BGU* 2347.5-6 (c.250). This papyrus contrasts the two terms well; see ed.n. for further refs. ὄξος is not always sour wine or vinegar; it may be cheap stuff ('vin ordinaire', LSJ, s.v.). Soldiers are not likely to have good quality wine on hand (Lk. 23.36, and parallels); but even if they did it would scarcely be wasted on a dying criminal (the incident is related, however, for the sake of the Scripture 'proof'). *P.Coll.Youtie* 66.30-31 (= **26**) offers another example where the words occur together.

43. ὀρθρίζω

This koine verb is very rare outside the LXX. A private letter on an ostrakon provides us with only the second documentary example encountered, to my knowledge. *O.Amst.* 22.7-8 (II) reads, ἵνα μίνης αὐτόν, ἐπὶ γὰρ | ὀρτίζει πρός σε αὔριον, 'Wait for him since he comes to you tomorrow.' (The translation is that of the editors of that corpus.) In *P.Mil.Vogl.* II, 50.13 (I) we read πορεύου οὖν ὀρθίσας εἰς ..., 'so rising early go to . . .' As in the case of the ostrakon the word is misspelled: read ὀρθρίσας (cf. LXX Ps. 126(127).2 where Cod.Sin. has ὀρθίζειν). The verb appears to have taken the place of Attic ὀρθρεύω (thus Moeris: ὀρθρεύει Ἀττικῶς, ὀρθρίζει Ἑλληνικῶς; for reference see **45**). ὀρθρεύω appears only once in LXX, at Tob. 9.6 (for which -ίζω occurs as a *v.l.*). It means 'lie awake at dawn', and the etymological link with ὄρθρος (dawn, cockcrow) is clearly felt. LSJ Suppl., s.v. (which replaces the inaccurate LSJ entry proper), cite biblical examples only, to indicate this verb's range. The main uses are—

      (a) rise up early in the morning;
      (b) (metaph.) be eager/earnest;
      (c) go eagerly/earnestly.

But the LXX examples listed in Hatch and Redpath suggest that the verb may possess a much more 'washed-out' meaning. With a verb of motion, ὀρθρίζω (in participial form) probably does mean 'rise early (and) go' (e.g. Gen. 19.2; Ex. 34.4; cf. the papyrus example above). But the etymological link with ὄρθρος appears to be no longer felt on several occasions, where τῷ πρωΐ occurs in the same context (e.g. Gen. 19. 27; 20.8; Jud. 19.5). The metaphorical force of the word, 'go with earnest zeal' does appear to be present at e.g., LXX Jer. 25.3, in view of the construction ὄρθρου ἀποστέλλων in the following verse. But a number of examples occur of the construction ὀ. + πρός + accusative (of a person); and at least some of these need mean no more than a bland 'come', e.g. Ps. 62(63).1; Hos. 6.1 (5.15); Is. 26.9 (though the etymological association may be felt here in view of the phrase ἐκ νυκτός). The verb occurs in a graffito quotation from Nubia of the first-mentioned of these three passages — no doubt the psalm was used liturgically. See S. Donadoni (*art.cit.*, **94**), 37.

This brings us to the only NT occurrence, Lk. 21.38. A verb of motion is required, but the only verb in the sentence is ὤρθριζεν. BAGD renders 'the people used to get up very early in the morning (to come) to him . . .' (similarly, the translations). In view of our ostrakon example, and the LXX usage of ὀ. + πρός + accus., this verse may be rendered by, 'the whole people used to come/kept coming to hear him in the temple'. However, the preceding verse may perhaps imply that the etymological link is not entirely forgotten (note τὰς δὲ νύκτας, and cf. the Isaiah passage mentioned above).

44. παγανός

— 'civilian'. *O. Florida* 2.8 provides an early example of this word in a letter from a decurion of a Roman garrison at Edfu in Upper Egypt (II). The decurion requires to have sent to him 'the civilian who set fire to the reeds near the new praesidium', τὸν παγανὸν τὸν κατακαύ|σαντα τὰ θρύα ἐγγὺς τοῦ πραι|σιδίου καινοῦ ... (trans.,ed.). The word is found more frequently in the later Roman and Byzantine periods. See. R.S. Bagnall's introduction to *O. Florida,* 26-27, especially n.66, for discussion of the term, which 'is often used precisely where distinctions between "soldiers" and "civilians" are made' (J.F. Gilliam, *AJP* 73 [1952] 77). C.J. Kraemer, *Excavations at Nessana* III (Princeton, 1958), takes the several occurrences of the word in a Byzantine daily record of sales and dates (no.90; VI/VII) to mean 'layman' (cf. his n. to *l.* 63 on p.284). *P.Oxy.* 3204 (1/1/588) refers to a woman who holds the position of pagarch.

45. παιδάριον

— 'slave' (clearly an adult male) at *BGU* 2347.3 (c.250), an order from one man to another to hand over to a slave a quantity of wine and vinegar: δὸς Ἅλᾳ παιδαρίῳ. There is nothing in the context of Jn. 6.9 to clarify whether the word means 'young child' or 'slave', nor indeed whether the person is male or female; all of which senses are attested elsewhere for the word. MM (a very useful entry) and BAGD allow the possibility of 'slave' for this NT passage, but it is rarely even taken up in the commentaries. The second-century grammarian Moeris claims that only in Attic was παιδάριον used of a female (G. A. Koch, *Moeridis Atticistae Lexicon Atticum* [Leipzig, 1830] p.293; for Attic examples see LSJ, s.v.); and Clement of Alexandria held the same view (*Paedag.* 1.4, quoted in Pearson's n., ad loc.). But παιδάριον occurs with considerable frequency in the LXX, and with a wide range of meanings. Thus at 2 Ki. 13.22 and 14.21 παιδάριον = 'young man' (clearly not servile); at 1 Ki. 30.17 the word is used to refer to soldiers. At Tob. 7.11 (A*+) παιδάριον is used of a woman (Sarah), either in the sense 'young woman' — she had already been given in marriage to seven husbands (in passing, is this the source of the story recounted in Mt. 22.23 ff.?) — or meaning 'child', for the speaker is her father. See G.M. Simpson, *A Semantic Study of Words for Young Person, Servant and Child in the Septuagint and other early Koine Greek* (diss., Sydney, 1976), 95, 182f., to which I am indebted for these references. Moeris' claim may be generally correct, but in view of this example from the Greek bible, his statement does not necessarily dispose of the possibility of παιδάριον referring to a female in Jn. 6.9. There is nothing *against* rendering this word by 'lad', 'boy' (*puer,* Vulg.); but the possibility of its meaning 'girl' or 'manservant' should be borne in mind, if only to avoid restricting the semantic range of this NT *hapax,* and as an antidote to sentimentalizing the passage. The use of ἡ παιδίσκη at Jn. 18.17 need not narrow the semantic range of παιδάριον at all.

46. φιλαγαθία

— *I. Kyme* 19.34 (2 BC-14 AD). MM mention that this noun occurs very commonly in (honorific) inscriptions. In this text, the *demos* of Kyme is according to L. Vacceius Labeo a series of privileges, ἀρετᾶς ἕνεκα | καὶ φιλ{ι}αγαθίας τᾶς εἰς ἑαυτόν. Tit. 1.8 employs the adjective in a list of criteria for an *episkopos.*

47. φιλανθρωπία **and related forms**

This noun appears twice in the grammarian's petition (**26**), *ll.* 46 and 69a. In both places Lollianus uses the noun in relation to imperial magnanimity. This is not dissimilar to the occurrence of the noun at Tit. 3.4 (quoting LXX), used of God. The verb in -έω is not attested in the NT, but MM include brief treatment of it s.v. φιλανθρωπία. *P. Stras.* 606 (Arsinoite nome, early II) is a letter in which a man about to depart on a journey finds he has been designated for a liturgy. He sends a sailor, a client of his, to make a written declaration (χειρογραφῆσαι, 5) about the matter for him. The recipient of the letter is requested to treat the sailor well (φιλανθρωπῆσ[αι] αὐτόν). For the adverb, only at Acts 27.3 in the NT, note *IG Aeg.* 9284 (270-46 BC), an honorific text which mentions that the honorand τοῖς τε τεχνίταις φιλανθρωπῶς ἅπαντα χρῆται (8). In 1976 texts the adjective is found at *ISE* 77.5 (Delphi, 256/5?), 78.17 (Delphi 247/6), and *I. Assos* 11A.20, 23-24 (Thasos, c.80-70 BC). All these are honorific texts. For the sense at *I. Assos* 11A.20 ('concessions, grants'), cf. *LSJ,* s.v., III.

On the word *philanthropia* in hellenised Jewish writers, see A. Pelletier in *Paganisme, Judaïsme, Christianisme. Mélanges offerts à Marcel Simon* (Paris, 1978), 35-44.

48. φιλοτιμία

— *I. Assos* 7.19 (c.100 BC), *ISE* 76.2 (260/59 BC?). The notion behind this word in the classical and earlier periods is quite fundamental to Greek thinking. It is ambition, love of honor, which is one of the basic drives in the Homeric hero, and no less so in a Demosthenes or an Alexander. Yet in the later Hellenistic period the word appears to be losing that strong force, such that MM speak of the verb in the NT meaning simply 'strive eagerly' (Rom. 15.20; 2 Cor. 5.9; 1 Thes. 4.11).

49. Agape

This name of a wife occurs in a Latin epitaph (*AE* 73) from a catacomb in the Via Appia, Rome (III). Only a few other occurrences of the name are listed in E. Jory's Index to *CIL* VI (pt. 7, fasc. 1, p.173). The Lexicon of Greek Personal Names currently in preparation (see **55**) will provide the most efficient way to investigate the spread and the period of the rise to popularity as names of such nouns descriptive of virtues (cf. Pistis, Eirene).

50. Apollos

Several examples from 1976 texts are listed below for this name which is fairly common in Egypt (see Preisigke, *NB*). *SB* 10999.6 (early I) mentions an Ἀπολλῶς in a list of names: cf. 11016.7 (private letter, 17/4/13), 11130.13 (private letter, III/IV), 11231.12, 22 (certificate, 29/10/549). The information about Apollos at Acts 18.24, Ἀλεξανδρεὺς τῷ γένει, accords well with the fact that the name is virtually unattested outside Egypt, though hypocoristic names are naturally commoner in the less stereotyped papyrus documentation. Given his name and city of birth, he is not at all unlikely to have been thoroughly Hellenised in his Judaism. It is tantalising to wonder whether this man, whom the Acts passage describes as ἀνὴρ λόγιος and δυνατὸς ὢν ἐν ταῖς γραφαῖς, may have been a one-time pupil of Philo; it is certainly possible chronologically.

51. Demas

Three attestations of this Greek name in 1976 texts, from diverse locations. Δημᾶς is mentioned in *SB* 10908, a tax certificate dated 9/12/120. Preisigke, *NB,* lists *BGU* 2.426.12 (II/III) as its only papyrus example; Foraboschi provides several more. A Latin inscription, found last century at Suvodol (in modern Yugoslavia) and republished as *IMS* 123, is an epitaph for Aurel(ius) Demas set up by his grandchildren and heirs. This epitaph is the only occurrence of the name as a cognomen listed in the *Thesaurus Linguae Latinae. Onomasticon* III.1 (1918) col.94. (Almost all the very few other references in *TLL* are to the NT [Vulgate].) Yet this should not occasion surprise. The man's nomen probably means that he received his citizenship under the Constitutio Antoniniana, whereupon his Greek name would have become his cognomen. Thirdly, in *P.Oxy.* 3197.10 Demas is a servile name (see **24**). 'Demas' is not attested in the Jory/Moore index to *CIL VI*; for the reason (hypocorism), see **50** above.

52. Didymos

Δίδυμος writes to Διδύμη — *BGU* 2351 (late II). Others with this name at no. 2364 in the same vol.; *P.Coll.Youtie* 31; *SB* 10800 [= **83**], 10842; cf. Didumianus in a Latin papyrus *(P.Coll.Youtie* 64). Didyme ἀειπάρθενος is mentioned in a certificate *(P.Lips.* [1906]60; 371?); another Didyme at *CPR* 5.16 (III). These names are especially common in Egypt, according to É. Bernand, *Recueil des inscriptions grecques du Fayoum* I (Leiden, 1975), 102, who provides nearly a dozen epigraphical references. Cf. the similar comment in L. Robert, *Hellenica* 2 (1946) 8. In the Fourth Gospel Thomas is ὁ λεγόμενος Didymos (11.16; 20.24; 21.2): here simply it is the Greek equivalent for Thomas (םואת = twin). Another with Didymos as an element in his double name is Didymos ὁ καὶ Ptolemaios, son of Didymos (*CPJ* III.459; 149 AD).

53. Evangelos

Εὐαγγέλῳ τῷ καὶ Ἡρωδιανῷ — *BGU* 2346 (20/11/181). The by-name formula makes certain that Evangelos is a name here. *CIJ* I.207 gives Ἄγριους Εὐάγγε(λ)ους as a name (Rome, no date given); *PGM* 32.1-2 attests another Evangelos, in a magical text. The person called Evangelos at *P.Stras.* 638 (IV) is clearly a Christian.

54. Onesimos

Used of a woman who with her husband Paulus set up an epitaph for their children (*AE* 37; Rome, late III/early IV). *P.Coll.Youtie* 27.1 (cf. *verso, l.*1) refers to Onesimos τῷ καὶ Herakleides (26/7/165).

55. The use of a double name

Bib. — G. A. Deissmann, *Bible Studies* (ET, Edinburgh, 1903²), 313-17; M. Lambertz, *Glotta* 4(1913) 78-143; id., *Glotta* 5(1914) 99-170; R. Calderini, *Aeg.* 21(1941) 221-60; id., *Aeg.* 22(1942) 3-45.

Of the more than 4000 texts in the two dozen or so volumes read to prepare this review well over one hundred examples were met of people with an alias, or alternative name. There is nothing at all uncommon about such occurences: see Calderini, 3-5, on the chronological spread of the phenomenon — papyrus examples are most frequent in II, though very common still a century either side of it. Amongst the 1976 texts covered, the two basic styles in which the alternative name is given are

    (a) Α ὁ/ἡ καὶ Β;

    (b) Α ἐπικαλούμενος Β.

In addition several other types occurred occasionally or only once:

     (c) A ὁ διὰ λόγων B;

     (d) Λ/B;

     (e) A ἀνθ' οὗ B.

For a full list of the different phrases attested in the papyri see Calderini, 224. As an example of how very common the double name is, *IG Aeg.* 33028 (Karnak c.200) is a fragmentary list of 54 complete or partly preserved names of which 17 are double names using the ὁ καί formula.

Women have additional names no less than men. The fact that only one example in Latin was encountered is merely an indication of the far greater preponderance of Greek inscriptions and papyri over Latin texts. Further, far more of the examples occur in papyri than in inscriptions — though they should not be thought rare in the latter — and this reflects the different function of the two writing mediums and the different nature of the texts placed upon them. Legal documents (texts, census returns, bills of sale etc.) require as exact a description as possible of the persons concerned (including physical identification such as "with a scar on the left arm"): they are on papyri because they are documents of an administrative, ephemeral, or private nature (see Calderini, 258-60, for the types of papyrus texts in which by-names occur). On stone are carved such texts as treaties, public honorific decrees, and epitaphs: and in the case of gravestones, there is of course not the same need to specify the deceased by an additional name if he had one. Names of relatives, age, and gnomic comments are more in order.

A sample of the texts published in 1976 will illustrate various aspects of this subject. What follows in no way seeks to provide a complete survey of the use of double names. But Jewish non-literary examples and Josephus' evidence has been included by way of comparison before the by-names in the NT are dealt with.

I. Selected 1976 texts.

1. *AE* 419 — *Paula sivi Vstathia* (= Eustathia). This is the sole Latin example noticed, but by no means the only one referring to a child (here, less than two years old). This epitaph from Gaul — date given as 'bas-empire' by G. Barruol, *Gallia* 33 (1975) 506 — is very likely to be for the child of Christian parents in view of the epithet *fidelis* used of her.

2. *BGU* 2263 (mid-II) — This list of canal workers from Soknopaiu Nesos demonstrates the synonymy of the phrases used to express a double name. At *l.*7 we have [Π]αβοῦς ὁ διὰ λόγων Π... .The same expression is employed for other people at *ll.* 15, 20. According to the editor (note on p.85), the phrase is 'equivalent to ἐπικαλούμενος and distinguishes the official name (preceding) from the sobriquet (succeeding).' Cf. Calderini, 243f. At *l.*19 another phrase occurs which the editor equates with ὁ καί: Σαταβοῦς ἀνθ' ⟨οὗ⟩ Παβοῦς Π[. On the form ἀπάτωρ in this papyrus see no.5 below.

3. *BGU* 2223 (175 AD) — Property for Isidora τῇ καὶ Harpokratiane is listed by her *kyrios* (?) for an official return. This woman is a Roman citizen and an ἀστή (i.e., a citizen of Alexandria; on this word see P.M. Fraser, *Ptolemaic Alexandria,* II [Oxford, 1972] 116-17). Given her status as citizen and property-owner, her additional name is probably to be regarded as a familiar name, used by those with whom she is on close terms. But because it is a further means of specifying this particular woman to the exclusion of the other Isidoras, it is included in this administrative document. Cf. no.6 below.

4. *BGU* 2224 (175 AD) contains two aliases in separate census returns. The first is a joint return made for Apollonarion τῇ καὶ Sarapias and her brother, who is simply called Sarapion. This text appears to show that the by-name is not used in every case for racial reasons (i.e., by those wishing to be identified more fully with the Hellenic culture than their native Egyptian one). A religious factor could be at work in a text like this where both the woman's names are Egyptian: brother and sister may be linked with a cult of Sarapis, and she adopted the extra name to be identified with it more clearly (cf. no.8 below). While it may be more common for the by-name to reflect a different culture, other 1976 texts may be cited as examples of the double name from the same cultural tradition: *BGU* 2235, 2237 *(bis)*, *CPR* 5. 1,14 (all Egyptian); *BGU* 2213, *CPR* 5. 9,13, *P. Köln* 50, 51 (all Greek).

5. *BGU* 2251.17 — This late II AD letter refers to Didymos ἐπικαλ(ούμ.) ὁ τῆς Ἀχιλλίδο[ς]. Here a metronymic acts as the by-name. Metronymics without accompanying patronymics may often imply bastardy, slavery, or polygamy. No slur is necessarily implied by illegitimacy, for Didymos uses it of himself. While not mutually exclusive (e.g., *P.Oxy.* 3189), an alias occurs quite often when no patronymic is given. Now, since the latter is a fundamental element in a free person's name in the Graeco-Roman world and also in the Near East, it may be that the additional name was used when the father's identity was unknown as an alternative way of defining relationships. The word ἀπάτωρ is relevant here. At *BGU* 2263.16-17 (no.2 above) a certain Πωλίων ἀπάτωρ μητ(ρὸς) Ἡ[is mentioned. For discussion of the term see H. C. Youtie, *Scriptiunculae,* I (Amsterdam, 1973) 330. For the name Didymos, see **52**.

6. *P.Coll.Youtie* 65 includes several double names. Of these, the one in *ll.*12-13, Marcus Vibius Horigenes alias Magnus, shows that the by-name may be merely a nickname. Informal as its origin may have been, it is added to official documents for it aids a more secure identification of the person (cf. 3 above). In the case of a graffito example, *SEG* 1843 (Zawiet Msus, Kyrenaike, I AD), the nickname for a soldier may have special point: Gaius Julius Capito ὃς καὶ Odysseus may have been so called to reflect his mobility while in service.

7. *P.Coll.Youtie* 67 deals with the return of a dowry. On p.450 a family tree is given in which Sarapion ὁ καὶ Apollonianos is the name of a grandfather, father, son, and one other relative alike. Examples like this which show the by-name being passed from one generation to another indicate that it was regarded by some as in no way different from the person's "main" name. Some families cultivated the use of the double name: see Calderini, 17-20.

8. *CPR* 14 — This quite possibly Christian text from later fifth-century Herakleopolis in Egypt gives a man's name thus: Aurelius Jonah Skim son of John . . . iabenis. Both father and son here have a biblical name and an unusual Egyptian name (cf. no.4 above). An intervening ὁ καί or similar phrase is lacking from the man's name and also from his father's. So, too *CPR* 18, where the editor regards 'Jacob, Symeon' in a list of names as possibly 'Jacob alias Symeon.' For further discussion of the name and by-names side by side like this, see Calderini 254f. See below, no.10.

9. *P. Vindob. Tandem* 11.20-22, 44-46. The name here is that of Aurelius Theodoros τοῦ καὶ Herakleios ἐπικαλουμένου Nikon — the only double by-name encountered in the 1976 texts covered (for other examples see Calderini, 254f.). This text appears to show the equivalence of the two most common ways of supplying an extra name. K. L. McKay has suggested to me that while the phrases as here are commonly

synonymous, they may not necessarily be in such an example. Possibly this man's second and third names had different standings in relation to his first. By way of contrast McKay has also drawn my attention to Rev. 12.9: ὁ δράκων ὁ μέγας, ὁ ὄφις ὁ ἀρχαῖος, ὁ καλούμενος Διάβολος καὶ ὁ Σατανᾶς, ὁ πλανῶν τὴν οἰκουμένην ὅλην, κτλ. Here a 'person' is identified by a double description, two names and a further description. For ὁ καλούμενος Διάβολος cf. *I.Kyme* 41.47-48 (see **2**), where Isis says of herself ἐγώ εἰμι ἡ Θεσμοφόρος καλουμένη.

10. *I. Bankers* 15. This lead curse tablet from Kourion in Cyprus (III) illustrates well the interchangeability of by-name formulae. It cites Alexandros τὸν καλούμενον Luscinius at *l*.7 (cf. 14-15, 20); but at *ll*.10-11 he is A. ὁ ἐπικαλούμενος L. T.B. Mitford, *The Inscriptions of Kourion* (Philadelphia, 1971), 260, believes that the curser is also called Alexandros (*l*.26), and is therefore careful to specify this particular enemy. In the same text Metrodoros ὁ ἐπικαλούμενος Asbolios the banker (12; cf.16) is also referred to as Metrodoros Asbolios the banker: the by-name formula is omitted altogether (9; cf.20, where restored). See no.8 above.

11. *I. Bankers* 17. An epitaph from Kelenderis in Asia Minor (Imperial period) was set up for a young banker, ᾧ ἔθοντο οὔνομα | μήτηρ ἠδ' ὁ πατὴρ | Συνέγδημον, οἱ δ' ἄλ|λοι πάντες ἐπωνό⟨μ⟩α|σαν Βίλλον ... (3-7).

II. Some Jewish evidence

A. Non Literary

Jewish inscriptions similarly attest double names for men, women and infants. E.g., *CIJ* I.14, 30 (restored), 47 (all of women); I. 86, II. 879 (both of men). I.362 reads Ἰώνιος ὁ κὲ Ἀκονε Σεφωρηνός, 'Ionios also called Akone from Sephoris.' Frey suggests in his note that Ionios may be a Greek form of Jonas; and he cites Juster's view that Ἀκονε may be simply a Greek transcription of הקנה, 'the zealot.' I.108 is an epitaph for an infant, Ἐρμειόνη τιγατρὶ | Πισίννα μήτηρ ἀνέθηκεν | ἣ ἀπέλωκεν μῆνη αι' (*sic*) ἡμ(έρας) ζ' | ἧ[τ]ινι ἐπίκλην βαρϢεοδα, 'To Hermione her daughter (read θυγ-), Pisinna the mother set up (the tomb); she lived (read ἀπέδωκεν) eleven months, seven days (stone has HMZ); she was surnamed Barseoda'. All these examples are from Rome, except II.879 (Tyre). For the use of ἐπικλήν cf. **23**.

From Egypt the papyri attest Jews with double names quite normally. Some of the double names in *CPJ* may not refer to Jews, but here are some examples from that Corpus. I.126.15, a Greek will from the Fayum (238/7 BC) in which a man leaves his possessions to various people, including Apollonios παρεπίδημον ὃς καὶ Συριστὶ Ἰωναθᾶς, 'resident alien, also known by the Syrian name Jonathas.' II.178 (28/4/79) mentions Theodoto(s) ὁ κ(αὶ) Niger, but in 249 the same man — apparently — is designated Niger ὁ καὶ Θεό[δωτος]. The latter text is dated 73/74; and both come from Edfu. III.462f. (13/9/157) makes mention of a Roman citizen in *ll*. 2-3, Marcus Clodius Alexandros τοῦ καὶ Γαιάνου |ἐπικ(αλουμένου). III.492.4 (171-74) uses the ἀνθ' οὗ formula. Other examples include II.223 (of a woman) and III.459 (two occurrences, of men).

I am grateful to W.L. Lane for bringing to my notice the occurrence of the term מתקרא in Nabataean inscriptions. E.g., *Corpus Inscriptionum Semiticarum* II 1, 1(1889) no. 158.2, ...זבדת מתקרא די ומרתי.. 'And Martai who is surnamed Zabdath'; II 1,3 (1902) no.486.1-2, עבדאלהי מתקרא די ... אבא בר חנינו, 'Honainu son of Aba who is surnamed Abdallahi' (see note on this text, p.346, where

equation is made with the ὁ καί formula); no. 488 B.1-2, מלכו די יתקרא בשמה
. . . 'Malku who is surnamed Bashamah (?) . . .'

B. Josephus

By way of comparison with this Jewish non-literary evidence, the use of the by-name in Josephus, a selection of references to which is given by Deissmann (314), is worth brief analysis.

1. *Ant.* 13.131 and 13.420 refer to non-Jews; both pairs of names are Greek.

2. Examples occur of Jews who have an additional, non-Semitic, name: *Ant.* 1.240; 12.385 (the same man is referred to in the passages from 1 *Macc.* to which Deissmann refers). To this group should be assigned *Ant.* 13.320, where two Jews are each accorded a second, and Greek, name; their first name is in each case a hellenised form of a Hebrew name (Jannaios/Yannai; Salina/Salome). The woman is cited as S. λεγομένη δὲ ὑπὸ Ἑλλήνων Alexandra.

3. Phraseology almost identical with this last example is used at *Ant.* 13.188, where Josephus mentions the double name of a town: Bethshan τὴν καλουμένην ὑπὸ τῶν Ἑλλήνων Skythopolis. At *Ant.* 5.85 another town is stated to have a Greek and a Semitic name, Arke/Ekdipous (= Heb. Achzib); but the identification of these two names with the one *polis* is mistaken (A. Schalit, *Namenwörterbuch zu Flavius Josephus* [Leiden, 1968], s.v., Ἀκή).

4. On two occasions this historian provides a reason why a man was accorded a nickname: Simon ὁ καὶ δίκαιος ἐπικληθείς, "because he was pious towards God and good-willed towards his compatriots": (*Ant.* 12.43; cf. 12.157); the treatment of Jews by Alexander Jannaeus was so particularly cruel on one occasion ὥστε ἐπικληθῆναι αὐτὸν ὑπὸ τῶν Ἰουδαίων Θρακίδαν (*Ant.* 13.383).

5. There remain two examples only where an indubitably Jewish person has an additional Jewish name. Frequently alluded to especially in *Ant.* XII is the famous Judas ὁ καὶ Maccabaeus (e.g. 12.285). Finally, there is Joseph ὁ (καὶ) Kaiaphas (*Ant.* 18.35; the MSS lack καί here, but it is an unremarkable omission in view of the first letters of the following name, and the by-name is confirmed in any case at 18.95, J. τὸν Κ. ἐπικαλούμενον). The gospel-writers never give this man's first name: Annas' son-in-law, high priest from 18-36, is referred to consistently simply as Kaiaphas (Lk. 3.2; Mt. 26.57; Jn.11.49; 18.13,14,24,28).

III. The NT

The following tabulation of most of the people with two names mentioned in the NT — not all necessarily by-names — shows the situation at a glance.

1. *Jewish name + Roman name:* Saul + Paul; John + Mark; Jesus + Justus; Symeon + Niger; Joseph + Justus.

2. *Jewish name/Greek (Roman) substitute name* (i.e. not a double name): Symeon/ Simon; Silas/Silvanus. (For a diminutive substitute of a Roman name, note Priska/ Priskilla.) G. Mussies reminds me that Jason at Rom. 16.21 is probably a substitute name for Jesus. He compares 1 Macc. 7.5, where Alkimos probably replaces Eliakim (cf. J. A. Goldstein's Anchor Bible *Comm.* [New York, 1976], 333).

3. *Jewish (nick) name = Greek translation name* (not really double names, though the second example has become so) : Kephas = Petros, Thomas = Didymos; Tabitha = Dorkas.

4. *Jewish name + (originally) patronymic used as a double name:* Joseph + Barsabbas; Judas + Barsabbas; Joseph + Barnabas; Elymas + Barjesus.

5. *Jewish name (graecised) + nickname/descriptive name:* Sym(e)on + ζηλωτής (Lk; Mt./Mk. have ὁ Κavavαῖoς, perhaps a Greek transcription of קנה, 'zealot'; cf. *CIJ* 1.362, quoted above, IIA).

6. *Jewish name + place of origin used as a name:* Maria + Magdalene (of Magdala); Judas Iscariot (man of Kerioth?).

7. *Jewish name + title* (which comes to be used as an alternative name): Jesus + Christos.

Some comments about certain of these names may now be offered.

a. The fact that two epitaphs for infants (I.1, IIA) accord them double names is of some interest for Saul/Paul. Although the by-name formula, Σ. ὁ καὶ Π. (Acts 13.9) occurs only once, he must be assumed to have had both these names from birth, in view of the statement about his Roman citizenship in Acts 22.26-29. In fact Paulus — an upper-class name in the Roman onomasticon — will have been only part of his full Roman name. But what is to be noted is his conscious decision to use his Roman name: Saul occurs nowhere in the letters he writes. It seems reasonably clear from the Acts narrative that this name became the one predominantly employed from early during the first missionary journey. Is the choice of name a very tangible expression of his goal to be 'all things to all men'?

b. In Sym(e)on's case the additional name given to him was merely a nickname which arose out of a pun (Mt. 16.15-18), for Kephas was Semitic too. (Symeon is the original form of his name; Simon is often substituted for it; cf. II.B.2 above.) There is no question here of a double name. But because the NT was written in Greek it was natural to use the Greek equivalent of Kephas, viz. Petros. (Almost certainly he must have come to be called by the Greek equivalent during his life, and this all but ousted Kephas from the NT writings.) Peter became popularised as the name for this disciple, rendering his true name all but redundant (cf. 1 Pet. 1.1; at 2 Pet. 1.1 Συμέων Πέτρος is the preferred reading). Yet we may notice an interesting feature in Acts 15. When the writer tells us about the Jerusalem debate, he says Petros rose to speak (15.7). But when James replies to this speech, the writer has James say, 'Symeon has told us . . .' (15.14). The distinction is carefully made by the writer. For the Greek readership, the disciple is referred to regularly by his Greek (nick-)name; when referred to by another Jew his Hebrew name is used. Whether or not Haenchen (*Comm.*, p.447) is right in thinking that 'Symeon' is used by Luke 'to show that James, the Lord's brother, is speaking Aramaic', the passage does at least suggest that this name continued to be favoured in Jewish circles. This same feature is evident in the Acts' use of 'Saul' in place of the more customary 'Paul' after 13.9 (note especially Ananias' quoted address at 22.13, with which cf. 9.17). Yet if the frequency of 'Peter' in preference to 'Symeon' reflects not merely an eye for his readers, the author of Acts may be unconsciously contradicting the overall contrast he builds up (with some exceptions: ch. 10 and 11) in that book between Peter the missioner to the Jews and Paul the apostle to the gentiles. For if the name Peter really became used too much in preference to Sym(e)on, it is a notable concession by the Jewish Christian to Hellenism. For a detailed study of usage in the NT of the various names of Peter see J. K. Elliot, *NovT* 14(1972) 241-56.

c. Example I.9 above provides us with a close analogy for Acts 1.23: Joseph τὸν καλούμενον Barsabbas, ὃς ἐπεκλήθη Justus. We have here a double by-name; although the second name is in origin a patronymic, it has virtually become a name in itself; cf. (f) and (g) below. It is surprising to observe how few genuine patronymics occur in the NT. K.L. McKay points out to me that the second formula here is equivalent to τὸν ἐπικληθέντα, which was presumably avoided on stylistic grounds after the participle in the preceding formula. Further, he suggests that the name Justus may have been significant, and was therefore a significant addition to the other names the man might possess. This could account for the different aspect in the second formula. McKay's suggestion receives some endorsement from the Josephus passage quoted above at II.B.4; and it is relevant as well for (f) below.

d. The young man who caused a difference of opinion between Paul and Barnabas is variously designated in Acts as John (13.5), Mark (15.39), and John Mark (τοῦ ἐπικαλουμένου, 12.12; τὸν ἐπικληθέντα 12.25; τὸν καλούμενον, 15.37). The overall synonymy of these different terms is plain, although K.L. McKay believes that there is an aspectual factor at 12.25 which sets it apart somewhat from the other two. The first and third are uncommon in non-literary papyri in respect of the article (Calderini, 236, 237), but cf. (e) and (i) below, and II.B.3 and 5 above. The usage found at Acts 12.25 is not attested by Calderini, but for another NT example, see (f). The fact that this man, Paul and Peter are referred to sometimes by one name, sometimes by the other, and occasionally by both, is not a matter to occasion surprise, even setting aside the feature noted in Acts — (b) above: for papyrus examples see Calderini, 249-252. It may be that the designation 'Simon Peter' (Mt. 16.16; Jn. 21. 2,3,7,11,15) is a by-name analogous to the example above at I.8. K.L. McKay, having considered all the passages where John Mark is referred to, reached the following conclusion (in a helpful note to me): 'It seems hard to escape the implication that he acquired the name Mark at some point between the two missionary journeys, and that it became the predominant name, at least in official Christian circles, although for full identification both names were used.'

e. Col. 4.11 refers to Jesus ὁ λεγόμενος Justus. This is simply another of the ways of giving a by-name, but on the basis of Calderini's study (p.239) it is not a style used very commonly at all. For Thomas ὁ λεγόμενος Didymos see **52**. Symeon is designated ὁ καλούμενος Niger (Acts 13.1), a rare (Calderini, 237) but quite analogous use. See (d) above and (i) below; also II.B.2 above.

f. Joseph ὁ ἐπικληθεὶς Barnabas is mentioned in Acts 4.36. On the form ὁ ἐπικληθείς see above, point (d). Barnabas' name is translated by the writer to mean υἱὸς παρακλήσεως though as in the case of point (g) below the rationale for this translation is obscure, and according to him this nickname was accorded to Joseph by the *apostoloi*. Everywhere else in the NT this man is known only by his by-name: his real name, Joseph, ceases to be used. Barnabas appears to be a patronymic which has developed into a name in its own right; see (c) and (g). The by-name of this Diaspora Jew is analogous with Symeon's Kephas, the only difference being that Kephas was readily transferable into Greek (Petros) whereas Barnabas was not. (G.J. Cowling refers me to the Hebrew subscript to the end of Sirach, which reads, 'Thus far the words of Simeon, son of Jesus, called Ben Sira . . .' [*Jerus. Bible,* 1958[2], p.1111, note p.]: the Hebrew text is dated c.190 BC by Eissfeldt [*OT Intro.,* p.507]. The writing of the book falls well within the Hellenistic period; and the name is thus another example of a patronymic which has become a by-name, thence employed as the name by which the individual is best known.)

g. The Jewish magician on Cyprus is called Barjesus, and the writer believes that his name could be translated as Elymas (Acts 13.6-8). This appears to be doubtful. Barjesus is another example of a patronymic which has become a name in itself; see (c) and (f) above. It is unlikely that the Acts passage is referring in a confused way to a by-name.

h. If Silas is the name used in Acts for Silvanus, then it is to be regarded as a substitute name, the former Semitic, the latter Latin. Philologically it is unlikely that Silas is an apocopated form of Silvanus: G. Dalman, *Grammatik des Jüdisch-Palästinischen Aramäisch* (Leipzig, 1905²; repr. Darmstadt, 1960), 157, n.5, regards Silas as an Aramaic form of Saul, not an abbreviated from of Silvanus. It is possible that Priska is an abbreviated form of Priskilla, but the latter is more likely a diminutive of the former.

i. When Jesus is accorded the title Christ, Ἰ. ὁ λεγόμενος X. (Mt. 1.16; 27.17,22), one may be reminded of the analogous application of titles to deities, as in the case of the Isis aretalogy from Kyme (I.9, above).

The prevalence of double names in the NT fits in well with non literary evidence for their popularity in II and the century on either side. Clearly Jews made use of by-names no less than other racial groups; and this brief survey has shown that whether or not the formulae gained currency originally in Ptolemaic Egypt, the geographical spread of the phenomenon was very wide by I. The NT examples demonstrate the great variety of formulae which are equivalent, overall, to the ὁ καί phrase. The use of names to differentiate rank is too large an issue to be taken up here. But studies of the NT onomasticon in relation to the contemporary non-literary sources ought to prove increasingly useful for those interested in the sociological background of the NT. The publication of the *Lexicon of Greek Proper Names* (funded by the British Academy; the project is under the general editorship of P.M. Fraser, of Oxford; anticipated publication date of vol.I is late 1984) will be of immeasurable help in this regard.

C. BIBLICAL AND RELATED CITATIONS

56. Miscellaneous citations from Psalms and Isaiah

An Eastern city, quite possibly Constantinople, may have been the original provenance of a sixth-century vase now in Italy, which carries quotations of parts of Is. 12.3 and Ps. 28 (29).3. D. Feissel, *AN* 47 (1976) 167-72, republished the text (*CIG* 8939; cf. *SEG* 792), and catalogues known examples of these passages preserved on vases, stone, and on a bronze statuette. Three others have this same pairing of Isaiah and Psalms: one from Carthage contains the Isaiah citation alone, while a number of others provide only the wording from the Psalm. Provenances of these texts include Syria, Carthage, Corinth, the Crimea, Bithynia, Caesarea, Jerusalem, Nessana, and three now in Italy (including the one which provides the focus of Feissel's discussion). These all appear to be Byzantine in date. Ps. 28.3 occurs alone on a wood tablet from Egypt (VI/VII) — van Haelst, 129 — and, in company with other verses from that book, on two parchments from Egypt whose date is unclear (ibid., 119,130). Is. 12.3 is not attested in the papyri.

IGLR has published several texts from Tomis (V-VI) which are citations from various parts of the Bible. No. 16 (first published in 1884; cf. I. Barnea, *Dacia* 1 [1957]) is an epitaph which quotes Is. 7.14 (cf. Mt. 1.23): Ἡμανουὴλ † Μ[εθ' ἡμῶν ὁ θεός]. The name Ἐνμανουήλ appears also on *IGLR* 25 (IV). The Is. passage is quoted on an ostrakon (VII; provenance unknown) — van Haelst, 884. Very fragmentary indeed is a quotation from Ps. 131.5-6, of which all that survives is ἄρτω[ν... (*IGLR* 61; the restoration is by Barnea, ibid., 267; cf. his pl. II.3 on p.277). Ps. 26.1 is cited in *IGLR* 60 and 118, the former written on a vase (cf. Barnea, ibid., 266, fig. 1). Ps. 26.1-14 appears on a parchment (VI; provenance unknown) — van Haelst, 128. Cf. the latter's cross-reference to other citations from this Psalm, though not the first verse.

Another Byzantine-period biblical citation from Psalms (120.8) was used on a stone placed above the entrance of a church in Djebel Akrum in Syria (541 AD): C. Ghadban, *MUB* 49 (1975/76) 566-73 (*non vidi*); cf. *SEG* 1632.

57. A cento of beatitudes

Provenance unknown   V
ed.pr. — H.A. Sanders, *HTR* 36(1943) 165-67

C.H. Roberts has republished 'a cento of biblical passages linked by the word μακάριος' (*P. Coll. Youtie* 6, pp. 74-75, at p.75; cf. K. Treu, *APF* 26 [1978] 158). The following citations occur: Mt. 5.11 (*ll*.1-2, very fragmentary); Mt. 5.6 (*l*.3); Ps. 118.2 (*l*.4); Lam. 3.27-31 (*ll*.5-9). In the last of these the papyrus reads μακάριος ἀ]νὴρ ὅταν, κτλ., but all MSS read ἀγαθὸν ἀνδρὶ ὅταν, κτλ. H.C. Youtie pointed out to Roberts, however, that Chrysostom cited this passage thus: μακάριος ὃς ἦρε ζυγόν, κτλ. Selected verses from Lam. 3.27-31 are only very rarely mentioned by patristic writers (*Bib.Pat.* 1.210; 2.210). This is the first occurrence of this particular combination of biblical verses; neither of the OT passages has appeared in papyrus texts before, while —

excluding large portions or whole gospels — Mt. 5.6 has been found only as part of Mt. 5.1-11 in a ninth-century parchment (van Haelst, 342). The function of this papyrus is uncertain: Roberts suggests two possibilities. It is less likely to be an amulet because there is no indication of folding on the sheet. A letter is suggested by ἐρρῶ]σθαί σε εὔχομαι (10), and if so the contents would require the form to be a literary epistle rather than a letter of a more private kind.

58. 'In the bosom of Abraham' (Lk. 16.22)

The conclusions of two 1976 Christian epitaphs of Byzantine date include a formulaic allusion to this parable from Luke. *IGAeg.* 9243.6-12 (Esneh, in Egypt; 30/4/890) is somewhat fuller than the damaged *BE* 756, no.7 (Nubia, VI — XIII). The former reads: ὁ Θ(εὸ)ς ὁ παντο|κράτωρ ὁ Θ(εὸ)[ς] ὁ τ⟨ῶ⟩ν πν(ευμ)ά|[τ]⟨ω⟩ν Θ(είω)ν (?) καὶ Κ(ύριο)ς πάσης | σαρκ[ὸ]ς ἀ[ν]άπαυσον | τὴ⟨ν⟩ ψυχ(ὴν) αὐτῆς ἐν κόλ[πῳ] | Ἀβραὰμ κ(αὶ) Ἰσαὰκ καὶ | Ἰακὼβ ...: 'Almighty God, the god of the divine spirits and Lord of all flesh, rest her soul in the bosom of Abraham and Isaac and Jacob ...'. *BE* 756 has εἰς κόλ]πους, while Luke's passage reads εἰς τὸν κόλπον Ἀβραάμ. For the *nomina sacra* here, see **69**.

59. 'Light and Life' in Christian epitaphs.

Tomis (Constanța)   from VI
ed. pr. — E. Popescu, *IGLR* 91, p.136 (pl.)

Bilingual limestone cross, *recto* inscribed in Greek, *verso* in Latin.

recto:	vertical arm	— Φῶ[ς]
	horizontal arm	— Ζωή
verso:	vertical arm	— *Hic* | *fa*|*cta* | *est* | *ora-*
	horizontal arm	— *tio episcoporum*
(same)	vertical arm	— *Ste*|*fa*|*ni*|[-----]

Bib. — *AE* 621

> **Light, Life. Here was delivered the speech of (prayer for?) bishops Stephen . . .**

Numerous examples of the Light/Life epitaph survive from the Greek East, Syria and Palestine. Without exception the formula occurs on Christian gravestones, and appears to be unattested before VI. The two words are taken to be an allusion to Jn. 1.4 (cf. 8.12). *AE* (1976) index, p.276, incorrectly lists Ζωή in the text above as a name. Other bilingual (Gk./Lat.) examples include *IGLR* 49, 94. The latter is heavily restored, only the Z being clear on the verso; the recto reads, *in mor*|*te re*|[*surrectio?*].

Other examples of the formula in *IGLR* are 50, 380. Popescu's n. on *IGLR* 49 gives references to other epigraphical examples from Syria and Asia Minor: *IGL Syr.* 1.671, 2.176, 479; 3.632; *MAMA* 4(1933) 99; H. Grégoire, *Recueil d'inscriptions grecques chrétiennes d'Asie Mineure* (Paris, 1922) 216, 265, 320. A painted text in a church near Hebron was published by B. Lifshitz, *Rev.Bib.* 77 (1970) no.17, pp.78-79 (pl. VIIb): † Ἐγώ εἰμι | τὸ φῶς καὶ | ἡ ζωὴ κ(αὶ) | ἄλ[φα καὶ ὦ]. This example links other Johannine passages together with the allusions from the Fourth Gospel: 1 Jn. 1.1-5; Rev. 1.8. But Lifshitz draws attention to the presence of the formula in the gnostic *Corpus Hermeticum.* Note esp. ὁ δὲ Νοῦς ὁ θεὸς ... ζωὴ καὶ φῶς ὑπάρχων (1.9); ὁ δὲ πάντων πατὴρ ὁ Νοῦς ὢν ζωὴ καὶ φῶς (1.12); φῶς καὶ ζωή ἐστιν ὁ θεὸς καὶ πατήρ (1.21). (For a text of the *Corpus Hermeticum* see the Budé edition by A.D. Nock and A.J. Festugière [Paris, 1945-]. H.I. Bell has a brief discussion of the corpus in *Cults and Creeds in Graeco-Roman Egypt* [Liverpool, 1953; repr. Chicago, 1975], 74-76.) Popescu, *ad IGLR* 49, says that the two terms came to symbolize the person of Jesus, and thus had an apotropaic function on tombstones, not unlike that of other words or letters on amulets.

60. Jn. 13.27 (Vulgate) on an oil lamp

Tomis (Constanţa)   IV
ed. pr. — J.D. Stefănescu, *Byzantion* 6 (1931) 571-74 (pl. 23); cf. I Barnea, *Stud. Teol.* 6 (1954) 96 *(non vidi); IGLR* 54; *AE* 619

The decoration on this clay lamp is unique. In the centre stands a bearded Christ wearing a toga; below his feet are crossed palm branches. Around him are written the words, *pacem meam do vobis* (Jn. 13.27, Vulg.). Surrounding this central figure is a border containing the busts of the twelve Apostles; though not named, individual features are portrayed to differentiate them. Above the figure of Christ, there is what appears to have been the figure of a woman, but this part of the lamp is damaged. The statement from the Farewell Discourse was used in the Gallican Liturgy, and Stefănescu suggests (572) that this may explain why it was well enough known to be written on a lamp such as this. It is surprisingly ornate, perhaps, for ordinary domestic use; may it have had a particular function at church services, for example? On the basis of other similar-shaped lamps, Stefănescu (573) dates this one IV. He doubts (574) whether the lamp was originally from the Tomis area: perhaps its origin was in the East. Whatever the provenance, the lamp offers possible evidence for a reasonably early Christian presence in the area. Apart from whole gospels or large portions of them, this verse appears only once on papyri, as part of a quotation from Jn. 13. 16-27 (van Haelst, 457, dated V).

61. The curse of Judas

Argos   post-Constantine
ed. pr. — D. Feissel, *BCH* 101 (1977) 224-28 (ph.225)

† Κυμητήριον διᾳ[φέρον – –]
νης καὶ τῆς ταύτη[ς – – – –]

λούσης· εἴ τις δὲ [ἀνορύξῃ αὐτὸ]
ἔξοθεν τῶν [κληρονόμων]
5   αὐτῆς, ἐχέτ[ω τὸ ἀνάθεμα]
τοῦ Ἰούδα [καὶ τῶν λεγόντων]
ἆρον ἆρον σταύ[ρωσον αὐτόν.]

One of a number of Greek sepulchral inscriptions, mostly from Argos and Athens, of later Roman and Byzantine date, containing a similar concluding warning against opening the grave. This inscription was inventoried in 1890, but is scarcely known at all, according to Feissel.
Bib. — SEG 437; BE (1978) 195 ·

(ll. 3-7) If anyone exhumes it apart from her heirs, let him have the curse of Judas, and of those who say 'Away with him, away with him, crucify him.'

This tomb appears to have belonged to two related women (l.2), perhaps mother and daughter (Feissel, 226). Feissel mentions another recently published inscription from Argos with remarkably similar wording: C. B. Kritzas. AD 27 (1972) B.207 (non vidi); cf. G. Touchais, BCH 101 (1977) 546-47 (fig. 76); SEG 434; BE (1977) 193. On that inscription — of pre-Constantinian date (Feissel, 226, n.109) — crosses precede and follow the wording; a fish sign appears after the writing as well. Other examples are assembled by Feissel, including IG IV.628, where the formula is ἐχέ[τω] τὴν μερίδα τοῦ Ἰούδα τοῦ προδότου. This anathema seems to have been popular at Argos: for a period in which only a dozen epitaphs are extant from that region, three contain this curse (ibid., 226). Athens has also yielded three: IG III, 2.1428, and two others which Feissel republishes — with revisions to one, which is not later than IV (ibid., 226, n.112) — in view of their inaccessibility.

Elsewhere, the formula has been found at Delphi, Naxos, Nicaea, Bithynia. In the ·west of the Roman world, there are a number of Latin.examples, mostly from Rome and Ravenna: Diehl, ILCV 1273, 1293, 3844-51, 3853, 3855, 3856, 3866 (cf. Feissel, 227, n.117). As with the Greek anathemas, these Latin ones vary slightly in their wording. For brief discussion of the Greek anathemas containing these formulae, see BE 256, with the references cited there.

The additional curse on the text printed above is an obvious allusion to Jn. 19.15 (cf. 19.6; Mk. 15.13, and parallels): cf. an inscription from Corinth (cited by Feissel, 228, n.124), which reads ἔστω αὐτῷ τὸ ἀνάθεμα Ἄννα κ(αὶ) Καιάφα. In addition to Feissel's references, note the Byzantine papyrus from Benghazi (SB 1 [1915] 5928) which urges Mary, παρθέν]ε θεοτόκε, to provide for desecrators of her shrine a portion μετὰ] τῶν θεοκτόνων Ἰουδαίων. The existence on gravestones of anathemas like the one printed above would seem to reflect anti-Jewish sentiment at a popular level, at least among Christians. W.A. Meeks and R.L. Wilken, *Jews and Christians in Antioch in the first four centuries of the Common Era* (Missoula, 1978), provides an examination of relations between the two groups in one locality. For a lease arrangement between nuns (?) and a Jew, see **82.** On anti-Semitism by Christians in the Roman World, see M. Simon, *Verus Israel* (Paris, 1964²), especially 239-474. E. M. Smallwood has argued that legislation concerning the Jews gradually alters from toleration by Pagan Rome to clear-cut discrimination by Christian Rome. The thesis is advanced in detail in *The Jews under Roman Rule* (Leiden, 1976), and briefly in *From Pagan Protection to Christian Oppression* (Belfast, 1979). On hostility from other quarters see J.N.

Sevenster, *The Roots of Pagan Anti-Semitism in the Ancient World* (Leiden, 1975).

C.J. Hemer draws my attention to two further anathemas on epitaphs to warn off potential disturbers of the grave : *MAMA* 6 (1939) 335 and 335a (for the latter see W.M. Ramsay, *The Bearing of Recent Discovery on the Trustworthiness of the NT* [London, 1915], 358-63). No. 335.14-20 reads as follows (κ- = καί):

$$ἔσται\ δὲ$$

$$15\ \ \ \ ἐπικατάρατος\ ὁ\ τυοῦ-$$
$$τος\ κ-\ ὅσαι\ ἀραὶ\ ἐν\ τῷ$$
$$Δευτερονομίῳ\ εἰσὶν\ γε-$$
$$γραμμέναι\ αὐτῷ\ τε\ κ-$$
$$τέκνοις\ κ-\ ἐγγόνοις\ κ-$$
$$20\ \ \ \ παντὶ\ τῷ\ γένει\ αὐτοῦ\ γένοιντο.$$

15 '. . . **Such a person shall be |accursed and may whatever curses stand written in**
20 **Deuteronomy come upon him and his children and his descendants and |all his**
    family.

The wording of 335a. 16-18 is similar but briefer: ... ἔσται αὐτῶ αἱ ἀραὶ | ἡ γεγραμμέναι ἐν τῷ Δευτερο|νομίῳ. The latter text is dated 248/49; both emanated originally from Akmonia in Phrygia (see edd.n. in *MAMA,* p.116). The curse invoked probably suggests that these epitaphs are Jewish (for the Jewish community at Akmonia cf. **5**). But Christian authorship ought not to be entirely ruled out, perhaps. At Gal. 3.10,13 ἐπικατάρατος is used on both occasions in allusions to Deut. The adjective also appears in the NT at Lk. 6.5D. L. Robert, *Hellenica* 11-12(1960) 399-400 (cf. T. Drew-Bear, *GRBS* 17[1976] 248), discusses another Akmonian curse epitaph which is to be seen as Jewish in view of its derivation from Zech. 5.2-4(LXX): ἔσ]ται αὐτῶ πρὸς τὸν Θεὸν τὸν ῞Υψιστον καὶ τὸ ἀρᾶς δρέπανον εἰς τὸν ὖκον αὐτοῦ [εἰσέλθοιτο καὶ μηδένα ἐγκαταλείψαιτο], 'He shall be answerable to the Most High God and may the curse's sickle enter his house and leave no-one behind'. Cf. **5**. For the Eumenian Formula here, cf. **86**.

62. Rom. 13.3 in a mosaic

B. Lifshitz published a mosaic inscription from Caesarea (*ZPE* 7 [1971] 163, no.22 [pl. 8f.]); cf. J. Reynolds, *JRS* 66 (1976) 196, n.293. The text quotes Rom. 13.3, omitting MSS δέ after the first word: θέλεις | μὴ φοβῖσθαι | τὴν ἐξουσίαν | τὸ ἀγαθὸν | ποίει. The mosaic was discovered in a monastic building of Byzantine date (cf. van Haelst, 501).

63. 1 Cor. 3.6-8 in a homily or commentary

Provenance unknown·   IV/V
ed. pr. — L. Koenen, *ZPE* 4 (1969) 41-42 (pl. 3b)

A very fragmentary — too much so, indeed, to be worth re-printing here — nine-line papyrus, which formed part of a codex.

Bib. — K. Treu, *APF* 22 (1973) 379, no.4; idem, *APF* 26 (1978) 157; B. Kramer, *P. Köln* 11, p.38.

Broken as it is, this text includes at *ll.* 6-9 a quotation from 1 Cor. 3.6-8 (text breaks off after the first four words of v.8). The NT passage is cited to illustrate the allegorical interpretation (*ll.* 1-6) that κῆπος καὶ πα[ράδεισος] stand for ἐκκλησία in the scriptures. This sort of interpretation occurs in Gregory of Nyssa and other patristic writers (see Koenen, p.41, nn. 1,2). In the NT quotation the divine name is abbreviated both times: θ(εό)ς (*ll.* 7, 9; the latter is restored, but the abbreviation is required by the line length, and is in any case likely in view of its occurrence two lines earlier). On *nomina sacra* see **69**. Kramer's apparatus claims that in *l.7* ἀ]λλὰ ὁ (= 1 Cor. 3.6) is a variant for NT codd. ὁ δέ, but Nestle/Aland²⁶ prints ἀλλὰ ὁ and marks no variants in its apparatus.

Another very fragmentary leaf from a codex (early IV) which may be part of a homily is republished by C. H. Roberts, *P. Coll. Youtie* 5 (pp. 71-74; *ed. pr.,* H. A. Sanders, *HTR* 36 [1943] 165-67; cf. K. Treu, *APF* 26 [1978] 158). Thirteen broken lines survive on either side of the papyrus. The passage appears to be interpreting the OT in the light of the NT: Moses (or Joshua?) is portrayed as a type of Christ: τῷ Μωήσῃ ὑπ[ήρε] | [τ ... (7-8); τύ]πος Χ(ριστο)ῦ κηρυσσόμεν[ος] (10). At *verso ll.* 23-25 several of the twelve tribes are named, largely in the order given by Origen (*Hom.* 23.1).

64. Christian amulet

Provenance unknown   V/VI
ed. pr. — O. Montevecchi, *P.Coll.Youtie* 91, pp. 585-88 (pl. 33a)

>].̣.[
>]ς κατὰ σοῦ [π]οιησαμ̣[εν
> εἰασά{σ}μενος πᾶσα̣[ν] νό[σ]ον .̣[
> [ ] X̅(ριστ)ὲ̅ εἴασε τὸν φοροῦντα{ν} ητη[
> 5   καὶ ψυχὴν καὶ σῶμα καὶ π̅ν̅(εῦμ̣)[α] · ο[
> τον ἀπὸ παντὸς κακοῦ [
> [.̣.]δ ιναυτο[.̣.̣.]σα̣.̣[
>]σικον[

A very fragmentary papyrus, lacking beginning and ending, of a text that is certainly Christian, and almost certainly an amulet.

(*ll.* 3-6) . . .healing every disease . . . Christ heal the wearer . . . and soul and body and spirit . . . from all evil . . .

The large size (13 x 8 cm.) suggests that this papyrus was not in actual use as an amulet; perhaps it provided a model of the formula used; thus Montevecchi restores ἡ] δ[ε]ῖνα (7), which the owner would replace with her own name (Montevecchi, 585). The presence of the *nomina sacra* X̅ε̅ and π̅ν̅α̅ (4-5) are indicative of a Christian origin (cf. **69**). The abbreviation of πνεῦμα here illustrates how, once the word was written in such a manner to refer to the Holy Spirit, the convention passed over to other uses of the word. This applies to a considerable number of words which can be treated as *nomina sacra*. τὸν φοροῦντα (4) is particularly suggestive of an amulet.

In *l*.5 the mention of soul/body/spirit immediately makes one think of I Thes. 5.23. Two papyrus letters of earlier centuries quote the same words: *P.Harr.* 107 (III), in the same order as this new papyrus; and *P.Oxy.* 8(1911) 1161 (IV) in the same order as the NT passage. These two letters are reprinted in Naldini, as nos. 5 and 60 (pp. 76-78, 254-55). The first of these has received a considerable amount of scholarly attention: in addition to the references in *P.Coll.Youtie*, p.586, or Naldini, 76, add J. O'Callaghan, *Aeg.* 52 (1972) 152-57. In that letter, a badly-educated man writes to his mother trusting that God will preserve her καιτά (= κατά) τε ψυχὴν καὶ σῶμα καὶ πνεῦμα. The trichotomy in this order (cf. F. E. Brightman, *JTS* 2 [1900/01] 273) is 'characteristic of Egyptian liturgies' (J. E. Powell's n. ad loc. to *P.Harr.* 107). H. Crouzel, *Aeg.* 49 (1969) 143, sees a possible link between Origen and the writer of this letter. *P.Oxy.* 1161 is a fragmentary letter written by a sick woman who hopes that God may help ἡμῶν | τῷ σώματι τῇ ψυχῇ, τῷ | π̅ν̅ι̅ (5-7). As with this papyrus, the new text is not consciously citing 1 Thes. 5.23 with its particular context in mind: closer to that may be *P.Harr.* 107. In the new papyrus Christ is asked to heal the 'whole man', every aspect of the wearer.

A corpus of Christian magical papyri is in preparation by J. van Haelst.

65. Negative Theology

Among a group of Christian inscriptions from Paros (*SEG* 1012-16; originally published by A.K. Orlandos, *Arch. Eph.* [1975] 34-35, no.69 [pl.]), it is possible that no.1014 is a very fragmentary citation from Chrysostom, ἀόρατε ἀ[κατάληπτε. For a further suggestion about this, see *BE* (1977) 345, where Orlandos nos.65 and 75 are attached to his no.69, yielding a little more of the Chrysostom passage.

66. Fragment of the Niceno-Constantinopolitan creed

Provenance unknown   V
ed. pr. — J. Kramer, *ZPE* 1 (1967) 131-32 (pl. III)

Legible on this papyrus are parts of seven lines from the creed formulated at the Synod of Constantinople in 381.

Texts of creeds are not frequent among pap. finds. Other quotations from the Niceno-Constantinopolitan Creed occur in *P.Oxy.* 15 (1922) 1784 (V²), and *P.Lit.Lond.* (1927) 239 (VI/VII). The latter is in fact a full text of the Creed, accompanied by an invocation to the Nile and Ps. 132(133), written on nine vellum sheets. According to H.J.M. Milne, the editor of that volume, the text was probably used as an amulet; i.e., it had an apotropaic function. The Creed of 381 was an enlargement of the Nicene Creed, which also is represented in the papyri: *P.Oxy.* 17(1927) 2067 (V); *P.Ryl.* 1(1911) 6 (VI). Our extract comes from the section which deals with the Son 'begotten, not made . . . enfleshed by the Holy Spirit.' That the papyrus text is citing the Niceno-Constantinopolitan Creed is clear from the fact that it omits one phrase which the Nicene creed contained: at *l.*3, δι' οὗ τὰ πάν[τα] | [ἐγ]ένετο, our text goes straight on with τὸν δι' ἡμᾶ[ς τοὺς] | [ἀνθ]ρώπους, omitting the explanatory τά τε ἐν τῷ οὐρανῷ καὶ τὰ ἐν τῇ γῇ. The Niceno-Constantinopolitan Creed was formulated by Gregory of Nyssa (Nicephorus, *Hist.Eccles.* 12.13); it was referred to in the *acta* of the Council of Chalcedon in 451, which reaffirmed the Creed agreed to at Constantinople in 381. On the creed see J.N.D. Kelly, *Early Christian Creeds* (London, 1960²), especially ch.10. Kelly's book does not deal with the papyrological evidence for the creeds, and accordingly not with the implications of such citations — their use as amulets for apotropaic purposes, for example. See van Haelst, 716-719, 938.

D. JUDAICA

67. Votive inscription to 'the god in Dan'

Tel Dan (Palestine)   late III/early II BC

$$\theta\epsilon\hat{\omega}\iota$$
$$\tau\hat{\omega}\iota\ \dot{\epsilon}\nu\ \Delta\acute{a}\nu o\iota\varsigma$$
$$Z\acute{\omega}\ddot{\iota}\lambda o\varsigma\ \epsilon\dot{v}\chi\acute{\eta}\nu$$

נדר זילס לא...

Bilingual text (3 lines of Greek followed by one of Aramaic) on a broken stone, 15.5 cm. x 26.5 cm. Date of text based on letter style (both Greek and Aramaic). The particularly good photo in *Rev. Bib.* (see below) shows up what appears to be some sort of grid incised on the stone (to align the letters?).

Bib. — No formal *ed. pr.* has appeared. A. Biran has mentioned the text briefly in reports of excavations at Tel Dan: *IEJ* 26 (1976) 204-05 (photo, pl. 35D); *Rev. Bib.* 84 (1977) 260-61 (photo, pl. VIIA); Greek text in *SEG* 1684; another photo in *BA* 39 (1976) 89. See also *Archaeologia* 107 (1977) 81 [*non vidi*]; *BE* (1977) no. 542.

To the god in Dan, Zoilos (discharges) his vow. (The Aramaic text appears to approximate to this in meaning.)

This text presupposes that the god worshipped here is well-known (at least locally). The plural may refer to the town, or possibly it points to "a tradition which linked the cult of this god with the tribe of Dan" (Biran, *Rev. Bib.* p.261). The stone appears to have been set up at a cult site, a temple or altar. The inscription appears to be complete; and it is therefore intriguing that this deity is not named. Such a text does not suggest any kinship with traditional OT cultus: perhaps it offers us a candlelight glimpse of the inroads made upon Hellenistic Palestine by Greek cults. The bilingual character of the inscription may be an indicator of this trend. F.I. Andersen suggested to me that an alternative interpretation ought not to be overlooked, the persistence of a local cult of non-Jewish Semites (Nabataeans?). As with **71** this inscription provides evidence for bilingualism in Palestine, and thus relates to a topic of some importance in NT studies. The name Zoilos may be an approximation for Silas (*BE* [1977] 542).

68. The Great Goddess of Samaria

Samaria (Sebaste)   late III/IV

ed. pr. — J.W. Crowfoot, et al., *Samaria-Sebaste* III (London, 1957), 37, no. 12 (pl V,3) *(non vidi)*

Εἷς Θεός
ὁ πάντων
δεσπότης
μεγάλη κόρη
5   ἡ ἀνείκητος

This painted inscription — the text is complete — was discovered in a cistern in the stadium at Samaria, together with a statue which probably depicts the goddess Kore (late II/early III).

Bib. — *D. Flusser, IEJ 25 (1975) 13-20 (pl. 2); J. Reynolds, JRS 66 (1976) 195, n. 275.

One god, the ruler of all things, great Maiden, the invincible.

The cult of Kore — which may well have reached Samaria in the Hellenistic period, although it is attested only from Roman times — appears to have replaced the worship of Isis in this area, although quite when this occurred is uncertain. Flusser republishes the above inscription in order to argue that the entire wording refers to Kore. If correct, this reinterpretation would provide significant testimony to 'the syncretistic monotheistic tendencies of later paganism' (Flusser, 20; cf.14, 17).

Kore was the only deity known to have had a cult at Samaria in Roman times in addition to those for the emperor and Jupiter Capitolinus. Several other inscriptions and graffiti referring to her were found in the same stadium; furthermore, she appears on two coins, the representation on one of which is not dissimilar in type to the statue found in the cistern. On all this see J. W. Crowfoot, et al., Samaria-Sebaste I (London, 1942; repr. 1966), 46-48; and for the temple of Kore, ibid., 62-67.

The phrase εἷς θεός has been considered briefly elsewhere (**69**); but it is to be noted that here at least it does not function as an acclamation, the prevalent Christian use. In this text it proclaims that Kore is the only god; it was thus appropriate — according to Flusser — to use masculine forms to secure her claim, which may have been left in doubt by use of the feminine. Kore is characterised by the epithet μεγάλη, used frequently of numerous gods in antiquity. For μέγας and its variants (μ.μ.; μέγιστος; etc.) in 1976 texts from Egypt note the following: P.Coll.Youtie 35; SB 10883, 10898; P.Tebt 1110-11, 1116-19; BGU 2216, 2221 (both partly restored); SEG 1801. In IGAeg. fourteen different gods are accorded this epithet (see Index IV, p.151, of that volume). The few Greek texts in P. Saqqara accord such epithets to Hermes, elsewhere known as Hermes Trismegistos. In Asia the epithet is common too, the best known example being the Great Mother; cf. Artemis in Acts 19.27, 28, 35. For other examples from Asia in literary sources, see M. Santoro, Epitheta deorum in Asia Graeca cultorum ex auctoribus Graecis et Latinis (Milan, 1974). Also well attested is the more general phrase θεοὶ μεγάλοι, e.g., SB 10883. 12-13; SIG³ 985.33 (Philadelphia in Lydia, II/I). In such contexts, μέγας does not imply a comparison with other gods. For modern bibliography on this matter see the refs. in L. Robert, Ath. Eph. (1969) 8, 10; cf. (briefly) Deissmann, LAE, 269, n.3. To speak of Kore as ἀνείκητος is arresting, for the epithet is usually associated only with Helios/Sol Invictus. According to Flusser (16, 18), the inscription sees Kore and Helios as two alternative manifestations — the female and male aspects — of the one god, ὁ πάντων δεσπότης.

Here Flusser's argument is at its least convincing. On Sol Invictus see G.H. Halsberghe, *The Cult of Sol Invictus* (Leiden, 1972).

Consideration is then given by Flusser (18-20) to what we know of Simon, the Magos who exercised a big influence in first-century Samaria, and who is encountered in Acts 8.9-24. Hippolytos, *Refutatio* 6.2, 14-15, includes quotations from Simon's work, *Apophasis* (on this see J.M.A. Salles-Dabadie, *Recherches sur Simon le Mage, I, L' 'Apophasis megalè'* [Paris, 1969]); further information occurs throughout [Clement], *Recog.* 1.72-4.3. When Acts mentions that Simon is called ἡ δύναμις τοῦ θεοῦ ἡ καλουμένη Μεγάλη the participle shows that the adjective is a title. However, τοῦ θεοῦ is a gloss (so Haenchen, Comm., ad loc.; cf. Salles-Dabadie, 125-29) which Lk. employs elsewhere (e.g., Lk. 22.69; contrast Mk. 14.62 = Mt. 26.64), but which misses the point. For in fact ἡ δύναμις here ought to be a synonym for God; and Acts may be avoiding the full force of the claim Simon was making for himself. On the term '(great) Power' as a synonym for God in Jewish thought, see G.G. Scholem, *Jewish Gnosticism, Merkabah Mysticism and Talmudic Tradition* (New York, 1965²), 67-69. Yet while the expansion of ἡ δύναμις by τοῦ θεοῦ does look like a gloss in Lk./Acts, the following two passages may be noted (both cited in F.F. Bruce's Comm. on Acts, *ad loc.*): PGM 4. 1225-29, ἐπικαλοῦμαί σε τὴν μεγίστην δύναμιν τὴν ἐν τῷ οὐρανῷ ὑπὸ κυρίου θεοῦ τεταγμένη and an inscription from Lydia, from W.M. Ramsay, *The Bearing of Recent Discovery on the Trustworthiness of the New Testament* (London, 1914), 117, εἷς θεὸς ἐν οὐρανοῖς Μὴν οὐράνιος μεγάλη δύναμις τοῦ ἀθανάτου θεοῦ.

The male/female aspects of the one god which Kore/Sol Invictus represent supply a further possible link with Simon's thought (Flusser, 19). He apparently saw himself as the manifestation of the *dynamis megale,* and his wife Helene as the female concomitant of that, viz., *epinoia.* Helene was also associated with Selene, a moon goddess. Now, as Isis had that function too, and Kore superseded an Isis cult in Samaria, it is intriguing to wonder whether these links are just coincidental. (Note that the identification of Isis with Selene is of Greek origin: see Y. Grandjean, *Une nouvelle arétalogie . . .* [= **2**], 58, n.119.) Flusser does not draw out the point explicitly, but if Simon were the creator (or propagator) of such ideas in the first century, and if there is a link to be made between his thought and the inscription, then his influence continued long after his death in the area in which he worked. Some support for this may be found in the fact that nearly 200 years later Hippolytos thought it necessary to counter Simon's views.

69. *Nomina sacra* in synagogue inscriptions

Beth-shan (Skythopolis), Palestine VI²
ed. pr. — B. Lifshitz, *Euphrosyne* 6 (1974) 27-29

π(ροσ)φορὰ ὧν Κ(ύριο)ς γ-
ινόσκι τὰ
ὀνόματ-
α· αὐτὸς
5 φυλάξι ἐν
χρό(νῳ)

A mosaic text, flanked by two pheasants. The synagogue building is older than the mosaic itself, which was provided by benefactors who retained an intriguing anonymity. Rcad γινώσκει (1-2).

Bib. — SEG 1683; BE 732

A gift of those whose names the Lord knows. He will preserve them in time to come.

The abbreviated *nomen sacrum* ΚΣ is very rare in Jewish inscriptions, though very common in Christian texts. Recent discussions of *nomina sacra* include E.A. Judge and S.R. Pickering, *Prudentia* 10(1978) 5-8; C.H. Roberts, *Manuscript, Society and Belief in Early Christian Egypt* (London, 1979), especially ch. 2. K. McNamee, *Abbreviations in Greek Literary Papyri and Ostraca* (*BASP* suppl. 3; Ann Arbor, 1981), App.*VI*, p.122, lists nine secular Greek literary papyri and ostraka containing Christian abbreviations. A trilingual inscription from Spain (*CIJ* I.661; VI) has Greek Κ(υρίο)υ corresponding to the unabbreviated Latin *domini* (the Hebrew text is not equivalent at this point). B. Lifshitz' Prolegomenon to the reprint of *CIJ* I includes two Jewish texts from Thessalonike. In 693b (cf. *Rev. Bib.* 75[1968] 377-78, and pl. 37; *BE* [1969] 370) we find a partial quotation from Ps. 46.8, 12: Κύριος μεθ' ἡμῶν. According to Lifshitz (ad loc.) this formula is unique in Jewish epigraphical remains, although it is frequently found in Christian texts. In 693b *kyrios* is not abbreviated, but the process of 'Christianisation' of Jewish texts is apparent: formulae distinctive of Christian texts are being incorporated in Jewish ones. The anonymity clause in the Skythopolis inscription above (*ll.* 1-4), current in Christian texts, occurs here for the first time in a Jewish one (cf. *BE* 732). For another possible example of Christian terminology permeating a Jewish inscription see D. Feissel, *BCH* 100(1976) 281.

Liftshitz' other text, *CIJ* I. 693a (= *IG* x 2 [1972] 789), first published in 1955 by S. Pelekidis (*non vidi*), is a bilingual inscription of a Samaritan synagogue from Thessalonike; discussed at greater length by Lifshitz and J. Schiby in *Rev. Bib.* 75(1968) 368-77 (with pl.35). The text is complete and has been dated IV-VI in view of the Samaritan script (J.D. Purvis, *BASOR* 221 [1976] 221-23 [correcting the earlier suggested date of IV; cf. *SEG* 779]). Lifshitz' *CIJ* discussion accepts the view (*BE* [1969] 369) that the text is complete: there is no need to posit αὐτούς or αὐτήν in a line 20. J. Schiby, *Zion* 42 (1977) 103-09 (in Hebrew; English summary, p.III) suggests it may be possible to locate the site of the synagogue. *Ll.*1 and 15 are in Samaritan, italicised in the translation below. The bulk of the inscription (2-14) consists of a quotation from Num. 6.22-27 (van Haelst, no.53); and the text concludes (16-19) with a dedication by the benefactor Sirikios.

ברוך אלהינו לעולם
καὶ ἐλάλησεν Κ(ύριο)ς μετὰ
Μουσῆ λέγων · λάλησον
τῷ Ἀαρὼν καὶ τοῖς υἱοῖς αὐτ[οῦ]
5   λέγων. οὕτως εὐλογήσ[ετε]
τοὺς υἱοὺς Ἰ(σρα)ὴλ · εἴπατε αὐτοῖς ·
εὐλογήσει σε Κ(ύριο)ς καὶ φυλάξει
σε, ἐπιφανεῖ Κ(ύριο)ς τὸ πρόσωπον
αὐτοῦ πρός σε καὶ ἀγαπήσει σε,

10 ἐπαρεῖ Κ(ύριο)ς τὸ πρόσωπον αὐ-
τ(ο)ῦ πρός σε καὶ ποιήσει σοι εἰ-
(ρή)νην καὶ θήσεται τὸ ὄνομά
μου ἐπὶ τοὺς υἱοὺς Ἰ(σρα)ὴλ κἀγὼ
εὐλογήσω αὐτούς.

15 ברוך שמו לעולם

ἶς Θεός· εὐλογία Σιρικίῳ τῷ
ποιήσαντι ἅμα συνβίῳ
κὲ τέκνοις. αὖξι Νεάπο-
λις μετὰ τῶν φιλούντων

Blessed be our God forever. And the Lord spoke with Moses, saying, 'Talk to
5 Aaron and to his sons. |Thus you shall bless the sons of Israel. Tell them the
10 Lord will bless you and will protect you. |The Lord will show his face to you
and favour you. The Lord will lift up his face to you and make peace for you;
and my name will be placed upon the sons of Israel, and I will bless them.'
15 |*Blessed be his name forever.* God is one. A blessing for Sirikios who made (this
inscription? synagogue?) together with his wife and children. May Neapolis
prosper with the friends.

This text makes clear that Thessalonike in Macedonia had a Samaritan community.
It is not merely that there are two quotations in Samaritan script. Lifshitz (and Schiby)
argued that the Greek in the biblical quotation, which constitutes the bulk of the
inscription, differs at numerous points from the LXX, and 'conforms to the Samaritan
Pentateuch, which gives here a text almost identical with that of the Hebrew *textus
receptus'* (*CIJ* Proleg., p.72). Thus, whereas this inscription follows the Hebrew verse
order, in the LXX v.24 follows immediately after v.27 (*Rev. Bib.*, p. 370). Lifshitz
lists verbal differences between LXX and this inscription: clearly they are deliberate
and cannot be attributed to careless laxity. That particular care was taken with the
inscribing of the biblical passage is clear if one compares the orthographical accuracy
of *ll.* 2-14 (the one exception being Μουσῆ for Μωυσῆ) with the phonetic spellings in
the dedication (16-19). Where this text has future indicatives, LXX uses aorist
optatives. Lifshitz/Schiby suggested — especially in their discussion of ἀγαπήσει (9)
— that the Samaritan Greek text of the Pentateuch provided a more literal and strictly
accurate rendering of the Hebrew than did the LXX. This inscription is thus 'of great
moment for the study of Greek translations of the Bible' (*CIJ* Proleg., p.71; cf. the
comments on pp. 74f.). This view, that our inscription provides a fragment of the lost
Greek translation of the Samaritan Pentateuch, was challenged by E. Tov, *Rev. Bib.*
81 (1974) 394-99. He believes that the text used in the Thessalonike inscription was
part of the LXX tradition and provides evidence of revision of the LXX — a revision
which sought to convey the Hebrew more exactly. Tov had earlier suggested (*Rev. Bib.*
78 [1971] 355-83) that the V/VI papyrus fragments of Deut. 24-29 found at
Antinoopolis (*P. Giss. Univ.-Bibl.* 13, 19, 22, 26) were similarly a revision of the
LXX, and therefore part of the LXX tradition, not fragments of a distinct Samaritan
translation written independently of the LXX.

In the biblical quotation we find ΚΣ four times (2, 7, 8, 10) and Ἰ(σρα)ήλ twice (6, 13); McNamee, op.cit. 44, attests the occurrence of ιηλ̄ twice in Greek literary papyri. In the case of ΚΣ̄ the Hebrew text uses the Tetragrammaton on each occasion. Tov argues (1971, p.375) that the use of Κύριος as a rendering of the Tetragrammaton could not have derived from a Samaritan source, since they did not pronounce it as *Adonai* (the equivalent of *Kyrios*); instead they said *Shema* or Ἰαβε when they met the Tetragrammaton. Therefore, the presence of ΚΣ in our inscription is based on the vocabulary of the LXX. That said, the suggestion made above, that abbreviation in Byzantine Jewish texts may reflect a process of 'Christianisation', may not be inapplicable to this inscription as well (cf. Roberts, 33), particularly if Purvis' date of IV-VI is to stand.

The 'God is one' formula at the beginning of the dedication (16-19) is more common in Christian inscriptions, though certainly attested in other Jewish texts (see **68**; cf. *CIJ* Proleg., p. 75, referring to E. Peterson ΕΙΣ ΘΕΟΣ. *Epigraphische, formgeschichtliche und religionsgeschichtliche Untersuchungen* [Göttingen, 1926]). Several examples of the formula were (re)published in 1976, mostly either from Egypt or Palestine: *BE* 756, no.8; *SEG* 1662,1690,1693,1697,1784,1810; note *ll.* 10-11 of the epitaph from Kommagene (325 AD), *SEG* 1617: Εἷς θεὸς ὁ δυνάῃ | τὰ πάντα. Magical texts occasionally include the phrase as well, e.g., D. Wortmann, *Bonn. Jahrb.* 168 (1968) 105, no.7 (amulet, V/VI provenance unknown), εἷς θεὸς ὁ θερα|πεύων πᾶ|σαν νόσον (which appears to be an allusion to Mt. 4.23); 107, no.10 (VII/VIII Fayum), a 'Hausschutz' on wood. The former of these parallels another amulet, *P.Oxy.* 8(1911)1077 (VI), which quotes Mt. 4.23-24 with a very idiosyncratic arrangement of the text upon the sheet of vellum (see pl. 1 in the ed.pr.).

Lifshitz/Schiby accepted as plausible the view of Pelekidis that Sirikios is to be identified with the fourth-century Sophist from Neapolis who taught at Athens. But the fourth-century date of the text posited by Pelekidis and accepted by later discussions depended on this identification. And Purvis has argued that on other grounds the text may well be rather later (see above).

It should be noted that the sense to be applied to τῶν φιλούντων (19) is quite different from that for ἀγαπήσει (9). L. Robert comments on *ll.* 16-19 in *Rev. Phil.* 48(1974) 222, n.249.

In *BE* (1969) 369, J. & L. Robert draw attention to several epigraphical attestations of the word Σαμαρίτης in the Greek world (those dated are II and III). They sound a caution that the word may not always refer to a person who is Samaritan by religious persuasion; Greek settlers from Samaria may be meant.

For a useful bibliography dealing with other Samaritan inscriptions and the Samaritan Pentateuch, see Purvis, 123. Purvis' examination of the Samaritan leads him to conclude that the lack of uniformity in the inscribing of the Samaritan letters, in contrast with the care taken with the Greek, may be indicative of a diaspora community whose acquaintance with Hebrew was limited. H.J. Leon's analysis of the Jewish inscriptions of Rome has shown that while knowledge of Hebrew was not entirely absent, the Roman Jews used Greek so predominantly that 'even in the synagogues the Greek language was employed for the ritual and the Torah readings' *(The Jews of Ancient Rome* [Philadelphia, 1960], 75; cf. 240-41).

With reference to S. Şahin's publication of a fragmentary inscription from a sarcophagus, *ZPE* 18(1975) 35, no.104, J. and L. Robert show, *BE* 684, that the word ἁγιωτάτη refers very commonly to a Jewish synagogue.

A. Ovadiah, *Eretz-Israel* 12(1975) 116-24 (in Hebrew; English summary, 122*; pl.), examines epigraphic evidence for Greek cults at Skythopolis in the Hellenistic and Roman periods, II BC-IIIAD (cf. *SEG* 1906). Several Greek gods are represented in the cults there, most notably Dionysos the patron god of the city. Of the six inscriptions, no.3 (p.120) is a dedication to Zeus Akraios Soter μετ' εὐχαριστίας (*l.*5). For this sense in the NT cf. Acts 24.3, Phil. 4.6, 1 Tim. 4.3f. and other references given by BAGD, s.v., 2. The verb εὐχαριστέω, common throughout the NT, occurs at *ISE* 77.13 (Delphi, 256/5?). S. Freyne includes a brief survey of the situation at Skythopolis in Hellenistic Galilee in *Galilee from Alexander the Great to Hadrian, 323 BCE to 135 CE* (Wilmington and Notre Dame, 1980), 108-113.

SEG 1683, with which this entry began, involved a benefaction to a synagogue. *I.Kyme* 45 (= *CIJ* II.738) may therefore be mentioned here. In this honorific inscription the synagogue members accord particular privileges to a woman who paid for the provision of certain parts of the synagogue.

> Τάτιον Στράτωνος τοῦ Ἐν-
> πέδωνος τὸν οἶκον καὶ τὸν πε-
> ρίβολον τοῦ ὑπαίθρου κατασκευ-
> άσασα ἐκ τῶ[ν ἰδ]ίων
> 5 ἐχαρίσατο τ[οῖς Ἰο]υδαίοις·
> ἡ συναγωγὴ ἐ[τείμη]σεν τῶν Ἰουδαί-
> ων Τάτιον Σ[τράτ]ωνος τοῦ Ἐνπέ-
> δωνος χρυσῷ στεφάνῳ
> καὶ προεδρίᾳ

Tation daughter of Straton, son of Empedon, having built (*or* furnished) the
5 **meeting room and the precinct of the *hypaithros* at her own expense, | bestowed a favour on the Jews. The synagogue of the Jews honoured Tation daughter of Straton, son of Empedon, with a gold crown and seat of honour.**

Originally from Phokaia or Kyme this stone record exemplifies the importance of philanthropy for the continued existence of voluntary associations in antiquity. The honours voted to the benefactor here are two very standard awards recorded often in epigraphic tributes from the Graeco-Roman world: the thorough-going hellenisation of the diaspora synagogue is thus apparent in these last two lines of the text. It is from such honorific contexts that the golden crown imagery in Rev. derives its point (4.4, 14.4; 9.7 seems to have a different point in view). Crowning as a mark of honour is not solely Greek, of course : in the NT cf. Heb. 2.7 (quoting LXX Ps. 8.6), 2.9. It is the award of a *gold* crown that is the distinguishing feature.

Engelmann's note to *l.*9 (p. 112) points out that the place of honour was where the Torah was. He refers also to Mt. 23.6. Cf. Jas. 2.2-3 where, E.A. Judge tells me, the gold ring identifies the man as being of equestrian census, and thus a potential benefactor. οἶκος here (*l.* 2) refers to the room where members assembled. The *peribolos* is an enclosure around the shrine area, the latter being open to the air. Engelmann provides a further bibliography for this inscription, first published just over a century ago. Wealthy women benefactors are by no means unheard of in the Roman period. The longest single text encountered in 1976, *I.Kyme* 13 (actually a series of five decrees), records the city's thanks for the extensive philanthropic aid provided by a certain Archippe (130BC). Cf. the support for Jesus' ministry by women of independent means (Lk. 8.2-3). Apart from Lydia's hospitality (Acts 16.15), Paul seems to have enjoyed the support of women influential in their own cities (Acts 17. 4,12).

70. The 'early Christian' ossuary inscriptions from Jerusalem

Jerusalem   I²/II¹
ed. pr. — E.L. Sukenik, *AJA* 51 (1947) 351-65 (pls), nos. 7 and 8

(7) Ἰησοῦς Ἰουδ[ο]ῦ   (8) Ἰησοῦς Ἀλώθ (*crosses*)

Two of several texts on ossuaries from a Jewish tomb in Jerusalem.
Bib. — *J.P. Kane, *PEQ* 103 (1971) 103-08 (fig.; for further bib. see his p.104, n.3); J. Reynolds, *JRS* 66 (1976) 195, n.281.

(7) Jesus son of Judas
(8) Jesus son of Aloth

The first editor claimed that these provided 'the earliest records of Christianity'. But Kane, having surveyed reactions to this view, argues that the writing on an ossuary will usually merely provide an identification of the deceased. No examples are known where magical formulae, pleas for divine aid, etc., are inscribed in lieu of the name of the dead person (105). As for the crosses in the second text, 'the cross shape of the Hebrew letter Taw was a sign of protection and deliverance used by Jews . . .' (ibid., 107). Kane's conclusion is that 'there is nothing among the finds in this tomb which can be related to the early Christians of Jerusalem. They are the normal contents of a Jewish tomb of the period' (108).

71. Bilingual ossuary inscription

Khirbet Zif, neighbourhood of Hebron   III
ed. pr. — L.Y. Rahmani, *IEJ* 22 (1972) 113-116 (pl. 18-19)

(a) Κυνωρὸς Διο-   (b)   קנרוס בר דוטוס רש(מ)רום
     δό[τ]ου πρω-
     τοπολείτη-
     ς.

The Greek and Aramaic texts above are carefully inscribed, one on either side of a broken ossuary lid, which is also decorated with palm branch, lilies, and wreath. *Bib.* — B. Lifshitz, *Euphrosyne* 6(1974) 44-46; *SEG* 1668; *BE* 737.

(a) Kynoros, son of Diodotos, first citizen,
(b) Kynoros, son of Dotos, head of the masters.

The Aramaic text is a translation of the Greek (see comment on **67**). Kynoros may be a Greek approximation to Semitic Caleb (Rahmani, 115, n.18). The provenance of this text is a district traditionally linked with Caleb (cf. Josh. 15.13-14). Diodotos is a name rarely attested in Palestine (ibid. 114): Dotos in the Aramaic text is a hypocoristic form of it. The epithet π. is rendered by the Aramaic 'head of the masters', or 'head of the citizens'. Usually π. = *princeps civitatis,* 'first or eminent citizen' (cf. LSJ, s.v.). And *P.Oxy.* I (1898) 41 (= Loeb *Select Papyri,* 239) uses the word three times in a late III/early IV acclamation for the prefect Dioskoros (for this text, cf. *BE* (1958) 105). Lifshitz refers to another III inscription, from Volubilis in N. Africa: E. Frézouls, *Acta V Internat. Congress of Gk. and Lat. Epig., Cambridge, 1967* (Oxford, 1971) 287-92 (and pl. 25); cf. *BE* (1977) 726. In the latter text, an epitaph, a certain Caecilianus is described as ὁ πρωτοπολίτης, πατὴρ τῆς συναγογῆς τῶν Ἰουδέων. Clearly he was the leader of the town's Jewish community. In that text the conjunction of the two terms is suggestive of the civic and cultic aspects of the body of Diaspora Jews living in the city (Frézouls, 290). The term, 'father of the synagogue', occurs in nine Jewish inscriptions from Rome, though whether it was merely an honorific one is uncertain: for references — all in *CIJ* — and discussion see H.J. Leon, *The Jews of Ancient Rome* (Philadelphia, 1960), 186-88. For discussion of the term πρωτοπολίτης see C. Vattioni, *Stud. Pap.* 16 (1977) 23-28. It is intriguing that the leader of the Jewish community has a Roman cognomen, one well known at Volubilis (ibid., 288). Caecilianus must be either a Jew who has Roman citizenship — cf. Paul — or a proselyte (Frézouls, ibid.).

72. *Talitha* (?) in a Jewish epitaph

Tiberias, Palestine
ed. pr. — M. Schwabe in M. Schwabe, K. Gutmann (edd.), *Commentationes Iudaico-Hellenisticae in memoriam J. Lewy (1901-1945)* [= *Sepher Johanan Lewy*] (Jerusalem, 1949) 211-216 (in Hebrew; *non vidi*)

Θαλεθθι Μαρα
θυγάτηρ Σαμ-
ουήλ, γυνὴ Λε-
[οντιου ?]

Bib. — M. Schwabe, *All the Land of Naphtali, the twenty-fourth Archeological*

Convention of the Israel Exploration Society, October, 1966 (Jerusalem, 1967), 182 f. (in Hebrew; *non vidi*); *B. Lifshitz *Euphrosyne* 6 (1974) 24-25; *SEG* 1686.

Thaleththi Mara, daughter of Samuel, wife of Le[ontius?].

From this brief text only the fourth line is probably lacking, which contains the rest of the name of the woman's husband. But it is the first word in the text which is of particular interest. It is very possibly a Greek transcription of Aramaic *talitha* (but can the change in final vowel be explained?). In Mk. 5.41 a translation is given for *talitha,* viz. τὸ κοράσιον. Now although girls were married at a young age, it is perhaps curious that the epitaph for Mara should emphasise her youthfulness in this way. Lifshitz suggests that the word may also mean 'young woman', or again that it is a proper name — a pet-name perhaps. If it is not a name then the word witnesses to 'the penetration of Aramaic words in the Greek spoken by Jews' in Palestine (Lifshitz). Mara is attested in Jewish (e.g., *CIJ* I.41, 372), as well as Christian and pagan texts: for references see Lifshitz, 24, nn. 8-10. No date for the text is suggested in Lifshitz or *SEG*.

73. Epitaph for a Jewish Archigerousiarch

Jewish catacomb, Via Nomentana, Rome   III/IV
ed. pr. — U.M. Fasola, *Riv. di Ant. Crist.* 52(1976) 36-37 (fig.15)

> ἐνθάδε κῖτε
> Ἀναστάσιους
> ἀρχιγερουσιάρ-
> χης, υἱὸς Ἀν[ασ-]
> 5 τασίου, οἱ[...

A menorah is drawn on either side of the text. In *l*.1 read κεῖται; the editor thinks the last word may have been intended as ἔτ[ων, followed by a number.
Bib. — *AE* 83; *SEG* 1178

Here lies Anastasius the Archigerousiarch, son of Anastasios, . . .

This is the first occurrence of the term *archigerousiarch* in a Jewish funerary inscription. There has been debate about the organisation of the Jewish community at Rome — see e.g., J.B. Frey, *CIJ* I, intro. pp. lxii-cxliv; H.J. Leon, *The Jews of Ancient Rome* (Philadelphia, 1960) 135-94 — but the *gerousiarch* appears to have been 'the chairman of the executive board of his congregation' (Leon, 183). Fasola suggests (37) that this new term may indicate that Anastasius had authority over the entire Jewish community of the city, or else that it was an honorific title conferred for distinguished service on a *gerousiarch* by his own synagogue. The formation of the word is presumably by analogy with, e.g., *archisynagogos*.

The father's name Anastasios is Greek, but his son has Latinised the spelling. *CIJ* I, index, lists several males and two females (Anastasia) with this name. Leon's analysis of the names of Jews at Rome (93-121), though helpful at times, needs to be used with some caution. Whether Anastasios is distinctively a Jewish and Christian name merits attention. In the case of the latter group were certain names resorted to as a means of mutual identification without attracting attention? More obviously 'Bible' names were becoming common by the fifth century. To the extent that the meaning of a name was consciously considered, Jews called Anastasios will have been ones who held to a belief in resurrection, i.e., non-Sadducees. A detailed onomastic study may help in the differentiation of certain beliefs within Judaism and earlier Christianity.

74. Epitaph for a Jewish Psalm-singer

Jewish catacomb, Via Nomentana, Rome III/IV
ed. pr. — U.M. Fasola, *Riv. di Ant. Crist.* 52 (1976) 19-20 (fig.7)

> ἐνθάδε κῖτε Γαια-
> νὸς γραμματέους
> ψαλμωδὸς φιλό-
> νομος. ἐν ἰρήνη ἡ
> 5   κοίμισις αὐτοῦ.

Above the writing a number of Jewish symbols are drawn. The *'aron* containing twelve rolls of the Torah is flanked by a shofar and a small oil flask on the left, and a menorah and an ethrog on the right. Read κεῖται (1), εἰρήνη (4), κοίμησις (5). *Bib.* — *AE* 79; *SEG* 1162

Here lies Gaianos, secretary, psalm-singer, lover of the Law. May his sleep be in peace.

Most of the symbols above the text occur with reasonable frequency in Jewish inscriptions from Rome. Especially common is the menorah, while the shofar, oil bottle and ethrog (citron) are certainly not rare. See *CIJ* I, index, p. 663; H.J. Leon, *The Jews of Ancient Rome* (Philadelphia, 1960) 195-228. More rarely depicted are the rolls of the Torah, which Fasola interprets (20) as contained in the Ark. Two other inscriptions which he publishes (pp. 25-26 and fig. 10; pp. 26-27 and fig. 11) include drawings of the *'aron* with nine and fourteen rolls respectively. Single rolls are occasionally included, without the *'aron,* e.g., *CIJ* I 193 (so Leon, p.201, correcting Frey's interpretation), 225, 361, 478. No. 520 shows the *'aron* empty with one roll beside it, while 518 has several inside and one beside. Further, there are occasionally depicted what appear to be boxes to contain rolls. Two of these have room for twelve rolls (*CIJ* I.221, 281a); 315 has space for six; others again could take differing numbers (see *CIJ* index, p.663). Pretty clearly the depiction of these scroll boxes is schematic, and the presence of one or many rolls is simply a general symbol of the importance of the Torah. Certainly nothing should be inferred from these sometimes crude drawings about the significance of the number of rolls for, e.g., contemporary views of the OT Canon (which varied in number: O. Eissfeldt, *OT Introduction* [Oxford, 1965] 569, discusses the Canons of 22 and 24 books; for the latter number see especially 2(4) Esdras 14.45, 'Make public the 24 books out of the 94 which were written').

Gaianos does not seem a common name. *CPJ* III lists only one, but that not a Jew. *CIJ* II.770 attests one Jewish woman with the name (Akmonia in Phrygia, 243/4). Gaianos is the secretary of his synagogue congregation. While we know little in detail about the functions of such an official, almost certainly it is not to be equated with 'scribe', the sense found most frequently in the NT. Of the 24 epitaphs from Rome containing this word — Leon's revised tally, p. 183; Frey had 28 in his index — eleven give an age at death: 99(27 years), 125(37 years), 145(70 years), 146(6 years), 148(22 years), 149(24 years), 180(7 years), 284(12 years), 351(50 years), 433(45 years), 456(35 years). Further, one of the two *mellogrammateis* recorded is aged 24(no.121). The striking feature of the list is the youthfulness of several of these people. In no.146 the child is called γραμμα(τεὺς) νήπιος, the latter word being an epithet of the title here; cf. LXX Is. 11.8 παιδίον νήπιον, the only occurrence in the LXX where νήπιος is used as an adjective. In no.284 a child of twelve was '*grammateus* (of the community) of the Augustesii.' Cf. no. 402 where a child less than three years old is designated *mellarchon* of the Volumnesii. Nos. 145, 146 and 149 all concern members of one family. The father Honoratos was a *grammateus* and died aged 70(145). His wife's epitaph is no.150. Their two sons were Rufus an *archon* (146) and Petronios a *grammateus* who was aged 24(149). Rufus' son Honoratos died at 6 years, but his epitaph includes the designation *grammateus* for him. Leon thinks (p.185) that such titles were accorded to deceased children as 'a tribute to their families.' But could it have been that in the early Christian centuries a Jewish son inherited the role of secretary of his synagogue from his father, and was accorded the title in anticipation? Certain families in the synagogue at Rome may have been able to monopolise some of the offices. This problem of official titles accorded to children confronts us elsewhere: *IGAeg.* 9314 (II) is a mummy label recording the decease of Anoubion ὁ καὶ Arion, son of Heron, γυμνασιαρχήσας ἐτελεύτησεν (ἐτῶν) ιαʹ. L. Robert, *Hellenica* 13(1965) 52, has shown that φιλόλογος — as also φιλογράμματος — is an epithet used on funerary texts of children who loved study; q.v. *BE*(1938) 362; *BE*(1965) 180; P. Roussel, *BE*(1926) p.287.

This inscription provides our first epigraphical example of ψαλμωδός, which refers to the deceased as a singer of psalms, cantor, in the synagogue liturgy (Fasola, 20). The word is very rare, LSJ citing only two examples, both from LXX Sirach (II, or perhaps I BC), and the former a *v.l.* — 47.9 (*cod.Sin.*; Heb. has 'harps'), 50.18. This new evidence occasions surprise for it is usually thought that there were psalm-singers only in the Second Temple; not until V, perhaps, does the Jewish song, the *piyyut,* appear. This view is not held universally, however, e.g., *Encyclopaedia Judaica,* s.v. 'liturgy' (as early as the Tannaitic period); 'prosody' (IV-VI). Fasola does not date this particular text although others from the catacomb (including **73,75,76,** in this review) are located as III-IV. Could the catacomb have been used over a wider span of time? Lampe cites three patristic references (Clement, Hippolytus, Gregory of Nyssa) for the use of *psalmodos.* In the late sixth century Gregory the Great decreed the removal to another locality of synagogues where the *vox psallentium* disturbed Christian churchgoers: see S.W. Baron, *A Social and Religious History of the Jews* II (New

York, 1952²), 283. Very infrequent, too, is φιλόνομος. Only one example is offered by LSJ, again an inscription from Rome: *SEG* 4(1930) 144 (= *CIJ* I.11). This text, seen complete a century ago, was later broken in two and the left part only published; the whole inscription was published by H.J. Leon in *AJA* 28(1924) 251-52: ἐνθάδε κεῖτε | Εὔκαρπος νή|πιος, ὅσιος, |φιλόνομος. |ʾΕν εἰρηνη κοίμη|σίς σου. This text may bear on the discussion about *grammateus* above. For the dead person is a child who is pious and loves the Law; or were his parents looking to the future? The epithet νήπιος in the LXX (49 occurrences) is predominantly that of a living child in the earliest stages of life (e.g., Joel 2.16; 3 Macc. 5.50), but it can be used of an unborn or stillborn child (Job 3.16), or of an older child (Ps. 23.13; Sir. 30.12), as well as metaphorically, 'babe in understanding' (Ps. 8.3, 18.8, 118.130). See G.M. Simpson, *A Semantic study of words for Young Person, Servant and Child in the Septuagint and other early Koine Greek* (diss. Sydney, 1976) 81-84. The use of φιλόνομος is confined to the Jewish community, according to *BE*(1951) 55. Virtually synonymous is φιλέντολος, attested at *CIJ* 132(of a female), 203(largely restored), 482(of a female; Latin text: *filentolia*), 509; cf. *BE*(1948) 258 where in a Jewish inscription from Alexandria ἐντόλιος apparently is equivalent in meaning. The epithet occurs on at least one Christian inscription (from Illyria): *BE*(1946/47) 46. Neither of these two rare words from Gaianos' epitaph is indexed in *CPJ,* for they are the sorts of epithets to be added to a funerary tablet memorialising someone, rather than to be found in everyday documents. However, the epigraphical appendix to *CPJ* III (= *CIJ* II.1424-1539), does not list them either. No instances are recorded in *WB* or in the *Spoglio.*

The question of hereditary positions having been raised above, brief mention may be made here of two papyri. *BGU* 2215 (Arsinoite nome, 113/14) is a partial census list of priests and pastophoroi in temples of a certain region. From this text it emerges clearly that a large number of such functionaries was supported at most temples; although some temples lack any priests and those from nearby are required to see to the continuing performance of the religious observances (θρησκεία{ι}ς, col.3, *l.*2). The sense here is different from the usage at Col. 2.18 or Jas. 1.26,27. The census tally does not include minors, but it appears that sons of priests and pastophoroi automatically became candidates for their father's respective offices (see ed. nn. to col.1, *ll.*4, 5). *BGU* 2216 (Soknopaiu Nesos, 156) provides the left-hand side of a papyrus published earlier this century. The document is a report of a request made to the high priest by a father to have his three sons circumcised. He has the necessary civil approval and the high priest, having determined that the boys have no blemishes (σημεῖα, *l.* 25), gives his consent. Ed. n. *ad l.*29 remarks on circumcision as an age-old custom in Egypt.

75. Epitaph for a 'lover of his brethren'

Jewish Catacomb. Via Nomentana, Rome   III/IV
ed. pr. — U.M. Fasola, *Riv. di Ant. Crist.* 52(1976) 11-13 (fig. 3)

ʾΕνθάδε κεῖται
Φίλιππος ὁ φιλάδελφος
ζήσας ἔτη τριάκοντα
τρία.

This small stone is set into the wall beside the place for the deceased. An axe is depicted above the writing.

Bib. — AE 78; SEG 1157

Here lies Philippus, lover of his brethren, who lived thirty-three years.

Such a placement of the epitaph is not common; in Christian catacombs the inscription is usually written on top of the flagstones which cover the tomb (Fasola, 12). The epithet φιλάδελφος (and cognates) occurs in other Jewish inscriptions, e.g., CIJ I.125 (largely restored), 321, 363; 2.815, 1488 (partly restored), 1489. On this basis Fasola regards the text as Jewish. In view of the contexts (e.g., association with words like φιλοπάτωρ, φιλότεκνος) in these examples the word refers to bonds of affection between members of an immediate family. But the word has an older history of course (see LSJ for classical Greek examples; in the Hellenistic world the epithet became a title for Ptolemy II), and was taken over by Jews and Christians, occurring in such writers as Philo and Josephus. 2 Macc. 15.14 is the nearest parallel to the sole NT occurrence at 1 Pet. 3.8, which refers to fellow-believers. Lampe does not record the adjective, but for the noun in -ια the NT sense is perpetuated and predominates.

76. The 'Divine Spirits' in a Jewish epitaph

Jewish catacomb, Via Nomentana, Rome   III/IV
ed. pr. — U.M. Fasola, Riv. di Ant. Crist. 52(1976) 38

> Dis
> Mani[bus]
> Cuspia[e filia-]
> e Cusp[ius]
> pa[ter posuit?]

Bib. — AE (1976) 85

To the Divine Spirits. For Cuspia his daughter Cuspius her father [set this up].

This fragmentary text is said by the editor to be pagan; and certainly there is nothing to make us think otherwise, except perhaps the place of burial. However, the conventional Roman term dis manibus occurs in several Jewish inscriptions, e.g. CIJ I. 524 (probably Jewish, in view of dae maetuenti [= deum metuenti]), 531, 678 (these two definitely Jewish), 287, 464 (these two possibly Jewish; for 287 see n. on p.204

of that corpus); in *CIJ* I Appendix, 63* is a likely candidate for inclusion, since the woman memorialised is Aurelia Sabbatia. (On the name Sabatius/-ia cf. B. Blumenkranz, in *Salo Wittmayer Baron Jubilee Volume,* I [Jerusalem, 1975] 232-33.) H.J. Leon's Appendix in *The Jews of Ancient Rome* (Philadelphia, 1960), 263-346, lists all *CIJ* inscriptions from Rome which he regards as indubitably Jewish. He omits all the above texts except no. 464. For strictures on Leon's selection see B. Lifshitz' *Prolegomenon* to the reprinted *CIJ* I (New York, 1975), 21-23. Further, we have a few recent examples of Christian texts with the same dedication *dis manibus: AE* (1975) 41 (Rome, no date given in *AE), D(is) M(anibus)* in an epitaph for a child who *decesset* [sic] *in pace; AE* 380 (Gaul, no date given in *AE*) begins with *DM,* the text being claimed to be Christian because of the phrase *memoriam (a)eternalem; AE* 434 (Lyon, III init.) is similar: *DM et quieti aetern(ae)* . . . Fifty-nine of the texts from *IMS* — one-third of that corpus — use *Dis Manibus* or some slight variant of it; and there is nothing to make us doubt that any of them are pagan. Of these note 149, $\theta(\epsilon o \hat{\imath} s) \ \Delta(a \acute{\imath} \mu o \sigma \imath \nu)$, and 176, where *DM* occurs, most rarely, at the end of the epitaph.

In the case of *IGLR* 17 (Tomis, III²/IV¹ [= *AE* 616]) it is unclear whether the text is Jewish or Christian. The woman's name is Aur(elia) Sambatis, which suggests that she may be Jewish (see Popescu, n. ad.loc.; cf. *CIJ* I, App. 63*, mentioned above). But *anima(m) re|dedit* (6-7) seems to be a phrase used by Christians (e.g., Diehl, *ICLV* 2.3326, 3328, and other texts printed by him, pp. 173-80). P.W. van der Horst mentions in a note to me that he doubts this statement, and refers to his *The Sentences of Pseudo-Phocylides* (Leiden, 1978), 189f. *(non vidi).* Apart from *DM* at the beginning of the inscription, that text is noteworthy because Aurelia says that she has the *ius (trium) li|berorum* (3-4); the relief above the writing shows three people, of whom two at least are children.

O. Montevecchi refers to an unusual Latin inscription from Salona (III) in her discussion of the 'nomen christianum', in *Paradoxos Politeia. Studi patristici in onore di Giuseppe Lazzati,* edd. R. Cantalamessa and L.F. Pizzolato (*Studia Patristica Mediolanensia,* 10; Milan, 1979) 485-500, at p.490. The text reads: *quitquit [Rom]ani sive Iudei sive Crissi[ani colunt] colent e[t deo]s manis,* 'whatever Romans or Jews or Christians worship, let them also worship the gods below'. For bibliography on this text see Montevecchi, 490, n.9. This orthography should not occasion surprise. Note, e.g., some names on inscriptions in *AE;* Crestio (dat. of Chrestius), 47 (Christian epitaph, Rome, IV); P. Verati P. l(iberti) Cresti (gen. of Chrestus), 220 (Italy, Augustan period); Cresti (probably gen. of Chrestus), 516 (graffito potter's signature on a vase from Germany, Augustan period). The names $X\rho\hat{\eta}\sigma\tau os$ and $X\rho\langle\eta\rangle\sigma\tau\epsilon\acute{\imath}\nu\eta$ occur in a metrical epitaph from Byzantion (*SEG* 788). *IGLR* 10 (Tomis, IV) is an inscribed altar reading ☧ $\Theta v\sigma[\iota a\sigma\tau\acute{\eta}\rho\iota o\nu] \ \chi\rho\eta\sigma\tau\iota[a\nu]\hat{\omega}\nu \ K\acute{v}[\rho\iota\epsilon \ \beta o\acute{\eta}\theta\iota]$, 'altar of Christians, Lord, help!'

There is no particular reason to question *IGLR* 5 (Tomis, III²/IV¹) as being pagan; but it is worth mention because when Aurelia Aemilia provides this bilingual epitaph for her husband, she sets it up *benemeri|to conpari virginio,* for which the Greek given as an equivalent is $\tau\hat{\omega} \ \grave{a}\epsilon\iota\mu\nu\acute{\eta}\sigma\tau\omega \ | \ \grave{a}\nu\delta\rho\grave{\imath} \ \pi a\rho\theta\epsilon\nu\iota\kappa\hat{\omega}$ [sic] (4-5, 9-10). The epithet *virginius/* $\pi a\rho\theta\epsilon\nu\iota\kappa\acute{o}s$ used of a husband is not common, although Popescu (n. *ad loc.*) cites a few Latin examples. *AE* 58 (Rome, IV) is a Christian epitaph in which . . . *c]um virgi[nio suo . . .* clearly means 'with her husband'. In the NT note Rev. 14.4 where $\pi a\rho\theta\acute{\epsilon}\nu o\iota$ is used of men. The phrase *bene merenti* and its variants is fairly common in epitaphs : thirty examples in *IMS.*

77. Some Jewish names (Abraham, Shime'on, Reuben)

N. G. Cohen, *JSJ* 7 (1976) 97-128, considers the problem why certain Jewish names are present in our sources from the Biblical period onwards, while others appear to have an intermittent popularity, sometimes confined to certain geographical regions. Three names and their variants are discussed at some length: Abraham (99-112), Shime'on (112-17), and Reuben (117-28). She suggests that Rufus is to be seen as a Greek/Latin transcription for Reuben (119); cf. Simon for Shime'on. A Rufus is mentioned in a Greek honorific inscription from Kyrene (*SEG* 1825); and Mk. 15.21 shows that the name is known from North Africa. Yet while in this NT passage Simon, the father of Rufus, may without too much hesitation be regarded as Jewish, the name Rufus is not at all uncommon among Romans of the Senatorial class, nor among veterans of the Roman army; and not merely in Africa, but also in Asia, and above all in Rome (as the Index to *CIL* VI makes abundantly clear). It may be that such a name enjoyed an overlapping vogue amongst a number of different national and class groups. Cohen deals at some length (125-28) with another related graecised form, Roube, on two inscriptions from Eumenia in Phrygia (cf. *SEG* 1377). She argues that this is 'virtually the only clearly so-called Jewish name yet found on an inscription from Phrygia' (127), but doubts that he was native to the area. He probably came 'from the semi-Jewish, semi-Christian, oriental urban milieu' of one of the Graeco-Roman cities of the Levant (128; cf. 127).

78. Jews in France in antiquity

In 1972 B. Blumenkranz published his *Histoire des Juifs en France* (Toulouse; *non vidi*); more recently in *Salo Wittmayer Baron Jubilee Volume,* I (edd. S. Ueberman and A. Hayman; Jerusalem, 1975), he has provided a survey of the ancient epigraphical evidence for Jews in France (pp. 229-35). The paucity of inscriptional testimony (compared with that for Rome for example) is in no small part due to the failure so far to discover any certainly Jewish burial place. There is archaeological evidence, however, for the presence of Jews from the end of the first century AD, then III, IV and early V. Blumenkranz publishes an epitaph (end II) from Antibes, ancient Antipolis, discovered last century but largely unknown. While unremarkable in itself — 'Justus, son of Silas, lived 62 years' — it does provide epigraphical testimony of a more probable kind to a Jewish presence there. The two names are associated particularly with Jews (cf. *BE* 798).

E. ECCLESIASTICA

79. Women office-holders in the Church

S. Şahin, *ZPE* 18 (1975) 46, no. 141 (pl.3), published an inscription from a sarcophagus in memory of Εὐγενείας διακόνου (Kirazlı, Turkey); cf. *BE* 684. A palaeochristian mosaic from Patrai in Achaia, first published in 1971 (reported in *BCH* 98 [1974] 625-26 [fig. 116]; *BE* 288), mentions ἡ θεοφιλεστάτη διάκονος Ἀγριππιανή. Further epigraphical and patristic references are provided by Lampe, s.v., C. A woman called Alexandra is described as a ὑποδιακόν(ισσα) in an inscription from Apollonia in Pontus (Thrace), reported in *BE* (1963) 152. The word is not attested in Lampe, although he does list the masculine form, which also occurs in a mosaic text from Beirut (*BE* [1961] 783). An epitaph for Kale πρε(σ)β(ῦτις) is reprinted in *AE* (1975) 454 (Centuripae, Sicily; IV/V). Another with this title is probably referred to in one of the so-called 'Angels of Thera' inscriptions, Ἄγγελος Ἐπικτοῦς πρεσβυτίδος (III-V): H. Grégorie, *Recueil des inscriptions grecques chrétiennes d'Asie Mineure* I (Paris, 1922), no.167; discussed by D. Feissel, *BCH* 101 (1977) 210, 212 (fig. 2, p.211). In an article discussing these 'Angels of Thera' texts, M. Guarducci doubts that this particular text is Christian (*Mélanges helléniques offerts à Georges Daux* [Paris 1974]), 150-52; contra, Feissel. Lampe, s.v., πρεσβῦτις B,2, includes this text as evidence of an office-bearer; for the sense 'elderly woman' (Lampe, s.v., A) cf. 1 Tim. 5.2; Tit. 2.3. M.Nagel, *ZPE* 18 (1975) 317-23, publishes a fourth-century Christian letter which mentions twice (5, 12) a woman called Κυρίαν τὴν διδάσκαλον. See Nagel's discussion, 320-23 (especially n.8). In *l.*11 there is a clear reference to 2 Cor. 13.13: ἡ χάρις τοῦ κ(υρίο)υ ἡμῶν Ἰη(σοῦ) [Χρ(ιστοῦ) μετὰ πάντων ὑμῶν]. On this see Nagel, 318. On the *nomina sacra* here, see 69. E.A. Judge suggests to me that the papyrus might be dated to the time of Licinius. Amongst the legal measures attributed to him during the period leading to the final confrontation with Constantine in 324, and designed apparently to curb the social effectiveness of the churches, is one which separated women from men for purposes of prayer and instruction (*Vita Constantini* 1.53.1). The catechisation of women was not to be done by bishops, but by other women. If we assume the historicity of the legislation (otherwise unattested), and there is no palaeographical obstacle, Nagel's text — inventoried as *P. Stras. Gr.* 1900 — might be assigned to this period.

These texts provide a continuity of evidence for women as office-holders in the Church (note διάκονος at Rom. 16.1).

AE 59 is a fragmentary Christian epitaph in Latin from fourth-century Rome for a man and his wife, the latter probably being the one to whom the epithet *exorcistae* (dative) should be applied. For Jewish exorcists in the NT cf. Acts. 19.13.

A 'Women in Christianity' project funded by the Volkswagen Foundation is under way, headed by Professor H. Küng (Tubingen). An analysis of the relevant non-literary data is to be undertaken by B. Brooten (Institute for Antiquity and Christianity, Claremont Graduate School, California).

80. A deacon's work contract

Provenance unknown early IV?
ed. pr. — J.R. Rea, *CPR* 11, pp. 24-26 (pl. 11)

Ἀμμωνοθέωνι ἐπισκόπῳ [..........
Αὐρήλιος Βῆσις Ἀκώριος ἀπὸ τοῦ . [..........
     (vac.)   χαίρειν. (vac.) [
ἐπειδὴ σήμερον ἐχειροτονήθ[ην εἰς τὴν σὴν
5   διακονίαν καὶ προφοράν σοι ἐξεδ[όμην πρὸς
τὸ ἀπαράβλητόν με εἶναι τῆς ἐπεισ[κοπῆς σου,
διὰ τοῦτο ὁμολογῶ διὰ τοῦδε τοῦ γρα[μματίου μὴ
ἐνκαταλείπειν σε μηδὲ μετέρχ[εσθαι.....
ἐπισκόπου ἢ πρεσβυτέρου ἢ κ[..........
10 μὴ συνπείθοι διὰ τὸ ἐμὲ ἐπεὶ το[ύτοις.....
ἐὰν δὲ θελήσω ἀποστῆναι .[............
σου ἢ καὶ χωρὶς γραμμάτων μ[..........
ρου τυχάνιν δῆθεν ἐγὼ τῆς δια .[..........
λα λαικῆς κοινωνίας μεταξιω .[..........
15 μην σοι τὸ γραμματῖον τοῦτο πρὸ[ς ἀσφάλειαν
καὶ — ὃ μὴ εἴη — ἐὰν πράξω τοῦτο ὑπεύ[θυνος ἔσο-
μαι τοῖς μεταξὺ ὡρισθῖσει καὶ ἐπερ[ωτηθ(εὶς) ὡμολ(όγησα).
καὶ μὴ ἐξε[ῖναι κοι]νωνῖν με μυσ[..........
γενομένῳ .[.....]. στη ἐὰν μὴ σ .[..........
20 τῷ προκειμέν[ῳ.....] (vac.) [
Αὐρήλιος Βῆσ[ις ὁ προκείμ]ενος τέτιμ[αι τὸ προκείμε-
νον γράμμα καὶ ὡ[μολόγ]ησα ὡς π[ρ]όκ[ειται.
Αὐρήλιος Ἱερακίω[ν] ὑπὲρ αὐτοῦ ..[
Μεσορὴ ιβ'.   (vac.) [

The right-hand edge of this papyrus is missing, and with it c.8-12 letters on
most lines. This missing section in the first line may have stated the bishop's
diocese and thus provided a provenance for the text. The restoration at *l*.16 is
virtually certain and thus provides an indication of the length of the lines.
Bib. — K. Treu, *APF* 26 (1978) 158.

To Ammonotheon, bishop . . ., Aurelius Besis son of Akoris, from the . . .,
5 **greetings. Since today I was ordained [into your] | diaconate and made a public**
profession to you that I should be inseparable from your bishopric, because of
this I agree by this document [not] to forsake you, nor to transfer [to the service
of another?] bishop or presbyter or [cleric], | [unless] you assent to it because of
10 **my [making the agreement] on these terms. If I want to leave [without your**
consent] and/or without a written [release, let me be unable] to retain the
diaconate [under you, but (merely)] hold lay fellowship with dignity (?). [I have
arranged] | this document with you for [security] and — may it not happen —
15 **if I do this I [will be] liable to the matters determined between us. And in answer**
to the question, [I have agreed]. And I am not allowed to share in [the
eucharist?] . . . unless . . . | to the aforesaid . . . I, Aurelius Besis, the aforesaid,
20 **have had the aforesaid document made and agreed as aforesaid. [I] Aurelius**
Hierakion [wrote] on his behalf [since he is illiterate]. Mesore 12th.

This is our only Greek papyrus example of what amounts to a formal contract of work between a deacon and his bishop. Coptic ostraca have yielded a number of similar texts (see Rea's introductory note), though none so full as this. The text confirms what was already known, that a deacon was appointed by his bishop (in contrast to priests, who were appointed by the bishop in concert with other priests in the see). Rea notes the general similarity which this text clearly has with contracts for work from other spheres of Egyptian life; see R. Taubenschlag, *The Law of Greco-Roman Egypt* (Warsaw, 1955²; repr. Milan 1972), 373-81. The form of the penalty clauses in this papyrus make this point of contact particularly marked. Although the lacunae leave some room for doubt, the main sanction seems to be that the deacon must return to lay status if he acts in some way without his superior's consent (8-14). Rea believes that the allusion cannot be to a transfer to another diocese, since a deacon being subject to a bishop makes it hard to explain the reference to the *presbyteros* and *k[lerikos]*. He therefore suggests that the papyrus is referring here to the promotion of the deacon to a higher order, and offers μετέρχ[εσθαι εἰς τάξιν] as a supplement in *l.*8. Yet if he is answerable to his bishop, how could the question of a deacon's promotion even arise without episcopal consent? One may note, further, that Lampe's entries s.vv., πρεσβύτερος and κληρικός both attest the meaning 'bishop', in addition to their other possible senses.

The bishop's name incorporates that of a pagan god. This was not felt unusual in the first couple of centuries of the Church (cf. Epaphroditus in the NT); but this attitude does eventually alter. Rea refers to the statement in Eusebius, *de martyribus Palaestinae* 11.8, where Egyptian Christians on trial surprise their judge because they had renounced their birth-name: ἀντὶ τῶν πατρόθεν αὐτοῖς ἐπιπεφημισμένων εἰδωλικῶν ὄντων εἰ τύχοι, μετατεθεικότων ἑαυτοῖς τὰς προσηγορίας, 'in place of the names belonging to idols which their fathers had given them, they called themselves after the names of prophets' (Trans. H.J. Lawlor and J.E.L. Oulton, vol.I [London, 1927], 385; Greek text, ed. W. Dindorf, *Eusebius* IV [Leipzig, 1890]). All five names given are OT ones, and this was very much the fashion among Christians — why is it that names of Christians prominent in the NT were apparently not popularised so quickly? Furthermore, it does seem curious that the Christians did not feel uncomfortable very much earlier in their possession of pagan theophoric names, for names undoubtedly had etymological significance in Graeco-Roman antiquity, whether as a description of a person's condition (e.g. Elektra, Oidipous), or as an indicator of servile status and geographical origin (e.g.., Onesimus, Chrestus, Thratta, Phryx), or as at least implying that something good was hoped for from the child (e.g. Demosthenes, Themistokles). The significance of one's name appears to have diminished in Roman times, however.

In view of the date of the papyrus the verb χειροτονέω (4) probably refers to ordination by the laying-on of hands (see Lampe, s.v., A.3 a,b). But in the NT it means simply 'elect', 'appoint' (BAGD, s.v.). In Acts 14.23 Paul and Barnabas perform this action to mark out πρεσβυτέρους in numerous congregations. At 2 Cor. 8.19 Paul mentions an unnamed Christian brother who is a companion of Titus and was χειροτονηθεὶς ὑπὸ τῶν ἐκκλησιῶν συνέκδημος ἡμῶν — a passage notable for the fact that the electing is done by 'the congregations' and that the man is appointed for a task, not to an office. However, Paul's terminology in this verse may be rather generalised. Rea concedes that the meaning he suggests for ἀπαράβλητον (6) is unattested (elsewhere, 'incomparable'), but it is hard to see how a meaning other than 'inseparable' can apply here; he bases his guess on one meaning of παραβάλλω (LSJ, s.v., VII, 2). The verb ἐγκαταλείπω (8) is attested quite frequently in the NT with the meaning 'forsake, leave in the lurch': Mk. 15.34 (= Mt. 27.46, quoting Ps. 22.2); at Acts 2.27 and 31 the allusion is to Ps. 16.10; Rom. 9.29 (quoting Is. 1.9); Heb. 13.5 (quoting Josh. 1.5 and other OT passages); elsewhere, 2 Cor. 4.9; Heb. 10.25; 2 Tim. 4.10, 16. συνπείθοι (10) is a phonetic spelling for συμπείθη (2nd pers., pres. subj. pass.). ἢ καί (12) is a standard 'and/or' phrase. In *l*.14 μεταξιω looks as though it has to be restored as μετ' ἀξιώσεως (cf. Rea's n.). It is difficult to resolve *l*.18 with confidence: μυσ appears to be μυστήριον, but whether the word 'here refers to the Christian faith in general . . . or to the eucharist . . ., it looks as if the present passage laid down a penalty of exclusion from the church, excommunication, in fact, for some contravention of the contract' (Rea, 26).

This is not the first text to mention an illiterate deacon; and here in any case that has to be inferred from the lacuna in the subscription (23). Rea refers to discussion of illiterate deacons in *RhM* 75 (1926) 426, which deals with *P.Princ.* 55.90, and alludes to *P.Cairo Masp.* 2 (1913) 67128.32 ff.. 'Illiteracy' in such contexts may mean only that the person cannot *write* Greek; the deacon here may have been able to read it, and of course he may have been literate in Coptic. But the point remains: a deacon is probably doing something more practical (e.g., financial responsibilities) than a lector.

The most comprehensive recent survey of the papyrus evidence for the Christian church in Egypt to mid-IV is E.A. Judge and S.R. Pickering, *JbAC* 20 (1977) 47-71, to which this *CPR* text should be added.

81. The earliest attested monk

Karanis   6/6/324
ed. pr. — N. Lewis, *P.Coll.Youtie* 77, pp.519-21

Διοσκόρῳ Καίσωνι πραιπ(οσίτῳ) ε πάγου
παρὰ Ἰσιδώρου Πτολεμαίου ἀπὸ κώ(μης) Καρ[α]νίδος
τοῦ ὑμετέρου πάγου· τῶν θρεμμ[άτ]ων Παμού-
νεως καὶ Ἁρπάλου καταλυμηνα[μέ]νων ἣν
5 ἔχω σπορὰν καὶ μὴν καὶ τῆς β[οὸ]ς α[ὐτῶν] πάλιν
ἐν τῷ αὐτῷ τόπῳ καταβοσκηθείσης ὥστε ἀχρή-
σιμόν μοι τὴν γεωργίαν γενέσθαι, καὶ καταλαβο-
μένου μου τὴν βοῦν καὶ ἀνάγοντος αὐτὴν
ἐπὶ τῆς κώμης ἀπαντήσαντές μοι κατὰ τοὺς
10 ἀγροὺς μεγά(λω) ῥοπάλω καὶ χαμαιριφῇ ἐμὲ ποι-
ησάμενοι πληγαῖς κατέκοψαν καὶ τὴν βοῦν
ἀφείλαντο ὥσπερ καὶ αἱ περὶ ἐμὲ πληγαὶ
δηλοῦσιν, καὶ εἰ μὴ βοηθείας ἔτυχο(ν) ὑπὸ
τῶν παραγενομένων Ἀντωνίνου διάκο-

15 νος καὶ Ἰσὰκ μοναχοῦ τάχα ἂν τέλεόν
    με ἀπώλεσαν. ὅθεν ἐπιδίδωμι τάδε
    τὰ ἔνγραφα ἀξιῶν αὐτοὺς ἀχθῆναι ἐπὶ σοῦ
    καὶ περὶ τῆς σπορᾶς καὶ περὶ τῆς ὕβρεως
    τηρεῖσθαι ἐμοὶ καὶ τὸν λόγον ἐπὶ τοῦ
20 ἡγεμονικοῦ δικαστηρίου ....
    τοῖς ἐσομένοις ὑπάτοις τὸ δ
    Παῦνι ιβ

A petition seeking to have a case of damages and assault brought before the prefect, written in a rapid cursive hand on a well-preserved papyrus sheet which had been folded; verso blank.

Bib. — E.A. Judge, *JbAC* 20 (1977) 72-89; R.S. Bagnall, *P.Col.* 7 (1979) pp.159-60;
    F. E. Morard, *VC* 34 (1980) 395-401.

To Dioskoros Kaiso, superintendent of the fifth district, from Isodoros, son of Ptolemaios from the village of Karanis in your district. The livestock of
5 **Pamounis and Harpalos trampled down |a crop I have and moreover their cow grazed a second time in the same place so that my work became useless. I seized**
10 **the cow and was leading it to the village when they met me in the |fields with a large stick, knocked me to the ground, beat me up and took away the cow, as the injuries on me show, and if I had not (by chance) found help from**
15 **Antoninos, *diakon*, |and Isak, *monachos*, who came along, they would probably have done me in. I therefore lodge this document asking for them to be brought before you and both in respect of the crop and of the assault for my**
20 **claim to be kept for the |prefectural court . . . Under the incoming consuls for the fourth time, on the 12th (of the month) Pauni.**

This is the earliest attestation of the term *monachos* (in its institutional sense of 'monk'), antedating the earliest allusion in ecclesiastical literature (Eusebius, *Commentary on Psalms,* 67.7 [*PG* 23.689B], written in the 330s); it is also the earliest secular reference to a deacon. The only earlier instance of an ecclesiastical position of any kind in a civil document is the 'reader' of *P.Oxy.* 33 (1968) 2665. (E.A. Judge and S.R. Pickering, *JbAC* 20 [1977] 47-71, list and discuss all the papyrological evidence to mid-IV for Christians in the public eye.) The date is of historical importance for two reasons (for the form of the date see L.C. Youtie, D. Hagedorn and H. C. Youtie, *ZPE* 10 [1973] 124).

In the middle of 324 the world was waiting upon the final showdown between Licinius and Constantine. Although Licinius enjoyed the support of (Arian) bishops, he was believed to have introduced a series of measures to break the social power and organisation of the churches (Eusebius, *Vita Constantini* 1.51,53). Given the new patronage Constantine claimed, the victory of Licinius would certainly have been hailed as the vindication of the old gods and would have led to the rapid disestablishment of the churches, to judge by the strength of the community support for the policy of Maximinus only 12 years earlier. Yet the petition of Isodoros (whom we know, from an extensive archive running back well over a generation, to have had nothing personally to do with the churches) shows that Christian institutions were so accepted in the Fayum (firmly within the territory of Licinius) as part of the normal social order, that he can cite them as a matter of course. The titles add nothing to his plea (though the names of the two are no doubt important as witnesses), but equally the reference to them is clearly no handicap to his cause. We cannot say that the Fayum was a backwater where Christianity had been able to flourish unnoticed, since this petition is going to the prefectural court, where the governor of Egypt would sit in person. It must mean that ecclesiastical styles are already the civilly accepted way of identifying people holding positions in church life, even minor ones. This in turn shows how swiftly the great 'sea-change' (Peter Brown's term) of late antiquity was running. The commitment which must have seemed at first to depend upon the arbitrary choice of the ruler was already revealing its deep-seated community character that was to frustrate Julian completely when he eventually attempted to revive the lost cause of Maximinus. The new petition of Isidoros neatly pinpoints the effective establishment of Christendom.

It also throws a shaft of documentary light into the legendary mists surrounding the origin of monasticism and into the modern debate over the meaning of the term *monachos*. The doubts inspired (e.g., in Reitzenstein) by the competition between Athanasius and Jerome to find an early début for monasticism have been progressively dissolved by papyrological finds. The appearance of Isak of Karanis (he is surely a local identity from the way he is referred to) now effectively confirms the date to which Athanasius assigns the creation of the public movement — c.305. An old-timer like Isidoros is hardly going to queer his pitch at the last by flourishing a new-fangled deacon and monk before the prefect. The implication surely is that they were long-familiar figures on the civil scene. The fact that we now have the name *monachos* in a secular document prior to any attestation in the ecclesiastical sources invites a new solution to the problem of its meaning. Whatever the significance of the word as a spiritual and philosophical ideal (thoroughly examined by Morard, *Freib. Z. f. Philos. u. Theol.* 20 [1973] 332-411), may it not be the case that its currency as an institutional term arises from the public reaction to a conspicuous social phenomenon (e.g. the change of dress, or of residence) which called for a new name? See the discussion in Judge, *JbAC* 20 (1977) 72-89, and for the whole body of papyrus evidence for monastic nomenclature in the fourth century see now Judge, *Proc. XVI Int. Cong. Papyrology* (Chico, 1981), 613-620.

                                                                                      (E.A. JUDGE)

82. Nuns as lessors of property

Oxyrhynchos   June/July 400
ed. pr. — M.W. Haslam, *P.Oxy.* 3203, pp.182-84

        μ]ετὰ τὴν ὑπατ[είαν Φλ(αουίου) Θεοδώρου
            τοῦ λαμπ[ρ(οτάτου) Ἐπεὶφ
        Αὐρηλίαις Θεοδώρ[ᾳ καὶ
        Ταύρι{ν} ἐκ πατρὸς Σιλβανοῦ

5 ἀ]πὸ τῆς λαμπρᾶς καὶ λαμπροτάτης

'Ο]ξυρυγχιτῶν πόλεως μοναχαῖς ἀποτακτικαῖς

παρὰ Αὐρηλίου Ἰωσὴ Ἰούδα Ἰουδαίως

ἀπὸ τῆς αὐτῆς πόλεως. ἑκουσίως

ἐπιδέχομαι μισθώσασθαι ἀπὸ νεομηνία[ς

10 τοῦ ἑξῆς μηνὸς Μεσορὴ τοῦ ἐνεστῶτος

ἔτους ο̅ς̅ μ̅ε̅ ἀρχῇ τῆ[ς] τεσσαρεσκαιδεκ[άτης

ἰνδικ[τ]ίονος ἀπὸ [τῶ]ν ὑπαρχόντων

ὑμῖν ἐν τῇ αὐτῇ Ὀξυρυγχιτῶν πόλει

ἐπ' ἀμφόδου Ἱππέων Παρεμβολῆς

15 ἐπίπεδον τόπον ἕνα ἐξέτραν κα[ὶ

τ]ὴ̣[ν] ἐν τῷ καταγείῳ καμάραν μία[ν

σὺν] χρηστηρίοις πᾶσιν, καὶ τελ[έσω

ὑπὲρ] ἐνοικίου αὐτῶν ἐνιαυσίως

ἀρ̣[γυ]ρίου μυριάδας χιλί[α]ς διακοσίας,

20 γί(νονται) (δηναρίων μυριάδες) Ἀς, καὶ ἐπάνα[γ]κ̣[ε]ς ἀποδώσω τὸ ἐνοίκιον

δι' ἑξαμήνου τ̣ὸ̣ ἥμι[σ]υ ἀνυπερθέτως,

καὶ ὁπόταν βουληθῆ̣[τ]αι παραδώσω τοὺς

αὐτοὺς τόπους καθα[ρο]ὺ̣ς ὡς καὶ παρείληφα.

† κυρία ἡ μίσθωσις δισσ[ὴ] γραφῖσα καὶ ἐπερ(ωτηθεὶς) ὡμ(ολόγησα).

25 (*m. 2*) Αὐρήλιος Ἰωσὴ Ἰούδα ὁ προκίμενος

μεμίσθωμαι τὸ συμπόσιον καὶ ἀποδώ-

σω τὸ ἐνοίκιον ὡς πρόκιται. Αὐρήλιος Ἠλίας

Ὀ̣π̣ε̣β̣α̣ί̣ο̣υ ἔγραψα ὑπὲρ αὐτο̣ῦ̣ γράμματα μὴ εἰ̣δ̣(ότος).

This virtually complete papyrus conforms to the pattern of property leases distinctive of the early Byzantine period.

After the consulship of Flavius Theodorus the most illustrious, Epeiph. To
5 **Aurelia Theodora and Aurelia Tauris, daughters of Silvanus, | apotactic nuns (?)**
from the illustrious and most illustrious city of Oxyrhynchos, from Aurelius
Jose, son of Judas, Jew from the same city. Of my free will I accept to lease
10 **from the new moon | of the next month Mesore of the present 76 = 45th year**
at the beginning of the fourteenth indiction, from the property owned by you
15 **in the selfsame city of Oxyrhynchos in the Cavalry Camp quarter, | one ground-**
floor room — a hall — and the single cellar in the basement, with all their
fittings. And for the rent of them I shall pay twelve hundred myriads of silver
20 **annually, | total: 1200 myriads of denarii. And I shall be required to pay the rent,**
half the amount forthwith each six months. And whenever it is wished, I shall
hand back the same rooms clean as I received them. The lease (and) two copies
25 **are valid: and in answer to the question, I have agreed. | (*2nd hand*) I, Aurelius**
Jose, son of Jose, named above, have leased the dining-room; and I will give
the rent as specified above. I, Aurelius Elias, son of Opebaios, wrote for him
since he is illiterate.

This papyrus brings sharply before us the fact of 'nuns' owning a building or part thereof, and entering into financial dealings with another party which will prove income-producing for themselves. On relations between Christians and Jews, see **61.** The text presupposes that the two women live in Oxyrhynchos — whether or not in the house, part of which they are now letting, is unstated — for no-one is acting on their behalf. Commenting on the phrase μοναχαῖς ἀποτακτικαῖς (6), Haslam says: 'Eremitic as opposed to cenobitic monastics were allowed to own property and engage in individual transactions.' This seems curious, for by virtue of the very name accorded them eremitics (or anchorites) ought not to be found together, as is implied by this papyrus, let alone residing in a town, but in groups on their own in the desert. Certainly Oxyrhynchos was full of monastics in this period, but by definition they ought not to be anchorites. Not everyone has accepted Haslam's view: E. Wipszycka reached the opposite conclusion — viz., that *apotaktikoi* are communal monks, in contrast with *anachoretai* — in her publication of a papyrus list of tax payments (367/8), which mentions at *l.*20 an ἀποτακτικ[ός connected with a monastery at Tabennese. See her discussion in J. Bingen, et al. (edd.), *Le Monde grec: pensée, littérature, histoire, documents. Hommages à Claire Préaux* (Brussels, 1975) 625-36 (pl. 18), especially 632-34. The word has also appeared in *P.Oxy.* 46(1978) 3311, a petition (c. 373/4) in which the claim is made that some disputed property was at one time under the control of an *apotaktikos* (*ll.* 4-5, 10). The editor, J.R. Rea, notes the differing views about the meaning of the word, but offers no firm conclusion of his own. An examination of the problem — 'Female Ascetics in the Greek Papyri', by A.M. Emmett — will appear in *Jahrbuch der österreichischen Byzantinistik* 32 (1982): *Akten des XVI. Internationalen Byzantinistenkongresses, Wien, 4-9 Oktober 1981. II. Teil : Kurzreferate.*

P.Vindob.Gr. G. 39847 (in *CPR* [1976]) provides us with the only other papyrus allusion to μοναχαί in the fourth century (unless we are to add women who are called ἀειπάρθενοι, e.g., Didyme in *P. Lips.* [1906] 60; 371?): in this lengthy tax list from Skar in the Hermopolite nome a μοναχή — her name is lost — is listed as a taxpayer. μοναχός occurs also among 1976 texts at *SB* 10926 (VI; provenance unknown). See, most recently, E.A. Judge, 'Fourth-Century Monasticism in the Papyri', *Proc.XVI Internat. Congress of Papyrology, New York, 1980* (Chico, 1981), 613-20, which lists in evidence a total of 17 (plus one possible) texts from the century. A considerable number of these include the term ἀποτακτικός; and of them note especially *P.Herm.Rees* (1964) 9.1-3 (Hermopolis, IV), where Chairemon writes a letter τῷ δεσπότῃ μου πατρί | Ἰωάννῃ ἀποτακτικῷ, requesting John to remember him in his prayers. This calls up the picture of the anchorite as a holy man who is trying to withdraw from things temporal to such a degree that others regard his prayers for themselves as especially efficacious. 'Given that the technical terms for monks seem typically to arise in formal documents, and that formal documents typically relate to property transactions of some kind, it is not surprising that the papyrus record appears to indicate a close involvement of monastics with property (only *P.Col.* 7[1980] 171, and *P.Herm.Rees* [1964] 9 contain no such suggestion). But that hardly invalidates the general picture we have from the literary sources of monasticism as a movement which renounced property. Those who did that will have been the ones who have left no trace in the papyrus record' (Judge, 617). Five of the texts in Judge's list refer to people as 'anchorites': *P.Lond.* 6(1924) 1925; *P.Herm.Rees* (1964) 7,10; *PSI* 13 (1953) 1342; *SB* 8 (1965) 9683. ἀναχωρεῖν without ecclesiastical connotations appears, e.g., in *P.Tebt.* 1099.4 (114 BC), in which tenants on crown land at Kerkeosiris are reported as having withdrawn to a temple at Narmouthis where they can gain asylum. This is a form of industrial action: see further J.G. Keenan's introductory note to the text, p.28; and M. Rostovtzeff, *The Social and Economic History of the Roman Empire* I (Oxford, 1957²), 274. A similar case — cited by MM, s.v. — is *P.Tebt.*1 (1902) 41.14 (119 BC). At *BGU* 2250. 6-7 (Lagis, 161/62 or 163/64) mention is made of farmers who are looking after land in place of those who have abandoned their holdings, ἀντὶ [ἀνακε]|χωρηκότω[ν]. For the verb in a non-ecclesiastical sense in the NT see, e.g., Mt. 2.14, and other references in BAGD, s.v., 2b.

For τὰ ὑπάρχοντα + dative denoting the owner (12-13) there are three NT parallels: Lk. 8.3, 12.15; Acts 4.32. A number of other property leases have been noticed among the 1976 texts. *P.Oxy.* 3200 (II/III) is a five-year lease of half a house, which specifies that upon expiry of the tenancy the building is to be returned, with 'the rooms free from filth and dirt of every kind . . . together with the existing locks and doors' (24-27). Also from Oxyrhynchos is a land lease, *BGU* 2340 (early III). Land suitable for the growing of flax is leased under the terms of *P.Coll.Youtie* 68 (probably Oxyrhynchos, Sept. 266). For the verb κυριεύειν in the two last-mentioned texts, see **24.** From Bacchias comes a rather more complicated document (*SB* 10779; ed. pr. G.M. Browne, *BASP* 7 [1970] 13-16), in which three sisters — acting through their *kyrioi* — allow a man to live in their share (⅑) of a house and courtyard, a proportion of which he already owns, in lieu of paying interest on a loan they have secured from him (13/4/71). The only epigraphical example encountered among 1976 publications is a fragmentary regulation concerning the lease of a garden (Thasos, c.330 BC), republished as *SEG* 1029. *P.Oxy.* 3203 shows that while there were standard clauses in leases from Oxyrhynchos, yet the wording of the agreement may include loose approximations, e.g., συμπόσιον (26) refers to the *exedra* (15), quite possibly because this document is a private arrangement, no officials being involved (24).

It is the *communis opinio* that the σχολὴ Τυράννου of Acts 19.9 refers to a building, viz., a hall used for lectures (so Lake and Cadbury, *Beginnings of Christianity* IV, p.239; Haenchen, *Comm.*, ad loc.). Whether Tyrannos was 'a lecturer or a landlord' (Lake and Cadbury) is unclear. If he were the latter, then documents not very dissimilar to the ones mentioned above will almost certainly have been exchanged, whether or not Paul himself were the lessee, since the apostle made use of the σχολή for two years (Acts 19.10). Yet the word may itself merit closer scrutiny. Of all the references in BAGD which are said to demonstrate σ. meaning a place, only Plut. *Mor.* 42A is beyond dispute. The other passages cited (all literary) are either clearly not referring to a place (e.g., Plut. *Mor.* 519F) or by no means necessarily do so (e.g., Jos. *Apion,* 1.53). Two of the references cited by BAGD (Dion. Hal. *Isoc.* 1, *Dem.* 44) were categorised by LSJ⁸ in this way; but in LSJ⁹, s.v., II.2, they are treated as alluding to groups of people to whom lectures were given. MM seem to imply that in *P.Giss.*1 (1912) 85.14 (Hermopolis: era of Trajan or Hadrian) σ. refers to a building. But again that sense is not required there: the writer asks to be provided with τὰ ἐπι|τήδια τῇ σχολῇ{ς}, οἷον βυβλίον εἰς ἀνα|γεινώσκειν Ἡραιδοῦτι, 'the things necessary for school (for the lecture?), e.g., a book to read for Heraidous.' Lampe, s.v., provides one example where the word means 'room' (Euseb., *qu. steph.* 16.3). Among the papyrus attestations the most common meaning is the primary one, 'leisure, relaxation' (for examples, see *WB* Suppl. 1 Lief.2 (1969), s.v., *Spoglio,* s.v.).

This query about the word may lead us to suspect that σχολή referring to a (lecture) hall, or some kind of building, is so uncommon that unless the context puts the matter beyond dispute we should not take it that way. In Acts 19.9 the preposition ἐν certainly does not require us to think of σχολή as a place. It may be suggested, then, that Paul embarks on his daily discussions and debate (διαλεγόμενος, 19.9) among those meeting under the aegis of Tyrannos. Paul is rubbing shoulders with others who have their own philosophies and *modus vivendi* to espouse. Each was competing for the attention of the same crowd, who by late morning or early afternoon were free of their other commitments and had time to relax and talk. Is there any reason why the noun in Acts 19.9 should not refer to a group of people to whom addresses were given during their leisure hours?

83. Letter from a Christian(?) tenant farmer to his patron

Provenance unknown   late III/early IV
ed. pr. — R.A. Kraft and A. Tripolitis, *BJRL* 51 (1968) 154-58

Κυρίῳ μου πάτρωνι
Διονυσίῳ · Βησαρίων.
Π[ολ]λὰ ἐν θεῷ χαίρειν.
Ἔγραψά σοι διὰ Διδύμου
5   τὴν διάθεσιν τῶν γηδίων
ὧν ‵περ′ ἔγραψάς μοι τῶν ἀποτᾱ(κ)-
των τῆς Πλελῶ καὶ οὐκ ἔγραψάς μοι περὶ αὐτῶν. εἰ τι σοι
δοκῖ ἀντίγραψόν μοι περὶ αὐ-
10   τῶν. καὶ δι’ αὐτὸ τοῦτο οὐκ ἐσχό-
λασα ἀναβῆναι πρός σου. ἀγόραζον σπέρματα ̣̣ · ἔπε[μ]ψα
διὰ τοῦ ἀδελφοῦ μου Συμε-
ώνος [[καὶ ἐπαγάθου]], ἀργυρίου
15   (τάλαντα) ΤΛΑ · τούτων φόρου προβά-
τω]ν τῆς Λιλῆ (τάλαντα) ΞΗ, καὶ ὑ(πὲρ) ἀργυ-
ρέκου φόρου τὰ λοιπὰ (τάλαντα) ΣΞ͞Γ.
καὶ πέμψον μοι τὸν μέλλον-
τα δοκιμάζιν τὰ σίπ’πια·
20   ἐτοίμασαν γὰρ αὐτά. ἔπεμ-
ψα δὲ διὰ τοῦ αὐτοῦ φοινίκια
πεταλίδια τέσ’σερα. οἱ δὲ τά-
κτονας εἰ μὴ μίαν κυκλάδᾱ(ν)
οὐκ ἐποίησαν. Πανηφ ̣ ̣ ̣ ̣ ̣ ση καὶ
25   Πασοῆρις μόνοι ἐποίησαν τὴν ᾱ(ὐτήν).
Ἐρρῶσθαί σε εὔχομαι πο̣λλοῖς
χρόνοις.

Numerous grammatical forms need resolution in this well preserved papyrus letter. At the end of *ll.*6, 23, 25 a horizontal bar above the final letter indicates abbreviation of the rest of the word. Apostrophes occur at *ll.* 16, 19 and possibly 22. The numbers in *ll.* 15-17 are not certain.

Bib. — *SB* 10800

To my lord patron Dionysios, Besarion: many greetings in God. I wrote to
5 **you via Didymos about |the disposal of the pieces of land concerning whose**
fixed rents at Plelo you wrote to me, but you did not write to me about them.
10 **If you think it a good idea write back to me about them. |And for this very**
reason I did not have the leisure to come up to you since I am buying seed. I
15 **sent via my brother Symeon [[also an honest man]] |331 talents of silver: of this,**
for rent of sheep at Lile, 68 talents; and the remaining 263 talents for rent in
20 **cash. And send me the man who is going to examine the hemp, |for I have it**
ready. And I sent via the same man four small dishes made of palm-wood. The
25 **carpenters made only one water-wheel: Pamphrese(?) and |Pasoeris made it on**
their own. I pray you will be well for a long time.

Is this a Christian letter? The editors seem to imply that it is: 'The opening and closing formulas (*ll.*1-3, 26-27) can be paralleled widely in Christian letters from the third to fifth centuries' (art. cit., 155). Certainly the presence of ἀδελφός (13) offers no real confirmation (see 18). S.R. Pickering tells me that to his knowledge the phrase ἐν θεῷ in a greeting does not occur in any private letter which is definitely non-Christian. As with *nomina sacra,* then, the presence of the phrase in this period should normally be a clue to the letter's Christian association. Rather less stress should be placed on the closing formula, however, as an indicator of a Christian authorship.

A number of features occurring in this letter have been noticed in other entries in this review. For the name Didymos (4), see **52.** Patron/client relationships have been represented in several other letters: **16, 19, 21.** Here Besarion — who appears to be leasing cattle and land from Dionysios — is offering to his *kyrios* and *patron* an account of the property under his care. The two villages mentioned (7,16) are in the Oxyrhynchite nome. Other texts in this review have mentioned the need to find a reliable courier to convey a letter or money (e.g., **17**); and here Symeon appears to be held in considerable trust. But the erasure in antiquity of the words καὶ ἐπαγάθου (14) is curious. A scribe might remove a mistake, or wish to alter his sentence; but why excise a commendatory epithet accorded to a man who is clearly regarded as reliable anyway?

Of words also found in the NT, a few may be listed here. For adversative καί (7) see Mt. 12.43 and other references in BAGD, s.v., 2g. The NT does not employ σχολάζω absolutely, as here (10-11). For ἀναβαίνω πρός σου (read σε) (11) cf. Acts 15.2. The form ἀγόραζον (11-12) may be imperfect, or a nom. pres. participle. In its literal sense the verb is fairly common, mainly in the Gospels. δοκιμάζω (19) is frequent in the NT, although usually with a personal object. ἑτοιμάζω τι (20), frequent in Synoptics.

84. A unique mention of Lent in a papyrus letter

Provenance unknown   IV

ed. pr. — G. Vitelli, *PSI* 7(1925) 831, pp. 134-36

κυρία [μο]υ μητηρ Συρα ..[.]
Εὐθάλις καὶ Μικης πολλὰ χαίριν.
πρὸ μὲν πάτων εὔχομαι τὴν
.ην ὁλοκλ[ηρία]ν σου παρὰ τῷ
5   κυ(ρίῳ) θε(ῷ). αἰθέλαισαν ἐλθῖν προσαι
πρὸ τῆς ἱορτῆς [καὶ] κατέσχε μοι
ἡ] ἀδελφή μου Μίκη, λαίγουσάν μου
ἵ]να φθάσῃ πρὸς τὴν μητέρα ἡμῶν
πρὸς τὴν λύσην τῆς νησίας.
10   ἐκτίνασον τὰ .ρόματα τὰ ἰς τὸ σφυριδὸν·
π]ροσδόκα τὴν ἀδελφή μου. ἔρχομαι πρό-
ς τῇ ἱορτῇ. αἰθέλαισα πέψο τινα ἵνα
ἔ]χοις αὐτὰ πρὸ τῆς νισίας καὶ οὐδάν-
α ἔχ]ω ἀνακέων ἄνθροπου. εὐθυμ-
15   ο]υ περὶ το[ῦ ν]αύλου Μίκκαις,
ὃ ἔ]χων δοῦναι ἀντὶ ὑμῶν.
ἀσπ]άδωμαι ὑμῖν. Νόνα ἀσπάδεται
ὑμᾶς] πολλὰ. Σιλβανὴ ἀσπάδαιται ὑμῆς.
Ἀννοῦτις καὶ Θεωνίλας καὶ Ἰσχυρίων
20   ἀσπαδωμαι ὑμᾶς. Ἀπίων' ἀσπάδωμαι καὶ τὸν' αἰπιστάτην καὶ τὴν σύ-
βιων αὐτοῦ καὶ τὰ πεδα. καὶ ἐγὼ Μίχη
ἀσ[π]άδωμαι τὸν αἰπιστάτην σὺ τοῖς
τέκνυς καὶ την συβίῳ αὐτοῦ.
25   γράφε σὺ οὖν Καλα.ἱδα περὶ τοῦ
κλυκυου τέκνον ὅτι νικηται. οὐδὲν δυνάμηθα πρὸς τῶν θάνα-
τον · οἶδες καὶ σὺ ὅτι α......εὔχομαι
σι καὶ ὁ οἱιο μου Δωρόθαιος. ἀσπάδωμαι
30   τὸν κύριώ μου πατέρα. Φαρμοῦτι ᾱ.
ἐ[ρρῶ]σθαί σαι εὔχομαι π[ο]λλοῖς χρόνοις.

     The Greek of this letter is so full of error that Rea, who re-edited it (see bib. below), has placed alongside it 'a corrected version preserving the normal characteristics of the late vulgar Greek that the author intended to write' (Rea, 357). Read αι for ε, ι for ει.

Bib. — *J.R. Rea, *Chr. d'Ég.* 45 (1970) 357-63; *SB* 10840 (includes Rea's 'corrected' version as well as the re-edition).

       To my lady mother Syras (?), Euthalios and Mikke, many greetings. Before
5   **everything I pray for your good health before the | Lord God. I wanted to come**

10   to you before the festival but my sister Mikke restrained me, telling me, 'Go to our mother for the end of the fast.' | Shake out the aromatic herbs in the basket. Await my sister. I am coming for the festival. I wanted to send some things so you would have them before the fast but I have no trusty person. Cheer up

15 | about Mikke's fare for the trip, which I can give her instead of you. I greet you. Nonna sends you many greetings. Silvane greets you. Annoutis and Theonilla

20   and Ischyrion | greet you. I greet Apion, and the overseer and his wife and children. And I, Mikke, greet the overseer along with his children and his wife.

25 | So write to Kala ... idas about his sweetest child that he should endure it. There is nothing we can do against death. You know as well that ... I pray for

30   you as does my son Dorotheos. I greet | my Lord Father. Pharmouthi 1. I pray you will be well for a long time.

Despite the second line this letter is clearly just from Euthalios to his mother; at *l*.22 Mikke has her own greetings added. (No mention is made in *ed. pr.* or Rea's re-edition of a second hand here.) Rea re-dates the letter to the fourth-century (*ed. pr.* — V/VI), on the basis of the lettering, but also on the basis of the simple style, uncharacteristic of Byzantine letters. The date at *l*.31 is 27 March, and so 'it is an obvious conclusion that the fast [9] and the festival [12] which the writer records are *Lent* and *Easter*' (Rea, 357). Rea thinks that the allusion to Lent may be unique in the papyri, although he lists two other, doubtful, candidates. In the fourth century Lent was 'not a forty day fast but confined to Holy Week' (Rea, 361). The style of salutation and especially the *nomen sacrum* at *l*.5 (cf. **69**) confirm the Christian association in this letter. The familial terms in the letter do seem to be used with reference to blood-relations (cf. **18**); but the extended list of greetings (17-24, 29-30; cf. **15**) apparently includes friends at the sender's end known to the recipient and others at her end. Whether a Christian circle at either end is in view is impossible to say.

Rea, 360-63, offers useful philological notes on the text. Some words and constructions may be noted here. ὁλοκληρία (4), only at Acts 3.16 (MM offer several other papyrus examples). Read πρὸς σέ (5). For imperatival ἵνα + subj. (8) see BDF § 387.3; BAGD, s.v., III.2. offer bib. and several NT references, including Mt. 5.23 and Lk. 5.33. φθάνω (8) seems to require the meaning 'go' here; cf. comment on the verb in **15**. λύσις (9), not in this sense in NT; and, naturally, νήστεια in NT lacks the specific meaning implied here (9). Read ἐθέλησα πέμψαι (12; cf. 5). ἔχοις (13) may be a genuine optative, or simply a phonetic variant for ἔχῃς (Rea, 361). For adversative καί (13, [6]) see comment at **83**. ἐκτινάσσω (10) occurs at Mt. 10.14 and parallels, Acts 13.51, 18.6; while ἀρώματα — if it is the right word at *l*.12 — does not occur in the same sense in the NT — certainly the context is very different from the Passion narrative. The NT uses σπυρίς, a variant of the diminutive σφυρίδιον (10). Acts 10.24 is the only occurrence of ἀναγκαῖος related to the usage in this letter (14), but even so the meaning is probably to be differentiated somewhat. For the meaning here see LSJ, s.v., II.1. αὐθυμέω intrans. (14), cf. Acts 27.22, 25; Jas. 5.13. In *l*.20 Rea thinks that Ἀπίων' could be nominative, 'I, Apion, greet ...'. In his corrected version Rea interprets the verb in *l*.26 as ἐνείκηται, aor. midd. subj. of φέρω, 'let him endure it'. Read υἱός (29).

85. A Christian complains about an assault

Oxyrhynchos?   IV
ed. pr. — G. Vitelli, *PSI* 8 (1927) 972, pp. 180-81.

κυρίῳ μου ἀδελφῷ Γονατᾷ γεούχῳ Ἀντωνῖ-
[ν]ος πλεῖστα χαίρειν. πρὸ μὲν [π]άντων εὔχομαι τὴ(ν)
ὁλοκληρίαν σου παρὰ {παρα} τῷ κυ(ρίῳ) θ(ε)ῷ ὅπος ὁλοκληροῦ(ντά)
σε ἀπολάβω. ἀσπάζωμαι τὰ ἀβάσκαντά σου τέκνα.
5   γινόσσκειν σε θέλω, κύριέ μου πάτρων, ὅτι μέμφις
μοι περὶ τοῦ καμηλάτης σου ὅτι ὕβρικεν ἡμᾶς.
ἐγὼ δὲ ὕβρικα Τιθοῆν ἐκ λόγου῾ς, οὐ μετὰ ῥαὺ βδίν,
ἀλλὰ ἐκ λόγους. τί οὖν ἔχει πρᾶγμα ὁ Πάντηρ ἐμένα ὑβρίσε{ν}; ἐγὼ γὰρ ἐτήρησα τὴν φιλείαν σου τὴν
10   ἀρχέα[ν], καὶ μέχρει σήμερον ἔχω πάλειν τὴ(ν)
.[.]ν φιλίαν. εἰ μὲν σὺ θέλεις ἀποσπάσῃς τὴν φι-
λ[ί]αν, ἔστω. γνῶτι οὖν ῾ὅτι῾ οὐδὲν αὐτῷ τῷ Πάντηρι
ἐποίησα διὰ σέ. οὐκ ἐξῖς γὰρ δραπέτων καὶ ἀγενὶς῾
ἄνθρωπων῾ ὑβρίδι τὸ⟨ν⟩ κω⟨μ⟩ψώτερον αὐτοῦ. διὰ σὲ ταῦ⟨τα⟩ ἡμῖν ποιοῦ῾-
15   σιν. ἐὰν ὑβρίσω Τιθοῆν ἐξῖς [[αυτω]] μοι αὐτῷ{ν} ὑβρίζω καὶ αὐτὸς ἐμένα, ἐπιδὴ συν῾κληρονόμος μού {ε}
ἐστιν. ὁ ἀγενὶς γὰρ οὐκ ἐξῖς μοι ὑβρίδι, ἐὰν μὴ {ε}
ἐπιστρέψῃς αὐτῷ. γνῶτι οὖν῾ ὅτι δύναμε αὐτῷ
πεδεύσω. ἐγὼ διὰ σὲ οὐδὲν αὐτῷ ἐποίησα μέ-
20   χρι σήμερον καὶ ἐὰν ἔλθῃς δύνῃ{ς} μαθεῖν ἀπὸ
τοῦ ἀδελφοῦ αὐτοῦ. ἐρρῶσ{σ}θαί σοι εὔχομαι πολλοῖς χρόνοις.
κύριέ μου ἄδελφε.

Downwards along the left margin across the fibres:—
ἐγὼ γὰρ τὰ ἐμὰ ἐσήτησα, οὐκ ἃ ἀλλότρια ἐγδῶ-
25   μεν. ἀφῆκα τὸ πρᾶγμα ἔστ᾽ ἂν ἔλθῃς.

verso, downwards along the fibres:—
ἐὰν δὲ ἀκούσῃς τοὺς καμηλάτης σου, οὐκέτι φιλι-
ασησ.. μετα ἄνθρωπον τὸ οὐδὶς ἐποίησεν.
λέγω{ν} σου [[μαλλων]] μᾶλλων μὴ ἄνα ἀκούσῃς
αὐτοῖς ἔστ᾽ ἂν ἔλθῃς.

verso, upside down, upwards along the fibres:—
κυρίῳ μου ἀδελ Χ φῷ Γονατᾷ
π(αρὰ) Ἀντωνίνου

This virtually complete papyrus letter is full of grammatical and spelling errors. This causes some sections to be obscure, even apart from the allusiveness with which the writer presents his grievance. Read ω|ο, α or ι for η, ι for ει.

Bib. — Naldini, no.64, pp. 267-70 (further bib. cited at 267); *J. R. Rea, *Chr. d'Eg.* 45(1970) 363-68; *SB* 10841.

To my lord brother Gonatas the landowner, Antoninos, very many greetings. Before everything I pray for your health before the Lord God that I may receive you back in good health. I greet your children — may they be immune from the
5   evil eye. |I want you to know, my lord patron, that I have a complaint about your camel-driver, because he attacked us. I myself did attack Tithoes verbally — not with a stick, but verbally. Therefore, what business is it of Panther to
10   attack me? For *I* maintained your long-standing friendship, |and to date I have your friendship still (?; *lit.,* again). If *you* want to withdraw your friendship, so be it! Realise, therefore, that because of you I did nothing to Panther himself. For next time the base runaway won't assault a man who is more refined than
15   he. It is because of you they do these things to us. |If I assault Tithoes next time I make an attack on my very self; indeed I myself attack myself, since he is joint-heir with me. For the base fellow will not attack me next time (even) if you don't turn against him. So realise, then, that I am able to teach him a lesson. For your
20   sake I did nothing to him |to date, and if you come you can learn (the truth) from his brother. I pray you will be well for a long time, my lord brother. (P.S.) For I strove to retain my own property not things which we surrender as
25   belonging to another. |I have let the matter rest until you come. *(Verso)* If you listen to your camel-drivers no longer your friendship (?) with men (?), which no-one did. I tell you, rather, not to listen to them until you come. To my lord brother Gonatas from Antoninos.

The situation alluded to in this letter appears to be that Panther, a camel-driver in the employ (?) of Gonatas, has assaulted Antoninos, apparently in retaliation for a tongue-lashing which the latter gave to Tithoes. To his physical assault Antoninos reacted only verbally but was very offended. He took no stronger action against Panther out of deference for his friendship with Gonatas. Antoninos airs his grievance fairly allusively in this letter to Gonatas, and warns that next time he will act, not just use words, against Tithoes.

As with the previous entry a number of indicators make certain that this is a Christian letter: the opening salutation (on ὁλοκληρία see **84**; the verb does not occur in the NT) and use of the *nomen sacrum* (*l.*3; cf. **69**) are probably sufficient alone. But in addition in this letter the writer addresses Gonatas as both 'my lord brother' *(l.*30) and 'my lord patron' (5). The latter shows that the two men are not siblings and that the use of ἀδελφός in these lines indicates social relationship (cf. **18**). The presence of capital *chi* in the middle of the word ἀδελφῷ (30) is a further sign. This letter was not printed by Vitelli in the *ed. pr.;* but Naldini and Rea both include it. One further phrase, συνκληρονόμος (16), deserves consideration in this context. Naldini considers that there is an allusion here to the dispute referred to, Rea that the passage is cryptic (p.363). Is the sense here that Antoninos and Tithoes are joint-heirs of some estate or is it an allusion to their both being Christians? MM know no pre-Byzantine papyrus examples of the word, but refer to Deissmann, *LAE,* 92, for an inscription (Ephesos, imperial period) which speaks of a man's wife as his joint heir. Deissmann, ibid., refers to another inscriptional example of the same period from Thessalonike. This papyrus letter, then, provides our earliest non-literary epistolary parallel to the four occurrences in the NT. In three of these, Eph. 3.6, Heb. 11.9, 1 Pet. 3.7, the word is followed by a genitive of thing, and the meaning of each case must be 'heirs together of something'. But at Rom. 8.17 the word is followed by a gen. of person (Χριστοῦ), and the preceding phrase, κληρονόμοι μὲν Θεοῦ, requires the word to mean 'heirs together with Christ'. The phrase in our papyrus letter, then, ought to mean 'since he is an heir together with me'. What Antoninos meant by saying he harms himself if he attacks Tithoes since they are joint-heirs is obscure, but it is not impossible that in a Christian letter, such as this is, it serves as a allusive reference to their common bond as believers. This suggestion ought not to be pressed, but it is worth ventilating.

The links between Christians provides one level of relationship in this letter. Another is that between patron and client. This subject has been referred to elsewhere in this review **(16, 21)**. This letter draws attention to the importance of friendship in such a context (cf. **19**). For discussion of the cessation of friendship, clearly alluded to in this papyrus at *ll.* 11-12, see P. Marshall, *Enmity and other Social Conventions in Paul's relations with the Corinthians* (Diss. Macquarie, 1980), 35-40. A complicating factor here, however, is that φιλία ought to exist between social equals, but the whole tone of this letter is that Gonatas is the social superior of Antoninos. As the letter bears out by its general tone, once relationship is established between two people it can only be one of friendship or enmity. Friendship cannot simply dissipate into nothing, but has to be actively withdrawn and this creates a relationship of enmity. ἀποσπάω (11) is not found in the NT with quite this sense. Note how Antoninos clearly does not want to lose his relationship of φιλία with Gonatas: the use of the adjective ἀρχαῖος (10) is clearly intended to pressure Gonatas into retaining φιλία. For the epithet in this sense, 'of long standing', cf. Acts 21.16. Several other words in the letter offer indications of status differentiation: δραπέτης (13; Rea, 366, says that the writer regarded δραπέτων as nom. sing.); ἀγενής (13, 17), for which MM offer little. The one NT occurrence, 1 Cor. 1.28, is a neuter plural which in its context probably refers to people and is thus being used there also as a status word. In contrast to these two words, Antoninos implies that he is κομψώτερος (14). The NT uses the comparative adverb at Jn. 4.52, where the sense required has nothing to do with status.

Some other words present in this letter may be mentioned briefly. For the construction used with ἀπολαμβάνω here (4), cf. Lk. 15.27. The meaning there may fit here in view of Antoninos' expectation that Gonatas will come to see him (25, 29). On ἀβάσκαντος (4), see **24**. Rea reads μέμψις for pap. -φις (5), found in the NT only at Col. 3. 13D. ὑβρίζω (6, 7, etc.) is found in numerous places in the NT, as is τηρέω (9), ζητέω (24: see BAGD, s.v., 2a), and ἀφίημι (25; cf. BAGD, s.v., 4). The diminutive force of ῥαβδίον (7) — in ECL only in Hermas — is not felt here. For θέλεις + subj. Naldini (269) refers to Mt. 13.28; cf. Jn. 18.39 and BDF, § 366.3. Rea points out that the literal translation of *ll.* 17-18 is illogical, and suggests κἂν μὴ ..., 'even if . . .' BAGD cite several NT examples of παιδεύω (19) used figuratively, s.v., 2b; of these none is exactly parallel with a context such as this letter gives. Note δύναμαι + aor. subj. (18-19). Neither the NT nor other ECL uses ἐκδίδωμι in the sense required here (24-25). *Ll.* 27-28 are very difficult to restore confidently. Rea offers a number of alternatives, including φιλία σή, μετὰ ἀνθρώπων which have been rendered in the translation above merely *exempli gratia,* not because they make real sense out of the passage. For μὴ ἵνα = ἵνα μή (28) see Rea's n. on p.368.

86. The Eumenian Formula with a cross

Upper Tembris Valley, N. Phrygia   early IV
ed. pr. — E.P. Gibson, *BASP* 12 (1975) 151-57 (pl.)

Cross

A(ὐ)ρ(ηλίου)
μνῆμα Εὐστ-
αθιαν-
οῦ μακελάρει-
5   ως κὲ εἴ τι-

ς εἰπιβουλε-
ύσι ἔ[[σ]]τη αὐ-
τοῦ πὸ[[σ]] τῶν
παντωκράτ-
10   ωρα θεόν.

The text above represents a second use of the stone. In *ll.* 1-4 the name and occupation have replaced another name, Abaskantos; for discussion of this name see **24.** A cross is carved above the text.
Bib. — BE 675

Monument of Aurelios Eustathianos, butcher. And if anyone contrives anything against it he will be answerable to the all-powerful God.

This inscription provides a late example of the so-called 'Eumenian Formula', ἔσται αὐτῷ πρὸς τὸν θεόν, a third-century warning quite frequently found on tombs from Eumenia, and in some other parts of Phrygia. Although pagan in origin and although it was used occasionally by Jews (an example is given in **61**), nevertheless the formula has normally been seen as a cryptic indication that the deceased was a Christian in a period before Christianity became legalised. The texts would thus provide evidence for the expansion of the Church in the third century. Dated occurrences are confined to the period 246-73; only one other text is known from Northern Phrygia (W.M. Calder, *Anat. Stud.* 5 (1955) 36, no.5). What makes Gibson's inscription unique is the presence of the cross on the stele together with the formula. 'It is one of the earliest occurrences of the cross on an orthodox (i.e., non-Montanist) monument' (Gibson, 155). Use of the cross by orthodox Christians is rare before mid-IV; it flourished in the post-Nicene period. Also unique to the formula is the verb ἐπιβουλεύειν.

The butcher's trade was of special significance to the Christian communities, since most meat reached the meal table via pagan ritual ceremonies and sacrifices (cf. Acts 15.29; contrast 1 Cor. 10.20-29). Gibson, 155, n.10, mentions five other epitaphs for Christian butchers from three places.

The epithet of God, παντοκράτωρ, was largely a Jewish usage (in NT cf. 2 Cor. 6.18 — an LXX quotation — and nine times in Rev.), and not common in Christian epigraphy until IV AD. Another indication of date may be the mistaken use of cases (according to Gibson, 154, with n.3), But μακελαρείως (nom.) instead of -είου is probably simply a slip, or carelessness of the kind seen repeatedly in the papyri; while as for αὐτοῦ, genitive for dative, the loss of the dative starts generally in Koine in I BC. C.J. Hemer in a note to me suggests that the irregular phonetic spellings where vowels differ — ἔστη for ἔσται (7) — and such features as πός for πρός (8) indicate that the text is characteristically Phrygian Greek, erected by Phrygian speakers.

Fuller treatment of the Eumenian formula will be reserved for discussion of the texts in E.P. Gibson, *The 'Christians for Christians' Inscriptions of Phrygia* (Missoula, 1978), in a later volume of this review. Bibliography for the subject: W.M. Ramsay, *Cities and Bishoprics of Phrygia* I, 2 (Oxford, 1897) 484-538; W.M. Calder, *Anatolian Studies Presented to W.H. Buckler* (Manchester, 1939), 15-26; idem, *Anat. Stud.* 5 (1955) 25-38; idem, *MAMA* 7 (1956) intro. p.xxxvii; L. Robert, *Hellenica* 11-12 (1960) 393-413, 429-39.

87. Two Christian bankers

a. Syracuse   b. Ephesos   a. Advanced Imperial Times;   b. V
ed. — a. IG XIV.88; b.H. Grégoire, *Recueil des inscriptions grecques-chrétiennes
d'Asie Mineure,* I (Paris, 1922; repr. Amsterdam, 1968), 29 no.98 *quater.*

(a)   ἐνθάδε κῖ-
      ται Βονι-
      φάτις παῖς
      Εὐσεβίου τοῦ
5   τραπε(ζίτου) κοιμη-
      θεὶ⟨ς⟩ πρὸ α' ἰδ(ῶν)
      Νοβενβρί(ων).
                P

(b)   † Ἡρῷον διαφέρον †
      Ἰωάννῃ τῷ ⟨ἐ⟩δ⟨ε⟩σι⟨μ⟩(ωτάτῳ)
      τραπεζίτῃ κὲ ἀργυρο-
      πράτῃ. †

Bib. — **I. Bankers* 19, 20, pp.21-22 (further bib. provided there)

**a. Here lies Bonifatios, child of Eusebios the banker, who fell asleep on the day
before the Ides of November.**
b. Tomb belonging to Johannes the very respected banker and dealer in silver.

With the Christianisation of the Roman Empire it became the norm to add a cross
or some other Christian symbol even on perfectly mundane administrative documents.
Similarly the introduction of distinctively Christian names (as in these epitaphs) soon
became conventionalised.

Words meriting brief comment here are all confined to Johannes' epitaph. In the
classical Greek period a *heroeion* was a shrine for a hero; but by at least the third
century AD the word was coming to mean merely a tomb for an ordinary individual.
In the sense in which it occurs here, 'belong to' + dative, διαφέρω is not found in the
NT or the Fathers; see *LSJ,* s.v., III.8. The adjective αἰδέσιμος is an honorific epithet
frequently used in the Byzantine period, according to L. Robert, *Hellenica* 11-12
(1960) 51, who holds that it appears to accord with the status of a *zygostates,* a public
weigher. Such an office may well fit with a man who is by profession both a banker
and a silver merchant. Although the same man often carried on both these trades, the
two words are not synonymous. Thus R. Bogaert, *Ancient Society* 4 (1973) 263, n.146,
points out that a slave could be an ἀργυροπράτης but not a τραπεζίτης.

The date of (a) is given in Roman style and equates with 12 November.

88. A new phrase referring to baptism

A Latin metrical epitaph for an infant from Julia Concordia (Venice), discovered
in 1961 and published the following year, has been re-examined by A. Degrassi, *Scritti
vari di antichità,* III (Venice, 1967), 345-52 (photo opposite p.352); cf. *AE* 243. The
inscription consists of four elegiac couplets, followed in ll. 9-10 by ΑΡΩ and part of
a date (late IV/early V). In *l.*2 the phrase *nova lux animae* occurs for the first time
as a periphrasis for Christian baptism. On this text note most recently A. Grilli,

RCCM 20(1978) [1980] 953-55. P.L. Zovatto, *Epigraphica* 8 (1946) 84-90 — referred to by Degrassi — reprints four inscriptions from the same city which include the word νεωφώτιστος used of recently-baptised people (*IG* XIV, 2325, 3226, 2328, 2334 = *CIL* V, 2.8725, 8727 [8728, wrongly, Zovatto, 88, n.17, followed by Degrassi, 347, n.7], 8729, 8732).

IGLR 428(V-VI?) is an inscription engraved inside a circular gold vessel, which appears to be referring to baptism: Ρ δεὰ (= διὰ) ὕδατος ἀνάπλυσον Κ(ύρι)ε εἰς ζοὴν ἀΐδιον, 'by means of water wash (me), Lord, for eternal life'. The verb ἀναπλύνω is not attested in LSJ or the Suppl.

89. A palaeochristian (?) bronze lamp shaped as a ship

'Mezul', 13 km. S-W of Smederevo (Yugoslavia)   III[1]
ed. pr. — L. Pavlović, *Starimar* 17 (1966) 123ff. (*non vidi*)

Dei in domu Termogenes votum fecit.

The prow of this somewhat damaged, ship-shaped lamp is in the form of a dragon's head: it holds a man in its mouth. The votive text is written on both sides of the prow and the stern.
Bib. — *IMS* 83, pp.89-90 (pl.), which includes further references.

Termogenes fulfilled his vow in the house of God.

The decoration on this lamp has been the object of diverse interpretations. The first editor suggested neo-pythagorean symbolism; V. Popović, *Starimar* 20 (1969) 323ff. (*non vidi*) felt it may have been a palaeochristian object. On that view the combination of a boat and a monster swallowing a man alludes to Jonah (cf. **90**). M. Mirković in *IMS* appears to accept this latter interpretation, and points out that *domus = ecclesia,* 'rare dans les provinces occidentales, sauf en Afrique du Nord, est assez fréquente en Asie Mineure et en Syrie'. Cf. H. Leclercq, 'Domus dei, ecclesiae, orationis', *DACL* IV.2 (1920) cols. 1442-43. The *Thesaurus Linguae Latinae* V.1 (1934), s.v., *domus* IA2a, col. 1970, registers numerous occurrences of this sense in the Latin Fathers and the Vulgate, but there are also examples from classical writers such as Cicero, Martial and Statius where *domus = templum* or *fanum*. In Greek patristic writing οἶκος may mean a church building (Lampe, s.v., 3), but οἶκος in the sense of shrine, temple, is common enough in non-Christian texts too (see S.C. Barton and G.H.R. Horsley, *JbAC* 24 [1981] 15).

Two hoards of Roman coins, dated 247 and 250, were discovered close by this find. If a Christian interpretation for this lamp is to be entertained, it may have been cached away during the Decian persecution in 250 (so, Mirković). Further, in view of Mirković's comment quoted above, this object may not be a local product, but imported perhaps from somewhere like Syria (cf. **60**). It would therefore provide very early evidence for the spread of Christianity in this area. But on balance there does not appear to be enough information to allow us to be even reasonably confident that the lamp has Christian associations.

The name Termogenes is not elsewhere attested, and an alternative suggestion, Hermogenes, is mentioned in *IMS*.

90. An early pictorial representation of the Crucifixion

Tomis (Constanța)   IV/V
ed. pr. — C. Smith, *ABSA* 3 (1896/7) 201-06 (fig.)

This carnelian intaglio was dated by Smith (206) as hardly later than III; *IGLR* 53 gives IV/V as the date, and provides a large bibliography. In the centre of the gemstone hangs the naked figure of Christ on the cross. The cross appears to have been in the shape of a T, with no vertical bar above the cross-beam; but a fragment chipped away from the gem above Christ's head makes this uncertain. Christ has been presented naked quite deliberately; for he is flanked on either side by six diminutively sized apostles who are clothed. According to Smith (204-05), this way of presenting Christ indicates a pre-Byzantine date for the portrayal. Around the top of the stone run the letters ΙΧΘΥΣ. Such depictions of crucifixion are not treated in M. Hengel, *Crucifixion* (London, 1977).

This same abbreviation occurs on another gemstone, this one of onyx, which has received much attention since its publication in the nineteenth century, and is republished in *IGLR* 435 (late III/early IV). Here we are given a representation of a man carrying a sheep with another at his feet. Various other animals and symbolic designs are portrayed: a tree with a bird in it, a sea monster, a man falling out of a boat; and the 'Fish' acrostic. The most comprehensive discussion of the ΙΧΘΥΣ idea is still F.J. Dölger, ΙΧΘΥΣ. *Das Fisch-symbol in frühchristlicher Zeit* (5 vols.; Rome 1910-43); see also J. Engemann, 'Fisch', *RAC* 7 (1969) 959-1097. The significance of the other elements is plain. Although Th. Klauser has argued that the sheep-bearer was a familiar secular symbol of philanthropy, and cannot on its own be taken as an expression of Christian belief (*JbAC* 1[1958] 20-51), the associations in this case put it beyond doubt. As well as Christ the Good Shepherd, we have the Dove, the Tree of Life (perhaps), and the Jonah story — this latter included perhaps because it was the one 'sign' given by Christ (Mt. 12.39-40; 16.4). This gemstone — now lost — offers one of the earliest indications known of the spread of Christianity into Dacia, brought in all probability by individuals in the Roman army.

IGLR 173 is a bilingual inscription referring to the 'cross of death and of resurrection': † Σταυρὸς [θανάτου καὶ] | ἀναστάσεως | † *Crux mort*[*is et*] *resurrect*[*ionis*].

91. An archdeacon's runaway slave

Sardinia   V²/VI¹
ed. pr. — G. Sotgiu, *Arch.Class.* 25/26 (1973/79) 688-97.

S[*ervus sum*] Felicis arc(hi)diac(oni): tene me ne fugiam.

A nearly complete bronze slave collar.
Bib. — J. Reynolds, *JRS* 66 (1976) 196

I am the slave of archdeacon Felix: hold me so that I do not flee.

In addition to listing other examples of inscribed slave collars (690-91), Sotgiu argues (694) that the use of this restraint constituted an amelioration of treatment for runaway slaves, who prior to Constantine underwent branding on the face. Paul's letter to Philemon perhaps envisages financial compensation (18).

92. The hammer as a hidden cross in Christian epitaphs

I. Kajanto, *Arctos* 10 (1976) 49-58 (cf.*SEG* 1911), has examined the occurrences of identifiable tools on texts in *ICUR* I-VI. He concludes that while the tools may often indicate the occupation of the deceased, nevertheless their inclusion on some tombstones may have been of symbolic import. In particular he considers the hammer, which is found on *stelai* of several women and children. He suggests that the shape of the hammer led to its adoption as 'a *crux dissimulata* in a period when the cross as such (had) not yet appeared on Christian epitaphs' (57).

93. The spread of Christianity in the Sinai

Recently published inscriptions and graffiti from the Sinai (34 Nabataean and 10 Greek in A. Negev, *Eretz-Israel* 10 [1971] 180-87; in Hebrew with English summary, p.xv; seven plates) have served to confirm the theory suggested in 1953 (M. Schwabe, *HTR* 46 [1953] 49-55, esp. 54-55) that Christianity spread into the Sinai and the far south of Palestine from Egypt. The earliest Christians in this area of whom we have (epigraphical) record were Egyptians. B. Lifshitz, *Euphrosyne* 6 (1974) 41-44, republishes several of the Greek texts first presented by Negev (cf. *SEG* 1657-64; *BE* 738). See Lifshitz' nn. 64-66 for further discussion about the spread of Christianity in this region; for the northern Sinai in particular see id., *ZPE* 7(1971) 157-61; cf. *ZPE* 8(1971) 160. Negev has since published the material more fully in *The Inscriptions of Wadi Haggag, Sinai* (*Qedem* 6, Jerusalem, 1977); and in view of its date of publication this volume will be covered in the next volume of *New Documents*.

Christianity's penetration of southern Palestine was not certainly prior to the end of IV: it probably arrived in the Sinai well before then. Schwabe (52) mentions that a bishop of Aila (Eilath) took part in the council of Nicaea in 325. The evidence for the Egyptian origin of the authors of these inscriptions lies in the names, e.g., Petteri(o)s [≠ Petros] (Negev no.43 = Lifshitz no.2); Sovairo(u)s (N. no.42 = L. no.3); Mouse/Mouses (N. nos. 38, 42 = L. nos. 4, 3); Isis (N. no.38 = L. no.4); Theone (N. no.37 = L. no.6). These texts were written by pilgrims travelling the caravan route from Aila westwards across the Sinai desert to Arsinoe. Some plates accompanying Negev's article show clearly drawings on the rocks of people leading camel caravans. In Lifshitz no.1 (= Negev no.35), L. reads the last line thus: $T\rho\iota(\acute{a})\delta o\varsigma$ $\grave{o}\lambda\epsilon\phi a(\nu)\theta\hat{\eta}\varsigma$ (gen. absol.); he claims (p.41) that it reflects some current polemic against another Christian group which denied the notion of the Trinity. D. Feissel's proposal to read the text much more innocuously is attractive (*BCH* 100 [1976] 275-76). The text is a standard appeal for help to the Lord by Timotheus (*l*.2) $\kappa a\grave{\iota}$ | $\tau\hat{\eta}\varsigma$ $a\grave{v}\tau o\hat{v}$ $\acute{o}\rho\mu a\sigma|\tau\rho\acute{\iota}\delta o\varsigma$ $`O\lambda\epsilon\phi\acute{a}\theta\eta\varsigma$, 'and his fiancée Olephathe' (apparently a semitic name). Cf. *BE* (1977) 545.

Further evidence of a rather different kind may be adduced to support Schwabe's hypothesis. J. Kubińska, 'La prière nubienne pour les morts et la question de son origine', *Nubia.Récentes Recherches* (see **94**), 83-84, considers briefly the formula used in Nubian prayers for the dead found on epitaphs (cf. *BE* 776). She draws attention to an identical formula in a liturgical papyrus text (late VI/early VII) from a village in the Negev: C.J. Kraemer, *Excavations at Nessana, III. Non-Literary Papyri* (Princeton, 1958) no.96, pp.309-10. Cf. *BE* (1961) 818 which provides other epigraphical references to such prayers. Kubińska implies (84) that this type of prayer came to Nubia from S. Palestine. But the fact that there are numbers of texts from Nubia and only the one from the Negev would surely suggest the opposite conclusion. A movement in this direction, from Nubia towards Palestine, would provide a good parallel to the graffito texts considered above.

94. Christianity in Nubia

Nubia. Récentes Recherches, ed. K. Michalowski (Warsaw, 1975), contains the *acta* of the second international conference on Nubian Studies held in Warsaw in 1972. Several of the papers bear on Christianity in Nubia, and three may be referred to specifically here. W.Y. Adams, 'The Twilight of Nubian Christianity' (pp. 11-17), offers a survey of reasons for the decline of the Nubian Church. Its heyday was VIII-XII, but a series of factors saw its gradual demise. These included the persecution of the parent Coptic Church in Egypt; the political weakness of the Nubian Kingdom; the increasingly esoteric character of church ritual, from which the laity were cut off; and the arrival in the land of 'secular military feudalism' (p.12) and the 'islamisation' of the monarchy.

S. Donadoni, 'Les graffiti de l'église de Sonqi Tino' (pp. 31-39), offers comment on the very varied texts found scribbled on various parts of the church (cf. *BE* 775). The texts are mostly in Nubian (30) or Greek (37) with a couple in Coptic. Few of those named include a patronymic; titles accompany the name instead. Tottina is ἀρχιπρεσβύτερος καὶ ἀρχιμανδρίτης (abbot) παρὰ ζῷα. Simeon is ἔπαρχος (governor, prefect), πρεσβύτερος μέγας καὶ χαρτουλάριος (keeper of archives). Gortnod has among his titles ἀναγνώστης μέγας. Most of the common titles are ecclesiastical. Of these διάκονος is to be noted; for it occurs with other titles, such as ἱερεὺς μέγας δ., δ. ἀβ(βα) ... ἐπίσκοπος, in a way that suggests it does not refer to a specific ministry. It may merely be a way of contrasting the ordained with the laity. One text in Donadoni's collection appears to include an allusion to the '24 elders' of Rev. 4.10. No date is offered in the article for these texts, but one may hazard the guess that the span of centuries will have included VI; few if any of these texts are likely to be much earlier. In the *acta* of the First Colloquium *Kunst und Geschichte Nubiens in christlicher Zeit,* ed. E. Dinkler (Recklinghausen, 1970), Donadoni discussed features of the church where these graffiti were found (*non vidi*).

M. Krause, 'Die Formulare der christlichen Grabsteine Nubiens' (pp. 76-82), examines 314 inscriptions from the cemetery at Sakinya in Nubia to see what variety existed in the conventions of epitaph phraseology (cf. *BE* 777). He uses the edition by T. Mina, *Inscriptions coptes et grecques de Nubie* (Cairo, 1942). The ratio of Coptic to Greek texts was almost 4:1. Only nine of these texts are clearly dated: they span the two centuries from 796-987. Krause shows that the formulae on Christian epitaphs are to be paralleled by texts from the Church in Egypt; the formulae do not reflect influence from Byzantion, as had previously been thought.

94 *bis*. The date of Ezana, 'Constantine' of Ethiopia

Axum   IV or V?

ed. pr — F. Anfray, A. Caquot, P. Nautin, *JSav* 72 (1970) 260-274 (ph., 264)

Ἐν τῇ πίστι τοῦ θ[εοῦ καὶ] τῇ δυνάμι τοῦ [πα]-
τρὸς καὶ υἱοῦ καὶ [ἁ]γί[ο]υ [π]νεύματος, τ[ῷ]
[σ]ώσαντί μοι τὸ βασ[ίλ]ιον τῇ πίστι τοῦ υἱ[οῦ]
αὐτοῦ Ἰησοῦ χριστοῦ, τῷ βοηθήσαντί μο[ι]

5   τῷ καὶ πάντοταί μοι βοηθοῦντι ἐγὼ
Ἀζανᾶς βασιλεὺς Ἀξωμιτῶν καὶ Ὁμηρι-
[τῶν κ]αὶ τοῦ ΡΕΕΙΔΑΝ καὶ Σαβαειτῶν καὶ
τοῦ Σ[ΙΛ]ΕΗΛ καὶ τοῦ ΧΑΣΩ καὶ βουγαειτῶν
[κ]αὶ τοῦ Τιαμῶ, ΒΙΣΙ ΑΛΗΝΕ, υἱὸς τοῦ ΕΛΛΕ-

10   ΑΜΙΔΑ, δοῦλος χριστοῦ, εὐχαριστῶ Κυρίῳ
τῷ [θεῷ] μου καὶ οὐ δύναμαι εἰπῖν πλίρης
τὰς εὐχαριστίας αὐτοῦ, ὅτι οὐ δύναται
τὸ στό[μ]α μου καὶ ἡ διάνοιά μου πάσας
τὰς εὐχαριστίας ἅσπερ ἐποίησεν μετ' ἐ-

15   μοῦ, ὅτι ἐπ[οί]ησεν ἐμοὶ ἰσχὺν καὶ δύναμιν
καὶ ἐχαρίσ[α]τό μοι ὄ[ν]ομα μέγα διὰ τοῦ υἱοῦ
[α]ὐτοῦ εἰς ὃν ἐπ[ί]στευσα [κα]ὶ ἐποίησέν μαι ὁ-
[δ]ηγὸν πάσης τῆς βασιλίας μου διὰ τὴν πί-
στ[ι]ν τοῦ χριστοῦ τ[ῷ] θελήματι [αὐ]τοῦ καὶ

20   δυνάμι τοῦ χριστοῦ, ὅτι αὐτὸς ὁδήγησέν
μαι καὶ εἰς α[ὐ]τὸν πιστεύω καὶ αὐτὸς ἐγέ-
νετό μοι ὁδηγός. Ἐξῆλθα πολεμῆσαι
τοὺς ΝΩΒΑ, ὅτι κατέκραξαν κατ' αὐτῶν
οἱ ΜΑΝΓΑΡΘΩ καὶ ΧΑΣΑ καὶ ΑΤΙΑΔΙΤΑΙ

25   καὶ ΒΑΡΕΩΤΑΙ λέγοντες ὅτι κατεπόνη-
σαν ἡμᾶς οἱ ΝΩΒΑ, βοηθήσατε ἡμῖν, ὅτι ἔ-
θλιψαν ἡμᾶς ἀποκτένοντες. Καὶ ἀνέστην
ἐν τῇ δυνάμι τοῦ θεοῦ χριστοῦ, εἰς ὃν ἐπί-
στευσα, καὶ ὁδήγησέν με. Καὶ ἀνέστην ἀ-

30   πὸ Ἀξώμεος ἐν μινὶ κατὰ Ἀξωμιτὰς ΜΑΓΑ-
ΒΙΘΕ η΄ ἡμέρᾳ σαμβάτῳ πίστι τοῦ θεοῦ καὶ
ἔφθασα εἰς ΜΑΜΒΑΡΙΑΝ καὶ ἐκῖθεν ἐσιτάρχησα.

A limestone stele 1.63 x 0.605 m., with another inscription of Ezana in Sabaean characters on the other side, found along with two *stelai* of king Kaleb (VI) on the site of the palace, 'Enda Sem'on, in the heart of Axum.
Bib. — *SEG* 1813; F. Altheim and R. Stiehl, *Klio* 58 (1976) 471-79.

In the faith of God, and the power of the Father and Son and Holy Spirit, who
saved for me the kingdom by the faith of his son Jesus Christ, who helped me
5   **and always does help me, I, |Azanas, king of the Axomites and Homerites and**

10   of Reeidan (?) and of the Sabaites and of Sileel (?) and of Chaso (?) and of the
Bougaites and of Tiamo, a man (of the tribe) of Alene (?), son of Elle-| Amida
(?), servant of Christ, give thanks to the Lord my God and I cannot state fully
his favours because my mouth and my mind cannot (embrace) all the favours

15   which he has given me, | because he has given me strength and power and
favoured me with a great name through his Son in whom I believed and he made
me the guide of all my kingdom because of (my) faith in Christ, by his will and

20 | the power of Christ, because he has guided me and I believe in him and he has
become my guide. I went out to make war on the Noba (?), because there had

25   cried out against them the Mangartho (?), the Chasa (?), the Atiaditai (?), | the
Bareotai, saying that, 'The Noba (?) have ground us down; help us because they
have troubled us by killing.' And I rose up in the power of the God Christ, in

30   whom I believed, and he guided me. And I rose up | from Axom on the 8th day,
a Saturday, of the Axomite month Magabithe (?), in the faith of God and I
reached Mambaria (?) and there I fed my army.

This first emphatically Christian document of Ezana greatly sharpens the controversy over the date of the conversion of Ethiopia, for which see A. Dihle, *Umstrittene Daten: Untersuchungen zum Auftreten der Griechen am Roten Meer* (Cologne, 1965). The editors, accepting the authenticity of the letter of Constantius II to Ezana (c.356), resolve the date in *ll*.30-31, by means of the perpetual calendar, to one of the years 349, 355 and 360. E. Dinkler, *Études et Travaux* 9 (1976) 6-15 (*non vidi*) raises the possibility of the latter part of IV or even V for the foundation of the church in Axum. Altheim and Stiehl, however, claim that the theology of the new text must be post-Chalcedon (451). The only other Christian inscription of Ezana is *Deutsche Aksum-Expedition* IV (Berlin, 1913), no.11, an Ethiopian text also on his campaign against the Noba, with a vague monotheistic emphasis which led to the suggestion that the king had first been converted to Judaism, or that he belonged to a monophysite era in V. Now Caquot and Nautin not only suggest (268) an echo of 2 Sam. 7.9 in *l*.16 of the new text, but refer (266) for the structure of the theological language to Mk.11.22, Rom. 3.22, Rom.3.26, 1 Cor. 2.5, 2 Cor. 6.7, Gal. 2.20, Gal. 3.22, Phil. 3.9, Jas. 2.1. Altheim and Stiehl (473) claim that in *ll*. 1-2 God is conceived as a unity with three δυνάμεις. Appropriately, therefore, it is through the Son that God acts (*l*.16). The Son and Holy Spirit are assumed to be of divine nature from the fact that the help is attributed to God in *ll*. 3-5. A human nature for Christ is excluded by *l*.28. The Holy Spirit proceeds from God, but not also from the Son (implied in *ll*.1-2). The coupling of Christ and God in *ll*.10-11 reinforces the impression of monophysitism. Ezana must name Christ, because he follows the religion named after him, but 'in everything else there speaks a ruler who rejects the Chalcedonian creed' (473-4). Altheim and Stiehl therefore reject the supposition of F. Heyer, *Die Kirche Äthiopiens* (Berlin, 1971), 257, that monophysitism may not have been taken over in Ethiopia until the Islamic period. The church, they claim, can now be seen to have begun with that creed, which effectively delays its origin to the time of Chalcedon. When Athanasius (*PG* 25.636f.) names Frumentius 'bishop of Axum', he is adding that as a claim on his own part to the letter of Constantius II. Frumentius did not convert the Ezana of the letter, nor did he reach Axum (474). He was rather a missionary to India.

(E. A. JUDGE)

F. VARIA

95. The following Christian texts were encountered in 1976 publications but have not been treated at all in this Review. ('Christian' here is used very broadly to refer to a text which may be distinguished by the presence of certain signs, e.g., a cross on an official document, or by its content.) Nearly all of these are Byzantine in date, some are late Roman; epigraphic texts are nearly all epitaphs.

AE:	32-36, 38-46, 48-57, 60-72, 74-77, 129 (according to index, p.270, s.v. *Florentinus)* 241, 242, 246, 249, 363-65, 410, 450, 451, 510, 522, 617 (=*IGLR* 30), 618 (= *IGLR* 43), 630, 665;
BE:	486, 492, 527, 570, 756 (nos 6 and 8);
IG.Aeg.:	9257, 33026;
IGLR:	7-9, 11-15, 20,22,24,28,29,31,32,35,36,40,44,45,48,51,52,55, 63, (cf.106,217), 64,70,76,79,80a,87,88,95,98,99,106,112,120,124(?), 125-32,140,141,143,144,147-50,152(?),153-55,182(?),183,185-87,194, 195,199-203,210,211,214,215,217(?),219,234,243,246,251,255,261-63, 267,273,301,303,308,309,311-24,326,329-31,333,336,341,344,346-50, 374,382-87,389,391,392(?), 396,398e,399,400,433,433a(?),437,443(?), 444-46;
IMS:	131(?),166(?),177;
SEG:	373,384,405,406,435,436,725,776,778,789,790,791,1121,1153,1155, 1156,1281,1374,1446,1491,1493,1627-30,1656,1672,1676,1677,1782, 1783-91,1797,1798,1805,1806,1811;
CPR:	24,25;
SIA:	W. Peek, *Att.Grab. Inschr.* 171-173;
P.Coll.Youtie:	88(?)., 89,90;
P.Laur.:	7;
P.Vindob. Tandem:	17-19,28,30-33;
O.Amst.:	91-93;
SB:	10766, 10767, 10773, 10798, 10805, 10808, 10809, 10810, 10814, 10902-05, 10935, 10936, 10939, 10965, 10990;

96. J.M. Reynolds, 'Roman Inscriptions, 1971-75', *JRS* 66 (1976) 174-99, provides a very useful survey of new inscriptions from the Roman world. She refers to a number involving early Christianity, 195-96.

97. *BE* 50, 51 are two useful cross-reference entries, the former listing Jewish texts in Greek treated in *BE* for 1976, the latter listing Christian texts.

98. Bishops of Provincia Scythia. E. Popescu discusses these and other officials (governors, generals) of the province during the period IV-VI, in *Epigraphica. Travaux dediés au VIIe Congrés d'épigraphie grecque et latine (Constanţa,* 1977), 255-83 (cf. *SEG* 842).

99. W.O. Moeller argues in a short monograph, *The Mithraic Origins of the Rotas-Sator Square* (Leiden, 1973), that the SATOR is Saturn, and that in the light of significant numbers and word meanings the text has a Mithraic character. He includes a lengthy bibliography. Cf. J. Reynolds, *JRS* 66 (1976) 195f., who points out that one merit of Moeller's largely 'unconvincing' study is that he shows that a Christian interpretation is not the only possible one.

INDICES

1. Biblical Passages

1 Tim.	1.10	12		7.1	5			.5	8
	2.10	12		.11	2			.6	5
	4.3-4	69		.23	27			.7	2,19,85
	.14	19		.27	9			.8	75
	5.2	20,79		8.9	19	2 Pet.	1.1	55
	.10,13	12		.16	2			.4	19
	6.21	12		10.25	80			.19	13
2 Tim.	1.3	16		.29	12			.21	2
	3.3	2		11.9	85			2.8	36
	.10	20		12.10	18			3.4	16
	.16-17	2		13.3	16	1 Jn.	1.1-5	59
	4.10-16	80		.5	80			4.18	18
Tit.	1.8	47		.16	18	3 Jn.	15	15
	.9	12	Jas.	1.11	2	Jude	3	9
	.16	19		.17,25	18	Rev.	1.8	22,59
	2.3	79		.26,27	26			.18	8
	.5	8		2.1	94 *bis*			2.1	9
	.7	27		.2,3	69			.17	39
	3.5	21		.3	13			3.9	16
	.9	2		.25	6			4.4	69
Philem.	4	16,91		5.2	26			.10	94
Heb.	1.11	16		.7	19			9.7	69
	2.3	19		.13	84			.20	16
	.6	16	1 Pet.	1.1	55			12.9	55
	.7,9	69		.19	19			14.4	69,76
	.12	25		3.1	8			18.11	21
	3.14	40		.3	2			21.6	22
	5.9	5						22.13	22

2. Words

This index does not register all occurrences of words in texts printed in this review, but simply those words which receive some notice in an entry. Item numbers in bold type indicate more than a passing reference. An asterisk (*) indicates that comment is offered on the MM or BAGD entry. New words are marked with a dagger (†).

A. Greek

ἀβάσκαντος	— **24**	ἀνάθεμα	— 61	Ἀσιάρχης	— 32
ἀγαθός	— 11	ἀνάκειμαι	— 1	ἀσπάζομαι	— 18
ἀγαπάω	— **69**	ἀνακλίνω	— 1	ἄστοργος	— 2
ἀγγαρεύω	— 9	ἀναχωρέω	— 82	αὐγή	— 2
*ἀγενής	— **85**	ἀνείκητος	— 68	ἀφθονία	— 27
ἁγιωτάτη (of synagogue)	— 69	ἀνθρώπινος	— 20	ἀφίημι	— 85
ἁγνός	— 25	ἀντίγραφον	— 18	βιάζω	— 18
ἀγωνία	— 13	ἀπαράβλητος	— 80	βινέω	— 8
ἀδελφός	— 17,85	ἀπαρτίζω	— 21	βλέπω	— 2
ἀδόκιμος	— 19	ἀπέχω	— 3	βόλος	— 40
ἀδελφοσύνη	— 21	ἀπογραφή	— 28	βουλή	— 31
ἄδυτον	— 3	ἀποδείκνυμι	— 18	βρέφος	— 2
ἀηδία	— 18	ἀποδημέω	— 20	γενεαλογέω	— 5
ἀκούω	— 12	ἀπολαμβάνω	— 85	γομόω	— 21
*ἀκριβής	— 9	Ἀπολλῶς	— 50	γονεῖς	— 2
Ἄλφα	— 22,59	ἀπονέμω	— 19	γραμματεύς	— 24,**74**
ἀμελέω	— 19	ἀποσπάω	— 85	γράφω	— 15
ἀμέτοχος	— 6	ἀποτακτικός	— **82**	δαίμων	— **2**
ἀναβαίνω πρός	— 15	ἀποτάσσομαι	— 17	δεκαταῖος	— 15
ἀναγκαῖος	— 84	ἀπρόσκοπος	— 15	δέω	— 12
ἀνάγκη	— 2	†ἁρματοφορέω	— 2	Δημᾶς	— 51
*ἀνάγκην ἔχω	— 9	*ἀρραβών	— 33	δῆμος	— 23
ἀναγνώστης	— 94	*ἀρχή	— 22	διάγνωσις	— **12**
		ἀρχιγερουσιάρχης	— 73	διαγινώσκω	— 2
		ἀρχιμανδρίτης	— 94	διάκονος	— 79,94
		ἀρχιπρεσβύτερος	— 94	διάκων	— 81
		ἀρχισυνάγωγος	— 5,73	διάλεκτος	— 2
		ἄρωμα	— 84	διαλλάσσω	— 2

B. Latin (selected)

3. Subjects

4. ECL, Patristic and Jewish Writers

5. Texts Discussed

Listed below are all texts new or old appearing in 1976 corpora and conspectus volumes and referred to in this work. Of other texts only those discussed in a more than passing manner are listed. Bold type indicates substantial discussion of text at the item number given, or that a non-1976 text has been reprinted here. It will not be the normal practice of this Review to suggest new readings, but where they are offered an asterisk (*) beside the text in this index will indicate it.

Corrigenda

The following corrigenda which affect clarity have been noticed:

p.ii,   entry **60**: for 'Jn. 13.27' read 'Jn. 14.27'.

p.5,   beginning of entry **1**: for '*P.Coll.Youtie* 51-5' read '*P.Coll.Youtie* 51-52'.

p.15,   item (vi): for 'see **35**' read 'see **11**'.

p.36,   first new paragraph, *l*.2: for 'used' read 'use'.

p.44,   middle of last paragraph: for 'Clement 1.3, 14.1' read 'Clement 1.3, 41.1'.

p.54,   beginning of entry **15**: add date in right hand margin, 'I'.

p.56,   Greek text, *l*.15: for 'ὁγίαν' read 'ὑγίαν'.

p.75,   end of B: for 'ambiguous' read 'unambiguous'.

p.77,   last paragraph, *l*.3: for 'Keraklammon' read 'Heraklammon'.

p.83,   first line of entry **33**: for '2243' read '2343'.

p.99,   entry **60**, title: for 'Jn. 13.27' read 'Jn. 14.27'.

p.147,   first column, *l*.1: for 'Jn. 13.27 — **60**' read 'Jn. 14.27 — **60**'.

p.147,   third column: for '2 Cor. 2.5' read '2 Cor. 6.7'.
           for '2 Cor. 3.10,13' read 'Gal. 3.10,13'.

p.149,   first column, s.v. θεός, εἶς θ.: add '5'.

p.150,   subject index, s.v. bilingual inscriptions: delete 'Greek-Coptic — 58'.

p.152,   *nomina sacra*, on amulet: delete '22'.

p.155,   second column: for '*SEG* 1688' read '*SEG* 1668'.

p.155,   second column: delete '*SEG* 1716 — 58'.